T0295818

Transforming Public-Private Ecosystems

Transforming Public-Private Ecosystems

Understanding and Enabling Innovation in Complex Systems

William B. Rouse

OXFORD
UNIVERSITY PRESS

OXFORD
UNIVERSITY PRESS

Great Clarendon Street, Oxford, OX2 6DP,
United Kingdom

Oxford University Press is a department of the University of Oxford.
It furthers the University's objective of excellence in research, scholarship,
and education by publishing worldwide. Oxford is a registered trade mark of
Oxford University Press in the UK and in certain other countries

© William B. Rouse 2022

The moral rights of the author have been asserted

Impression: 1

Published in the United States of America by Oxford University Press
198 Madison Avenue, New York, NY 10016, United States of America

British Library Cataloguing in Publication Data

Data available

Library of Congress Control Number: 2022930879

ISBN 978-0-19-286653-0

DOI: 10.1093/oso/9780192866530.001.0001

Printed and bound by
CPI Group (UK) Ltd, Croydon, CR0 4YY

Preface

My research projects in recent decades have all involved complex ecosystems, including national security, healthcare delivery, higher education, and energy and climate, with a range of stakeholders from government, industry, academia, nongovernmental organizations (NGOs) and, of course, the overall public.

All have involved pursuing improved outcomes that society would be likely to endorse, except when the paths to those improvements affect a range of powerful vested interests. These vested interests included government bureaucracies; defense and technology companies; healthcare providers, payers, and suppliers; education constituencies; and entrenched competing ideas.

If we can make change work for everybody, we might gain support, although there is the ever-present risk of "not invented here." Thus, there is great risk of failure in terms of significantly impacting change. This book is concerned with understanding public-private ecosystems and, based on this understanding, thereby enabling innovations that facilitate change.

Why public-private ecosystems? In the United States, such ecosystems are central to the functioning and provisioning of security, healthcare, education, and environment. These ecosystems face challenges of governance, diverse constituencies, numerous advocacy organizations, incompatible outcome metrics, and persistent media attention, to name a few.

There is a wide range of public and private players involved in operating, sustaining, and investing in these ecosystems. Thus, transformation—fundamental change—involves understanding a wide range of interests and accommodating change strategies accordingly. Transformational change is not a spectator sport; further, it is a team sport.

Transforming these ecosystems easily qualifies as "wicked problems." Horst Rittel, almost five decades ago, characterized wicked problems as social or cultural problems laced with incomplete or contradictory knowledge, large numbers of people and opinions, substantial economic burdens, and the interconnected nature of these problems with other problems. This book addresses these challenges for four important ecosystems, and provides an integrated perspective for understanding and enabling change.

I have worked in these four ecosystems for many decades, conducting studies, performing analyses, prototyping solutions, and deploying decision support systems for strategy formulation, R&D investments, and planning new policies, products and services. Many of these efforts struggled to address the challenges associated with these public-private ecosystems. Some of these challenges thwarted successful deployment. Others were overcome.

In *Transforming Public-Private Ecosystems*, I outline an approach to systemically anticipating and addressing these challenges. Playing the game of change can be greatly facilitated if you understand the likely wickets you will encounter and how best to address them.

Transforming Public-Private Ecosystems is the third volume in a three-part series exploring model-based approaches to complex systems. *Computing Possible Futures* (2019) addressed the use of computational approaches for exploring the futures of healthcare delivery, higher education, and other domains. *Failure Management* (2021) considered how model-based approaches could enable detection, diagnosis, and remediation of malfunctions of technologies, organizations, and society. The result was a decision support construct that enables predictive surveillance and control of complex systems, organizations, and ecosystems.

Transforming Public-Private Ecosystems is concerned with the need to transform the complex system of interest. The concern is no longer only with predicting possible futures of the existing system. The system itself needs to change in terms of structure and processes. This is greatly complicated by the public-private ecosystems associated with national security, healthcare delivery, higher education, and energy and climate. A wide range of stakeholders needs to be understood and convinced of the merits of transformation.

There are essential relationships among these three books. Abilities to predict possible futures are central. Abilities to understand and manage things going wrong are critical. Understanding when and how an ecosystem should fundamentally change is the key to sustainable futures. The 36 case histories presented in *Transforming Public-Private Ecosystems* provide ample evidence of how such changes can be possible.

The solutions to our complex societal problems will not rely solely on engineering, i.e., will not simply be the computed optimal solutions of mathematical formulations. In contrast, these solutions will be socially negotiated, computationally explored, and behaviorally embraced as stakeholders come to understand, become involved, and deeply trust such explorations. These societal problems are laced with behavioral and social phenomena, hopefully enlightened but occasionally exacerbated by technology perspectives. This book aims to create the balance across these perspectives so as to enable progress.

William B. Rouse

Contents

List of Figures

List of Tables

1
Ecosystems, Innovation, and Transformation

This chapter addresses the following questions:

- What are public-private ecosystems?
- Why are they important?
- What is enterprise transformation?
- Why is it difficult?
- What is innovation?
- Why is it difficult?
- How will the rest of the book unfold?

Public-Private Ecosystems

Table 1.1 summarizes the key players in the four public-private ecosystems addressed in this book. These ecosystems are laced with governmental organizations, corporate organizations, academic institutions, and non-governmental organizations, typically non-profits. These organizations co-function to provide defense, healthcare, education, and energy, all crucial to the prosperity and safety of the country.

Transforming any of these ecosystems involves the values, perceptions, and concerns of the many players associated with the row of the table associated with that ecosystem. As is illustrated throughout this book, this can be a daunting process. The concepts, models, methods, and tools discussed in this book can help to facilitate addressing such challenges.

Ecosystems

What is an ecosystem? The term comes from ecology and usually refers to natural systems rather than the built environment. We can define an ecosystem as a community of living organisms that interact with the non-living elements of their environment, performing together as an overall system. Human activities are important in the

Transforming Public-Private Ecosystems. William B. Rouse, Oxford University Press.
© William B. Rouse (2022). DOI: 10.1093/oso/9780192866530.003.0001

Table 1.1 Four Public-Private Ecosystems.

Ecosystem	Public Players	Private Players
National Security	Dept. of Defense, Homeland Security, State, Energy; Intelligence Agencies, Federal Bureau of Investigation, State and Local Agencies	Aerospace & Defense Companies, Technology Companies, Research Universities
Healthcare Delivery	Dept. Health & Human Services, National Institutes of Health, Food & Drug Admin, Centers for Medicare & Medicaid Serv., Veterans Health Admin. et al., States, Cities, Public Providers	Private Providers and Payers, Pharma and Device Companies, Licensing & Accreditation Agencies, Advocacy Groups, Foundations
Higher Education	Dept. of Defense, Education, National Science Foundation, National Institutes of Health, et al., States, Public Institutions	Private Institutions, Publishers, Accreditation Agencies, Advocacy Groups, Foundations, Industry
Energy & Climate	Dept. Energy, Commerce, Environmental Protection Agency, National Labs, National Science Foundation, National Aeronautics & Space Admin. et al., States, Cities	Extractive Companies, Automobile Companies, Transportation Service Companies

ecosystems addressed in this book. These activities include operating the elements of the ecosystem. Their effects may also influence external factors like climate.

Ecosystems provide a variety of goods upon which people depend. These goods include tangible outcomes of ecosystem processes such as food, medicines, and vehicles. Ecosystem services, in contrast, include things like the maintenance of hydrological cycles, cleaning air and water, the maintenance of oxygen in the atmosphere, crop pollination and even things like beauty and inspiration.

Resource management as applied to whole ecosystems is called ecosystem management. Common principles include the long-term, intergenerational sustainability of the production of goods and services by the ecosystem. As human population and consumption grow, demands imposed on ecosystems lead to threats such as air and water pollution, and waste management challenges. The need to better understand long-term ecosystem health, as affected by human habitation and economic activity is essential and is now becoming urgent.

Business Ecosystems

A business ecosystem is an economic community supported by a foundation of interacting organizations and individuals within the business world. This economic community produces goods and services of value to customers, who are themselves members of the ecosystem. The member organizations include lead producers, competitors, suppliers, and other stakeholders. Over time, they co-evolve their capabilities and roles, and tend to align themselves with the directions set by one or more central companies. Those companies holding leadership roles may change over time, but the function of ecosystem leaders is valued by the community because it enables members to pursue shared visions, to align their investments, and to find mutually supportive roles (Moore, 1993, 1997).

Moore's adoption of this ecological view of business addresses "companies that co-evolve capabilities around a new innovation: they work cooperatively and competitively to support new products, satisfy customer needs, and eventually incorporate the next round of innovations." He illustrates these notions in ecosystems for personal computing, automobiles, and retail.

He summarizes cooperative and competitive challenges during his four evolutionary stages of business ecosystem development: birth; expansion; leadership; and self-renewal. A key idea is that members of a business ecosystem co-evolve in themselves—or they do not survive, as illustrated by my analysis of the cases of Kodak, Polaroid, Digital, Xerox, Motorola, and Nokia (Rouse, 2021).

Public-private relationships are not limited to particular markets such as personal computing. I have been involved in several industry alliances with universities in urban centers. IBM partnered with the Tennenbaum Institute at Georgia Tech in Atlanta to address healthcare. Accenture partnered with the Center for Complex Systems and Enterprises at Stevens Institute in New York City to address financial services and other practice areas, e.g., automotive. Asplund and colleagues (2021) report that

> [t]he ability of public innovation ecosystem leadership to act early on novel technology might be offset by the inability of involved firms to commit to bringing the technology to market and the individuals typically active during public-private ecosystem genesis are not ideal for handling this challenge. In fact, increasingly connected public leadership could smother the innovation ecosystem unless well-connected and multidisciplinary researchers are brought in as brokers.

Autio and Thomas (2014) characterize innovation ecosystems as "a network of interconnected organizations, connected to a focal firm or a platform, that incorporates both production and use side participants and creates and appropriates new value through innovation." These two reports emphasize the importance of the innovation network in terms of who participates and the roles they play.

Hileman and colleagues (2020) report on a "study of keystone actors and sustainability challenges that highlights an important source of influence largely not addressed in previous research: the presence of organizations that occupy strategic positions around keystone actors." They employ network analysis to identify players in these strategic positions.

Public-Private Collaborations and Partnerships

Some public-private ecosystems involve formal contractual relationships. Public-private collaborations often include collaborative governance: "The pursuit of authoritatively chosen public goals by means that include engaging the efforts of, and sharing discretion with, producers outside of government." (Donahue & Zeckhauser, 2006)

A public-private partnership "is a long-term contract between a private party and a government agency, for providing a public asset or service, in which the private part bears significant risk and management responsibility." (Roehrich, Lewis, & George, 2014) This extensive report reviews 1,400 articles published on public-private partnerships and addresses the question, "Are public-private partnerships a healthy option?" Their finding shows enormous diversity in what public-private partnerships mean and how they are organized in different domains and countries.

Maltin (2019) considers "What successful public-private partnerships do." She addresses public-private partnerships where "businesses supplement public investment in return for reaping rewards such as tolls and fees." Partnerships that are significantly over budget and late cause people to question the overall viability of public-private partnerships.

Focusing on ironclad contracts can portend difficulties. Intense focus on meeting milestones can undermine the health of the public-private working relationship. She suggests the following guidelines:

- Personal commitments that extend beyond contractual relationships
- Establish operating principles among the partner organizations
- Form cross-organizational teams to address challenging issues
- Hash out differences openly and authentically
- Admit to and correct setbacks quickly

Summary

As is quite clear from Table 1.1, there is no single formal partnership that links together all the organizations in each row of this table. There may be a variety of formal contractual relationships sprinkled across these organizations, but these relationships are not the focus of this book. Instead, I am concerned with the policies and rules of the game, procedures and practices, and values and norms that affect all the players in the ecosystem.

Historic Transformations

Most of the historical examples that I relate in this book are characterized as "past innovations." In this section, I discuss six clusters of innovations that, collectively, can easily be termed historic transformations. The panorama of these transformations sets the stage for the wealth of innovations addressed throughout.

Civil War (1861–1865)

Slavery was a major cause of the Civil War. The Confederates wanted to protect Southern society where slavery was an essential element of their economy. President Abraham Lincoln singed the Emancipation Proclamation as an executive order on January 1, 1863. The 13th (1865), 14th (1868), and 15th Amendments (1870) to the U.S. constitution were enacted to ensure equality for the emancipated slaves. Arrington (2011) summarizes the economic situation in the North and South.

> By 1860, 90 percent of the nation's manufacturing output came from northern states. The North produced 17 times more cotton and woolen textiles than the South, 30 times more leather goods, 20 times more pig iron, and 32 times more firearms. The North produced 3,200 firearms to every 100 produced in the South. Only about 40% of the Northern population was still engaged in agriculture by 1860, as compared to 84% of the South.
>
> Even in the agricultural sector, Northern farmers were out-producing their southern counterparts in several important areas, as Southern agriculture remained labor intensive while northern agriculture became increasingly mechanized. By 1860, the free states had nearly twice the value of farm machinery per acre and per farm worker as did the slave states, leading to increased productivity. As a result, in 1860, the Northern states produced half of the nation's corn, four-fifths of its wheat, and seven-eighths of its oats.
>
> The Southern lag in industrial development did not result from any inherent economic disadvantages. There was great wealth in the South, but it was primarily tied up in the slave economy. In 1860, the economic value of slaves in the United States exceeded the invested value of all of the nation's railroads, factories, and banks combined.

Trends during the war included (Arrington, 2011):

- Northern transportation industries boomed—particularly railroads.
- Northern industries, including weapons manufacturing, leather goods, iron production, textiles, grew and improved as the war progressed.
- The North took advantage of railroad lines and new, improved steamships to move soldiers and an endless supply of troops, supplies, and weapons.
- The North increased the influence and footprint of the federal government to transform industrial, economic, agricultural, mechanical, and financial sectors.
- The South had neither the ability nor the desire to develop a comparable industrial economy or centralized financial system.

Thus, beyond winning the Civil War, the North made investments that greatly enhanced the growth and competitiveness of the U.S.

Progressive Era (1897–1920)

The Gilded Age (1870–1900) set the stage for the Progressive Era. The Gilded Age was an era of rapid economic growth, especially in Northern and Western U.S. Some investors gained enormous wealth. Most people, however, experienced problems caused by industrialization, urbanization, immigration, and political corruption. The main objectives of the progressive movement were to address these problems.

Teixeira and Halpin (2011) summarize the tenets of progressive economics.

> The contours of progressive economics emerged in the late 19th century as a pragmatic attempt to deal with the realities of frequent depressions, workplace dangers, low wages, assaults on labor rights, mass unemployment, environmental negligence, public health issues, and political corruption at all levels of government. As with the transformation of philosophy and constitutional theory during this period, the original progressives charted a new and more realistic path in economics that preserved a market-based society and private enterprise while strengthening democratic control over the economy and employing the positive power of the state to advance human welfare and national prosperity.
>
> In contrast to a free-market approach of minimal state involvement in the economy and little to no social protections promoted by classical economists, and a state-controlled approach of extensive planning and public ownership of the major means of production favored by socialists, progressive economists embraced the concept of a "mixed economy"—essentially private economic freedom coupled with government regulation, social protections, and the maintenance of public goods.

It was an era of trust busting, led by President Theodore Roosevelt. President William Howard Taft, Roosevelt's hand-picked successor, presided over the culmination of several momentous changes:

- In 1911, the Supreme Court ruled that Standard Oil's aggressive pricing to push out the competition was in violation of the Sherman Antitrust Act, and ordered the company be divided into 34 companies. These companies would decades later engage in mergers that eventually led to Amoco, BP, Chevron, and ExxonMobil
- Also in 1911, the Supreme Court ruled that the American Tobacco had to be dissolved and the company divided into three major parts: American Tobacco, Liggett and Myers, and P. Lorillard

- The federal government attempted to use federal antitrust laws to break up U.S. Steel in 1911, but that effort ultimately failed due to the existence of innovative competitors in the 40 percent of the steel market U.S. Steel did not control
- The Panic of 1907 resulted in the Federal Reserve Bank being formed in 1913 by Congress to provide the nation with a safer, more flexible, and more stable monetary and financial system

New Deal (1933–1939)

President Franklin D. Roosevelt's New Deal involved a series of programs, public works projects, financial reforms, and regulations enacted in response to needs for relief, reform, and recovery from the Great Depression. Fishback (2017) provides an assessment of the economic impact of the New Deal.

> It was the largest peace-time expansion in federal government activity in American history. Public works and relief spending had state income multipliers of around one, increased consumption activity, attracted internal migration, reduced crime rates, and lowered several types of mortality. The farm programs typically aided large farmers but eliminated opportunities for sharecroppers, tenants, and farm workers. The loans to banks and railroads appear to have had little positive impact.

Dunleavy (2018), in contrast, takes a broader view that includes economic, social, and political impacts. Several programs created through the New Deal did have a lasting positive impact on the U.S. economy which was flagging throughout the 1930s:

- The Social Security Act, which provided income for the elderly, disabled, and children of poor families
- The Glass-Steagall Act of 1933 established the Federal Deposit Insurance Corporation, which effectively insured the savings of Americans in the event of a bank failure, which was all too common at the time
- The National Industrial Recovery Act of 1933 was enacted to foster "fair competition" through the fixing of prices and wages and the establishment of production quotas, among other measures
- The subsequent National Labor Relations Act of 1935 allowed for collective bargaining and essentially led to the development of the labor movement in the United States, which protected workers' rights and wages
- The Works Progress Administration, created in 1935, also had a positive impact by employing more than 8 million Americans in building projects ranging from bridges and airports to parks and schools

To an extent, the New Deal built upon the accomplishments of the progressive era to further balance the interests of big business with opportunities and a safety net for the overall population.

Infrastructure Development (1817–1956)

Infrastructure development is a classic and core example of public-private collaborations and partnerships. Three compelling examples include the Erie Canal, Rural Electrification Program, and the National Highway System. These investments had profound economic impacts far beyond the particular infrastructure created.

Construction on the Erie Canal began at sunrise on July 4, 1817. New York Governor DeWitt Clinton was largely responsible for this undertaking. The waters of the Great Lakes and the Atlantic Ocean were "wedded" on November 4, 1825. Over the 25 years following the opening of the canal, annual economic growth soared from 2.5 percent to 4.6 percent—"among the highest periods of economic growth in two centuries of American economic history." The canal enabled the establishing of manufacturing industries in Buffalo, Rochester, Syracuse, Utica, Schenectady, etc. because they had had easy access to markets to ship their manufactured goods. Prior to the Revolutionary War, New York City lagged Boston, Philadelphia, and Charleston as ports. New York City benefitted greatly from the Erie Canal—it now became the "commercial emporium of America." (Bernstein, 2005)

The Rural Electrification Act of 1936, enacted on May 20, 1936, provided federal loans for the installation of electrical distribution systems to serve isolated rural areas of the United States. The funding was channeled through cooperative electric power companies, hundreds of which still exist today. These member-owned cooperatives purchased power on a wholesale basis and distributed it using their own network of transmission and distribution lines. The Rural Electrification Act was one of many New Deal proposals by President Franklin D. Roosevelt to remedy high unemployment during the Great Depression. (Sablik, 2020)

The Federal Aid Highway Act of 1956, popularly known as the National Interstate and Defense Highways Act (Public Law 84–627), was enacted on June 29, 1956, when President Dwight D. Eisenhower signed the bill into law. With an original authorization of $25 billion for the construction of 4,1000 miles (66,000 km) of the Interstate Highway System supposedly over a 10-year period, it was the largest public works project in American history through that time. The impact on the U.S. economy was enormous. It also transformed the urban landscape of many cities (Weingroff, 1996).

Civil Rights Movement (1954–1968)

The civil rights movement in the United States involved a long struggle by African Americans and their allies to end institutionalized racial discrimination, disenfranchisement and racial segregation. It focused on the country's failure to deliver on the promise of the 13th, 14th, and 15th Amendments of the U.S. Constitution. Martin Luther King, Jr. was a central figure in this struggle. President Lyndon Johnson signed the Civil Rights Act in 1964.

Wright (2006) addresses the question of the extent to which the Civil Rights Movement provided economic benefits to blacks in South Carolina. His overall assessment is,

> First, the Civil Rights revolution was an economic as well as a political and social revolution, and its effects included economic gains for blacks in the South that were tangible and enduring; second, the Civil Rights revolution was a liberating economic breakthrough for the Southern regional economy as well as for its black population; and third, that the black presence in economic as well as political life continues to be a distinguishing feature of the South, another lasting consequence of the Civil Rights revolution of the 1960s.

Wright (2006) summarizes several trends.

- "The share of black employees in the South Carolina textiles jumped from less than 5% in 1963 to more than 20% in 1970, to more than one third by 1980."
- There are similar trends in manufacturing and paper industries, but nevertheless including denying blacks opportunities for advancement
- Black high-school graduation rate increased from 35% in 1960 to 57% in 1970 to 71% by 1977
- Blacks have steadily gained election and appointment to municiple offices and black firms have increased their share of municipal contracts
- Median black male income in the South caught up to the Midwest and Northeast
- These changes led by the 1990s to net black in-migration to the South, following several decades of net out-migration from the South."

The Economist (2020) recently reported on the ongoing impacts of segregation. Notable observations include.

- The incarceration rates of the criminal justice system tripled for black men and women from 1960 to 2010
- The household income gap and household wealth gap between whites and blacks have persisted over the past 50 years
- The "opportunity structure" still disadvantages blacks: 6% of white children live in high poverty neighborhoods; 66% of black children do
- Integrated schooling increases wages by 30% and reduces incarceration by 22%.

Clearly, the Civil Rights Movement remains a work in progress.

Connected Era (1991–2013)

It is difficult to address an era that is still playing out. Significant developments include AOL dialup in 1991, Netscape in 1994, Explorer in 1995, GPS in 1995, Google in 1998, Skype in 2003, Facebook in 2004, Twitter in 2006, iPhone in 2007 and Zoom in 2011. The era reaches formal closure, I argue, once mobile devices dominate in 2013. Other hallmarks include Motorola being sold to Google in 2011 and Nokia being sold to Microsoft in 2016.

The connected era has not really ended, as the civil rights era has not actually ended. However, our levels of connectivity are now seen as business as usual. Once mobile devices dominated, people were not going back to their desks to check emails or access their files. Thus, connectivity is like electricity almost a century ago.

The capabilities of the connected era have enabled many people to function despite the pandemic. Offices, classrooms, and medicine have embraced "tele" capabilities, often with no other choices. Of course, many people have not had such choices. Personal services are difficult to deliver remotely.

The connected era has also transformed public discourse. People can limit their information access only to outlets with which they already agree. Misinformation has become pervasive. Election results are subject to being dismissed as fake, fraud, or otherwise wrong.

This situation poses challenges for all of the four public-private ecosystems discussed in this book. Transformation requires engaging stakeholders in finding common ground on key issues, identifying opportunities, and exploring possibilities going forward. Lack of trust can completely undermine this process.

Enterprise Transformation

We tend to think of transformation in terms of a single enterprise, often a company but sometimes an institution such as a university. Individual enterprises tend to have leadership teams and boards of directors, or equivalent. Thus, there is ultimately a single decision-making authority.

Public-private ecosystems have multiple decision-making authorities that must negotiate shared decisions. A lack of consensus may lead to the courts for resolution. Elected officials who represent the public may lead some of these multiple authorities.

These complications result in transformation initiatives being much more complicated, as illustrated by the 20 historical case studies discussed in Chapters 3–6. Decision making becomes a negotiation process, which is elaborated in Chapter 2.

Nevertheless, the fundamentals of enterprise transformation still apply, with defi-nitions, concepts, and methods adapted to the context of public-private ecosystems. In this section, I discuss both these fundamentals and the adaptations.

Enterprise transformation goes far beyond business process improvement. Just getting better and better at what you are already doing is not enough. Motorola pioneered a version of Total Quality Management termed Six Sigma—a prod-uct or process that has just 3.4 defects per million units or opportunities. Six Sigma was not sufficient to overcome products that were no longer attractive to customers.

It is very difficult to successfully innovate when new offerings render your current offerings obsolete. It can require transformation of your enterprise. However, it has been suggested that transforming an enterprise is akin to rewiring a building while the power is on. How can we design and develop a transformed enterprise while also avoiding operational disruptions and unintended consequences in the process? To address this question, we need a deeper understanding of the notion of enterprise transformation.

Our earlier studies (Rouse, 2005a, 2005b, 2006) have led us to formulate a qualita-tive theory: "Enterprise transformation is driven by experienced and/or anticipated value deficiencies that result in significantly redesigned and/or new work processes as determined by management's decision making abilities, limitations, and inclina-tions, all in the context of the social networks of management in particular and the enterprise in general."

Context of Transformation

Enterprise transformation occurs in—and is at least partially driven by—the external context of the economy and markets. As shown in Figure 1.1, the economy affects markets that, in turn, affect enterprises. Of course, it is not quite as crisply hierarchical as indicated, in that the economy can directly affect enterprises, e.g., via regulation and taxation. The key point is that the nature and extent of transformation are context dependent.

There is also an internal context of transformation—the "intraprise" in Figure 1.1. Work assignments are pursued via work processes and yield work products, incur-ring costs. Values and culture, reward and recognition systems, individual and team competencies, and leadership are woven throughout the intraprise. These factors usually have strong impacts on an enterprise's inclinations and abilities to pursue transformation.

What changes does Figure 1.1 need to apply to the four public-private ecosys-tems addressed in this book? For national security, the economy might be re-placed by the current and projected geopolitical situation. Market could be-come anticipated military missions. Enterprise and intraprise easily fit national security.

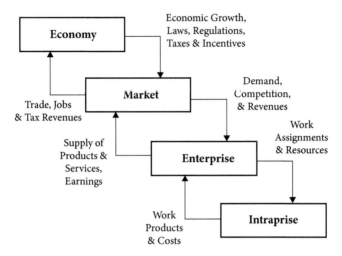

Fig. 1.1 Context of Enterprise Transformation

The original terminology works for healthcare delivery and higher education. For energy and climate, the current and projected global climate situation might replace economy. The energy market is fitting. Enterprise and intraprise easily apply to the players in this ecosystem.

Qualitative Theory of Transformation

Succinctly, experienced or expected value deficiencies drive enterprise transformation initiatives. Deficiencies are defined relative to both current enterprise states and expected states. Expectations may be based on extrapolation of past enterprise states. They may also be based on perceived opportunities to pursue expanded markets, new constituencies, technologies, etc. Thus, deficiencies may be perceived for both reactive and proactive reasons.

In the context of our four public private ecosystems, value deficiencies might involve declining technological superiority (national security), increasing chronic diseases (healthcare delivery), unsustainable increases in costs (higher education), or increasing global temperatures (energy and climate). A central issue is the inability of one actor to unilaterally address such deficiencies.

Transformation initiatives involve addressing what work is undertaken by the enterprise and how this work is accomplished. The work of the enterprise ultimately affects the state of the enterprise, which is reflected, in part, in the enterprise's financial statements, Balanced Scorecard assessment, or the equivalent. Other important elements of the enterprise state might include market advantage, brand image, employee and customer satisfaction, and so on. For public-private enterprises, public trust and confidence are key metrics.

Ends, Means and Scope of Transformation

There is a wide range of ways to pursue transformation. Figure 1.2 summarizes conclusions drawn from numerous case studies. The ends of transformation can range from greater cost efficiencies, to enhanced market perceptions, to new product and service offerings, to fundamental changes of markets. The means can range from upgrading people's skills, to redesigning business practices, to significant infusions of technology, to fundamental changes of strategy. The scope of transformation can range from work activities to business functions, to overall organizations, to the enterprise as a whole.

The framework in Figure 1.2 has provided a useful categorization of a broad range of case studies of enterprise transformation. Considering transformation of markets, Amazon leveraged IT to redefine book buying, while Wal-Mart leveraged IT to redefine the retail industry. In these two instances at least, it can be argued that Amazon and Wal-Mart just grew; they did not transform. Nevertheless, their markets were transformed and competitors were forced to adapt.

Illustrations of transformation of offerings include UPS moving from being a package delivery company to a global supply chain management provider, IBM's transition from manufacturing to services, Motorola moving from battery eliminators to radios to cell phones, and CNN redefining news delivery. Examples of

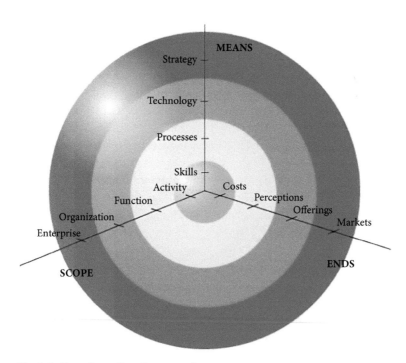

Fig. 1.2 Transformation Framework

transformation of perceptions include Dell repositioning computer buying, Star-bucks repositioning coffee purchases, and Victoria's Secret repositioning lingerie buying. The many instances of transforming business operations include Lockheed Martin merging three aircraft companies, Newell Rubbermaid resuscitating numerous home products companies, and Interface adopting green business practices.

Relative to our four public-private ecosystems, transformation often involves changing the rules of the game in the market, e.g., acquisition policies for military platforms for national security. Examples of transforming offerings include Social Security, Medicare, and the Affordable Care Act in healthcare delivery. Transformed operations include telemedicine in healthcare delivery and online education in higher education.

The costs and risks of transformation increase as the endeavor moves farther from the center in Figure 1.2. Initiatives focused on the center (in green) will typically involve well-known and mature methods and tools from industrial engineering and operations management. In contrast, initiatives towards the perimeter (in red) will often require substantial changes of products, services, channels, policies, laws, etc., as well as associated large investments.

It is important to note that successful transformations in the outer band of Figure 1.2 are likely to require significant investments in the inner bands also. In general, any level of transformation requires consideration of all subordinate levels. Thus, for example, successfully changing the market's perceptions of an enterprise's offerings is likely to also require enhanced operational excellence to underpin the new image being sought. As another illustration, significant changes of strategies often require new processes for decision making, e.g., for R&D investments.

I hasten to note that, at this point, I am only addressing what is likely to have to change, not how the changes can be accomplished. In particular, the success of transformation initiatives depends on gaining the support of stakeholders, managing their perceptions and expectations, and sustaining fundamental change (Rouse, 2001, 2006, 2007). Leading initiatives where these factors play major roles requires competencies in vision, leadership, strategy, planning, culture, collaboration and teamwork (Rouse, 2011). I will return to these issues in Chapters 2, 7 and 8.

Challenges

As indicated earlier, anticipated or experienced value deficiencies drive transformation, while redesigned or new work processes enable transformation. For public-private ecosystems, a central question concerns who invests in change and who gains the returns on investments. A related question is who pays the operating costs of new processes?

If one government agency invests in change while another government agency gains the returns, e.g., cost savings, progress can be impeded until a mechanism is created to, in effect, share costs and returns. This can be quite difficult as, unlike within a company, cross payments among agencies are quite rare. More typically, such issues are resolved in House and Senate committees in the U.S. Congress.

Two other challenges are quite important. First, measuring value deficiencies requires understanding the construct of value. Value is about outcomes or outputs, not inputs of budgets, staff, and facilities. I have had several senior executives in the government tell me that they spend most of their time securing their budgets, and the rest of their time defending their budgets.

Second, changing work processes requires understanding your processes. Government agencies, as well as healthcare providers and educational institutions, tend to think of themselves as a hierarchy of functions, supported by staffs and budgets. The notion of process flows does not come naturally. However, inadequate or faulty process flows are often the source of value deficiencies.

Finally, there is the threat of creative destruction (Schumpeter, 1942). From a broad perspective, creative destruction is a powerful, positive force. New value propositions, often enabled by new technologies, led by new, innovative competitors take markets away from established players. Jobs are created. The economy grows. People can, therefore, afford cars, TVs, smart phones, etc.

The story is not as positive for the incumbents. They are under constant pressure. They have to face the dilemma of running the organization they have while they try to become the organization they want. But, the organization they have is usually consuming all the money and talent. They need to address the balance between investing in getting better at what they are already doing versus investing in doing new things.

It is very difficult to achieve this balance. Most of the stakeholders are strongly committed to the status quo. They need resources and attention to keep the status quo functioning. Many of the stakeholders in the future have yet to arrive. Consequently, they are not very demanding. Creating a sense of urgency is usually essential to addressing this stalemate.

Various pundits express this in the sense of needing a "burning platform." A key is to identify leading indicators of both positive and negative changes. Then, one should look for evidence of these indicators, both externally in the economy and marketplace and internally in the enterprise and intraprise. The result can be stories of change that, hopefully, everyone can understand and find compelling (Yu, Serban & Rouse, 2013).

Creative destruction is much more likely to affect private sector players in a public-private ecosystem. Public sector players very rarely disappear. Nevertheless, creative destruction can upend an ecosystem when, for example, defense companies' workforces are unsustainable or fossil fuel companies lose revenues, and hence jobs, to renewable energy companies. Public sector players usually play key roles in sustaining the whole ecosystem.

Examples of Success

Fundamental change can be successfully pursued and achieved. IBM moved from relying on mainframe computer sales to selling software and services. Microsoft moved beyond milking Windows and Microsoft Office to embrace the Internet. Apple transformed itself from selling computers to providing elegant digital devices. IBM had its highest share price in 1990 but was on the path to losing billions in 1993. Louis Gerstner, IBM CEO,

. . . is widely credited with transforming IBM into a customer-focused global enterprise dedicated to leadership in services and technology. Mr. Gerstner joined IBM in April 1993. Through year-end 2001, the company's share price increased more than 800%, and its market value grew by $180 billion. The company also gained market share in key strategic areas, including servers, software, storage and microelectronics. IBM had received more U.S. patents than any other company for nine consecutive years. (IBM, 2002).

Microsoft at first dismissed the Internet and Netscape's web browser, introduced in 1994. By May of 1995, however, Microsoft CEO Bill Gates had thrown his company wholeheartedly into joining the "Internet tidal wave." They released Internet Explorer as an add-on for Windows 95. More recently, Microsoft introduced Azure cloud computing services in 2010 and now is second in market share behind Amazon Web Services.

Apple was on the brink of fizzling out, struggling to find a consistently profitable source of revenue. Instead of continuing to aimlessly pursue marginal product ideas, Apple, with Steve Jobs again leading, began to focus once more on creating beautiful consumer electronics, starting with the iMac in 1998. The iPod was an even bigger success, selling over 100 million units within six years of its 2001 launch. The iPhone, another smash hit, was released in 2007 and resulted in enormous year-over-year increases in sales. The iPad followed in 2010. Apple changed its name in 2007 from Apple Computer to just Apple.

Success is possible. However, as is evident from these three examples, leadership is crucial. If top leaders remain stewards of the status quo, fundamental change will not happen. Leadership is the most important competency along with vision, strategy, communications, and collaboration (Rouse, 2011).

Role of Innovation

Invention is the creation of a new process or device, while innovation is creation of change in the marketplace (Rouse, 1992, 1993). The marketplace can be for art, automobiles, computers, consumer products, or medicine, to name just a few ecosystems. From this broader perspective, innovation is context dependent. Some innovations are driven by inventions. Others are driven by needs—necessity is the mother of invention. New understanding drives others, e.g., discovery of bacteria.

In the context of public-private ecosystems, markets can be conceptualized as constituencies. Constituencies can be military missions, public health, or perhaps a targeted group, for example, patients or students. An intended innovation becomes an actual innovation once the targeted constituencies embrace it.

Consider the differences between automobiles and medicine. The underlying phenomena are quite different. Automotive is driven by inventions in terms of originations of technologies, manufacturing processes, and value propositions. Medicine is driven by epidemics, war and biomedical research. Both of these timelines are well documented and later discussed.

Measures of innovation depend on the context. Percent of sales from new offerings makes sense for automobiles, but not healthcare delivery. Number of deaths avoided is likely a better metric for medicine. Increased Quality Adjusted Life Years is another metric. Notice the contrast. For automobiles, the key metrics are about what *did* happen—sales—while for medicine, the key metrics are about what *did not* happen—poor quality of life and deaths.

Given the contrast I have drawn this far, what can be said about innovation in other arenas? Airplanes are much like automobiles. Education is much like healthcare. Let's add computing to the comparison. The following observations seem relevant.

- Automotive: Devising means to make automobile driving easier, less expensive, more enjoyable, and safer—for consumers
- Medicine: Discovering the causes of morbidity and mortality; and the understanding of how to thwart these causes—for patients
- Computing: Developing means to solve complex computational problems for business and government—later for consumers

In the next section, I elaborate these and other differences.

Differences Among Domains

Innovations in consumer or business markets have been subjects of much research, but there can be innovations in, for example, scientific techniques. Of course, one could argue that the scientific community is then the constituency. Perhaps innovation happens when a targeted population changes how it does things.

In automobiles, we look at what people buy. In science, we look at what people cite. For consumers, we might look at what people consume or buy. In medicine it may be clinicians voting, not patients. Same for expert service providers in general. Thus, the population of potential adopters targeted is key.

Another factor is the infrastructure needed to adopt something so it can become an innovation. This held up electricity but, once powerplants and utility lines were in place, eased the adoption of television—and many other inventions. A key to innovation, assuming needed infrastructure, is adoption by some population.

What does this mean in aerospace, automobiles, communications, computers, healthcare, medicine, etc., as well as art, education, economics, geography, history, humanities, politics, etc.? How do we measure innovation and visualize measurements in each of these domains? Let's start with just two domains.

Innovation in Technology

Does a technology trend change shape as the technology enables innovation, e.g., corporate and venture investments in AI? Gartner's "hype cycle" model exhibits an interesting shape change in terms of expectations rather than adoptions. Clearly, there is not always a linear path from idea to R&D to innovation.

It is interesting to understand what metrics are used to place a technology on this hype curve—"expectations" define the Y-axis and time the X-axis (Basole, 2018). It is also interesting that once it is successful, expectations are lower. When does something become an innovation and when does it cease to be an innovation, e.g., air conditioning, indoor toilets?

We analyzed ten years of **IEEE Spectrum**'s annual issue on "Top Ten Tech Cars" to assess their abilities to predict innovations. We employed a huge data set of the exact configuration of each car sold globally over a decade. There were mixed results, probably meriting a grade of C. However, these annual special issues do raise expectations. This analysis also led to the realization that a technology has "made it" when it is common on Honda Accords and Toyota Camrys (Liu & Rouse, 2015).

Gartner (2020) defines the phases of the hype cycle as follows:

- "A potential technology breakthrough kicks things off.
- Early publicity produces a number of success stories.
- Interest wanes as experiments and implementations fail to deliver.
- More instances of the benefits of the technology start to crystallize and become understood.
- Mainstream adoption starts to take off, as criteria for adoption are more clearly defined."

The hype cycle is an interesting representation of technological innovation. Expectations surge, propelled by exuberant marketing, plummet when expectations are not met, and eventually recover as value propositions mature and deliver real value. Eventually innovations are absorbed into everyday life and we no longer think of them as innovations. Indoor plumbing and electricity are good examples.

The exuberance of marketing is relatively recent. I could not find any **New York Times** articles portending the likely advent of indoor plumbing and electricity. It is interesting to imagine hype cycles for these important innovations. It took well over 50 years for Edison's vision to affect almost every home. It took over a century for the majority of homes in the developed world to have indoor plumbing. In contrast, the smart phone became ubiquitous in ten years.

How could the innovation of the smart phone happen so much more quickly? The answer, as noted earlier, is infrastructure. The smart phone could leverage the Internet and cellular technologies, not to mention electricity. Such infrastructure was not available to Edison, nor was it to Isaiah Rogers who first demonstrated indoor plumbing in 1829 in the Tremont Hotel in Boston.

The relevant metric here is quite straightforward. What percentage of the population is benefitting from the innovation? When every Accord or Camry comes with a rear-facing backup camera as standard equipment, camera technology has made it. When every vehicle has this capability, few could imagine a vehicle without it. Backup cameras, as this point, no longer seem like innovations.

Innovation in Art

Let's move from technology to art. Are there hype cycles for visual arts (painting, photography, sculpture), literature (fiction, non-fiction), performing arts (dance, improv, opera, symphony, theatre), and culinary arts? It is difficult to imagine anticipating the conceptual innovations of Picasso, Matisse or Warhol, or the experimental innovations of Mondrian, Kandinsky, or Pollack (Galenson, 2006). It is extremely unlikely that the usually prescient projections of *The Economist* would have heralded these innovations, or that Gartner would publish hype cycles for art.

Innovation in art differs from innovation in technology (Borstlap, 2016). Only occasionally do these innovations involve technology adoption, e.g., materials or techniques. Further, adoption does not mean that eventually everybody embraces it. For instance, after Cubism emerged in 1907–11, all the other artists did not become Cubists.

Orchestras that focused on Baroque music, e.g., Bach, in the 17th century did not anticipate subsequent Classical music, e.g., Mozart and, later yet, Romantic music, e.g., Chopin. There were no European fan magazines heralding the possibilities of these innovations. Yet, all three musical forms have endured as has indoor plumbing and air conditioning.

Innovation metrics for art might be adoption by art museums and orchestras. Once almost all orchestras included saxophones, invented by Adolphe Sax in 1841, one could argue this instrument was a genuine innovation. Similarly, once almost all major museums included exhibitions of Cubist art, you could say it had arrived.

I hasten to note that this is not how art historians view innovation. Instead, they would assess how the invention affected the artistic community. If other artists extolled the invention, despite not necessarily adopting it themselves, it would over time be seen as an innovation.

There are several significant differences between innovation in art and technology. Aesthetic innovation can involve creative adoption and extensions of old paradigms, sometimes abetted by technological innovations. Some artistic innovations involve leveraging technological innovations, e.g., robots, to the purposes and intentions of these domains. However, technology is inherently different because of constant progress—few people want an innovative new outhouse.

A fascinating crossing of borders between technology and art involves the impact of Poincare's famous book on geometry, which led to Einstein's relativity theory and Picassos' cubism (Miller, 2008). Science and art drew on the same intellectual roots to invent new conceptualizations of space and time. It would be quite difficult to imagine anyone having predicted these outcomes—unlikely that there would have been a hype cycle for geometry.

Measures and Timelines

Various innovation timelines have been published:

- Arts (Wikipedia, 2020b)
- Automotive (Jardine, 2020)
- Computing (Zimmermann, 2017)
- Consumer Products (Felton, 2008)
- Medicine (Wikipedia, 2020a)

All the timelines have the dates when successive innovations happened and often the name of the innovators. What are not presented are hype cycles, or equivalent, for how these nascent innovations emerged, struggled, gained acceptance and were finally fully adopted. It is also important to note that many of these innovations displaced earlier innovations. For example, electric motors in factories displaced steam engines that drove belts among machines.

These five domains can be contrasted in terms of the characteristics of innovations and measures associated with these characteristics. It is very clear that no one set of metrics applies across all domains. Clusters of metrics, with domain-specific instances within each cluster, are defined in the next section.

Nevertheless, there are common behavioral and social underpinnings of innovation. All of the domains of interest involve similar biological, physiological, psychological, and social phenomena, as they all involve people interacting and performing (Rouse, 2003; Rouse & Rouse, 2004). While there are variations of cognitive abilities, attitudes, and motivations, all the players are humans, perhaps recently with AI-based cognitive assistance.

Creativity can be important for inventing something new, and also be central to facilitating its adoption to become an innovation. In a review of studies of creativity (Rouse, 1986), it was found that people judged to be creative had three common tendencies. They were broad information seekers across a wide range of sources. They mixed multiple approaches to processing information. Finally, they perceived connections and distinctions that others did not. Picasso and his colleagues reading Poincare's geometry treatise seem like a good example.

Reviewing and contrasting innovations in technology and art, and considering how these observations apply to business, education, government, and law, the range of metrics has to broaden. For example, while innovations often involve adoption of technologies, they can involve new value propositions such as bundling or un-bundling offerings, customer services, etc., and new approaches to marketing, sales, and service, as well as brick and mortar stores versus online.

For example, Nokia dominated the cell phone market providing less and less expensive phones globally. Apple came out with a $500 iPhone and took the market away. One could argue that Apple's innovation reflected the recognition that people wanted a general-purpose digital device that also included a phone; even though people did not yet fully know they needed this.

Technology innovations are the best documented with lots of plots of adoption curves. The rate of adoption is highly dependent on available infrastructure, for example, as noted earlier, power plants and utility lines for Edison and charging stations for battery electric vehicles. These adoption curves, such as with hype cycles, usually start from when the capability is first introduced to the market rather than when the enabling technologies were researched and invented, often many years earlier.

Typical measures on innovation include:

- Number of users or units sold/population of potential users—more people adopted smart phones than surgeons adopted robotic surgery
- Total revenues—very few aircraft carriers are sold, but they cost many billions of dollars
- Extent to which a technology, process, technique etc. enables something that was previously impossible—a new medical device or new musical sound
- Extent to which humans' workflow, performance, safety, and health are significantly improved—reduction of medical errors and safety in crashes
- Extent to which performance and appreciation of performance are substantially enhanced—speeds of race cars and quality of music

Metrics are concerned with how well innovation happens in terms of both timing and magnitude. Figure 1.3 illustrates this for consumers' adoptions of technology.

These contrasts emphasize the need to identify "markets" for inventions, ideas, new paradigms, etc. Whose acceptance and endorsement of an idea matters to an idea being deemed an innovation? Related issues are the size of markets and what other ideas are competing for adoption. Betamax would have become an innovation if VHS had not emerged from JVC and, in contrast to Sony, shared the technology with other firms.

Measures Versus Domains

Table 1.2 presents three clusters of measures and maps them to six different innovation ecosystems. The three clusters are:

- Performance—new, better, faster, cheaper
- Market—market share, revenues, profits
- Change—perceptions, attitudes, commitments, behaviors

Innovations in medicine and technology relate to performance metrics. Innovations in autos and technology relate to market metrics. Innovations in art, education, and

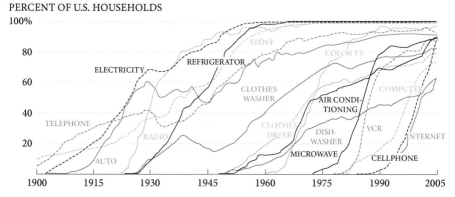

Fig. 1.3 Consumers' Adoption of Technologies (Felton, 2008)

Table 1.2 Relevance of Clusters of Measures to Different Domains.

Metrics	Domains					
	Arts	Autos	Educ.	Gov't	Med.	Tech.
Does something new					✓	✓
Does it better					✓	✓
Does it faster					✓	✓
Does it cheaper					✓	✓
Impacts "market" significantly		✓				✓
Impacts market share		✓				✓
Impacts revenues		✓				✓
Impacts profits		✓				✓
Changes people's perceptions	✓		✓	✓		
Changes people's attitudes	✓		✓	✓		
Changes people's commitments	✓		✓	✓		
Changes people's behaviors	✓		✓	✓		

governments relate to change metrics. Within each cell of Table 1.2, especially for the change metrics, the perceptions, attitudes, commitments, and behaviors whose change would warrant designation as an innovation will depend on context.

Innovation in Public-Private Ecosystems

Innovation may or may not involve one or more inventions in a classical sense of technology inventions. It is useful to think in terms of interventions when the context is a public-private ecosystem. It is also important to think of mechanisms whereby an intervention can be implemented. Mechanisms can include policies, regulations, incentives, and investments.

Important mechanisms also include communications and education. Often, many of the stakeholders in potential innovations are not participants in open forums and discussions and debates of decision alternatives. The overarching concern is with employing mechanisms that will result in well-informed, as well as correctly informed, stakeholders.

As shown in Table 1.2, the measures of innovation of interest include the extent to which interventions and mechanisms result in

- Changes of people's perceptions
- Changes of people's attitudes
- Changes of people's commitments
- Changes of people's behaviors

Chapter 2 discusses approaches to these changes. Chapters 3–6 illustrate these approaches in four public-private ecosystems.

Summary

The phenomenon of innovation seems broadly applicable, but the context matters in terms of the nature of what is considered innovative and how it is measured. New products, services, ideas, experiences, etc. have to be assessed and measured differently. Such considerations concern monitoring and projecting potential innovations.

Another essential concern is how best to foster innovation. In all domains, the vast majority of inventions do not lead to innovations. Most people and organizations are much more inventive than innovative, despite the claims on resumes and marketing brochures. Innovation is hard work.

Edison famously said, "Genius is one percent inspiration and ninety-nine percent perspiration." The perspiration is central to transforming a creative invention into a true innovation. The enthusiasms of many people and organizations wane when they come to realize this, whether they are artists, clinicians, engineers, or politicians.

Yet, there is another phenomenon that I have encountered working with hundreds of organizations. Many inventors simply do not believe that the inherently low probabilities of success apply to them. Consequently, they doggedly invest themselves, almost irrationally, in getting their creation to "market," whatever that means in their domain. While the odds remain very low, we all benefit from this determination and the few that actually become innovations.

Overview of Book

This chapter has set the stage by defining and illustrating the concept of public-private ecosystems. The notion of enterprise transformation was introduced and fundamental findings summarized. The broad construct of innovation was reviewed and its relevance in public-private ecosystems discussed.

Chapter 2 outlines the analytic framework I have employed to address transforming public-private ecosystems. The idea of "wicked problems" is reviewed and informs how best to think about public-private ecosystems. The methodology of human-centered design is discussed as it applies to such ecosystems. The result is a nominal approach for addressing all ecosystems. Finally, I discuss how to perform economic valuations of transformation-level innovations.

Chapters 3–6 address the four public-private ecosystems central to this book:

- National Security
- Healthcare Delivery
- Higher Education
- Energy & Climate

I define and illustrate each of these ecosystems, summarize past innovations, propose alternative future innovations, and apply the analytic framework from Chapter 2 to these candidates.

Chapter 7 crosses ecosystems. Lessons learned from past innovations in the ecosystems are summarized and elaborated. An investment portfolio that crosses the four ecosystems is elaborated and evaluated. The focus is on the economic and technical validity of this portfolio.

Chapter 8 is concerned with enabling change. How can we get society to buy into and support transformation of these ecosystems? This is the realm of behavioral and social science, leavened by economics and politics. Key elements include leadership, vision, strategy, collaboration, and communications.

Conclusions

This book is about understanding and enabling innovation in complex organizational, political, and social systems. These systems are such that no decision authority can unilaterally decide and implement particular policies, regulations, incentives, or investments without first cultivating sufficient stakeholder support to overcome objections and impedances to progress.

This book does not argue for specific solutions to transforming the four ecosystems addressed. Instead, it suggests alternative transformative paths and outlines a systemic process for developing solutions with substantial involvement of key stakeholders. In this way, transformation is a behavioral, social, and political process of identifying, refining, and gaining commitments to productive ways forward.

References

Arrington, B.T. (2011). Industry and economy during the Civil War. In NPS, ed., *The Civil War Remembered* **(pp 1-8)**. Washington, DC: National Park Service

Asplund, F., Bjork, J., Magnusson, M., and Patrick, A.J. (2021). The genesis of public-private innovation systems. Bias and challenges. *Technological Forecasting & Social Change*, 162, 120378

Autio, E., and Thomas, L.D.W. (2014). Innovation ecosystems. In M. Dodgson, D. Gann, and N. Phillips, eds, *Oxford Handbook of Innovation Management*. Oxford, UK: Oxford University Press

Basole, R.C. (2018). Visualizing ecosystems of hype. *Proceedings of the 51st Hawaii International Conference on System Sciences*, pp. 4964–4973

Bernstein, P.L. (2005). *Wedding of the Waters: The Erie Canal and the Making of a Great Nation*. New York: Norton

Borstlap, J. (2016). Is innovation in the arts a good thing? *The Imaginative Conservative*, March 15

Donahue, J.D., and Zeckhauser, R.J. (2006). Public-private collaboration. In M. Moran, M. Rein, and R.E. Goodin, eds., *Oxford Handbook of Public Policy* (Chapter 24). Oxford, UK: Oxford University Press

Dunleavy, B. (2018). Did New Deal programs help end the Great Depression? *History* https://www.history.com/news/new-deal-effects-great-depression

Economist (2020). Segregation still blights the lives of African-Americans. *The Economist*, July 9

Felton, N. (2008). Consumptions spreads faster today. *New York Times*, February 10.

Fishback, P. (2017). How successful was the New Deal? The microeconomic impact of New Deal spending and lending policies in the 1930s. *Journal of Economic Literature*, 55 (4), 1435–1485

Galenson, D.W. (2006). *Analyzing Artistic Innovation: The Greatest Breakthroughs of the Twentieth Century*. Cambridge, MA: National Bureau of Economic Research.

Gartner (2020). *Gartner Hype Cycle* https://www.gartner.com/en/research/methodologies/gartner-hype-cycle. Accessed 08-07-20

Hileman, J., Kallstenius, I., Hayha, T., Palm, C., and Cornell, S. (2020). Keystone actors do not act alone: A business ecosystem perspective on sustainability in the global clothing industry." *PLOS One*. 15 (10), e0241453

IBM (2002). Samuel J. Palmisano Elected IBM CEO; Louis V. Gerstner, Jr. to Remain Chairman Through 2002. IDM Press Release, January 29

Jardine (2020). *Timeline of Innovations in Automobiles*. Lancaster, UK: Jardine Motor, https://news.jardinemotors.co.uk/lifestyle/the-history-of-car-technologyAccessed 06-17-20

Liu, C. and Rouse, W.B. (2015). Ten years of Top Ten Tech Cars: An analysis. *IEEE Spectrum*, April 1

Maltin, E. (2019). What successful public-private partnerships do. *Harvard Business Review*, 98(1), January 8

Miller, A.J. (2008). *Einstein, Picasso: Space, Time and the Beauty that Causes Havoc*. New York: Basic Books

Moore, James F. (1993). Predators and prey: A new ecology of competition. *Harvard Business Review*, 71(3),May–June, 75–86

Moore, James F. (1997). *The Death of Competition: Leadership & Strategy in the Age of Business Ecosystems*. New York: Harper Business

Roehrich, J.K., Lewis, M.A., and George, G. (2014). Are public-private partnerships a healthy option? A systematic literature review. *Social Science & Medicine*, 113, 110–119

Rouse, W.B. (1986). A note on the nature of creativity in engineering: Implications for supporting system design. *Information Processing & Management*, 22 (4), 279–285

Rouse, W.B. (1992). *Strategies for Innovation: Creating Successful Products, Systems, and Organizations*. New York: Wiley

Rouse, W.B. (1993). *Catalysts for Change: Concepts and Principles for Enabling Innovation*. New York: Wiley

Rouse, W.B. (2001). *Essential Challenges of Strategic Management*. New York: Wiley

Rouse, W.B. (2003) Invention and innovation in technology and art. In B.B. Borys and C. Wittenberg, ed., *From Muscles to Music: A Festschrift to Celebrate the 60th Birthday of Gunnar Johannsen* (pp. 140–151). Kassel, Germany: University of Kassel Press

Rouse, W.B. (2005a). Enterprises as systems: Essential challenges and approaches to transformation. *Journal of Systems Engineering*, 8 (2), 138–150

Rouse, W.B. (2005b). A theory of enterprise transformation, *Journal of Systems Engineering*, 8 (4), 279–295

Rouse, W.B. (ed.). (2006). *Enterprise Transformation: Understanding and Enabling Fundamental Change*. New York: Wiley

Rouse, W.B. (2007). *People and Organizations: Explorations of Human-Centered Design*. New York: Wiley

Rouse, W.B. (2011). Necessary competencies for transforming an enterprise, *Journal of Enterprise Transformation*, 1 (1), 71–9

Rouse, W.B. (2021). *Failure Management: Malfunctions of Technologies, Organizations, and Society*. Oxford, UK: Oxford University Press

Rouse, W.B., and Rouse, R.K. (2004). Teamwork in the performing arts. *Proceedings of the IEEE*, 92 (4), 606–615

Sablik, T. (2020). Electrifying Rural America. *Econ Focus*. First Quarter, 24–26 https://www.richmondfed.org/publications/research/econ_focus/2020/q1/economic_history

Schumpeter, J. (1942). *Capitalism, Socialism, and Democracy*. New York: Harper

Teixeira, R. and Halpin, J. (2011). *The Origins and Evolution of Progressive Economics*. Washington, DC: Center for American Progress

Weingroff, R.F. (1996). Federal-Aid Highway Act of 1956: Creating the Interstate System. *Public Roads*, 60 (1). Summer

Wikipedia (2020a). *Timeline of Innovations in Medicine*. San Francisco: Wikipedia, The Free Encyclopedia, https://en.wikipedia.org/wiki/Timeline_of_medicine_and_medical_technology, Accessed 06-17–20

Wikipedia (2020b). *Timeline of Invention in the Arts*. San Francisco: Wikipedia, The Free Encyclopedia, https://en.wikipedia.org/wiki/Timeline_for_invention_in_the_arts, Accessed 07-19-20

Wright, G. (2006). The economics of the Civil Rights revolution. In W.O. Moore, Jr. and O.V. Burton, eds, *Toward the Meeting of the Waters: Currents in the Civil Rights Movement of South Carolina During the Twentieth Century* (pp 1-27). Columbia, SC: University of South Carolina Press

Yu, X., Serban, N. and Rouse, W.B. (2013). The demographics of change: Enterprise characteristics and behaviors that influence enterprise transformation. *Journal of Enterprise Transformation*, 3 (4), 285–306

Zimmermann, K.A. (2017). History of computers: A brief timeline, *Live Science*, September 7

2

Wicked Problems and Human-Centered Design

This chapter addresses the following questions:

- How should we think about public-private ecosystems?
- What are multi-level models and how can they help?
- What are complex adaptive systems?
- How can wicked problems be addressed?
- What is human-centered design?
- How can human-centered design be applied to wicked problems?
- What are interactive visualizations and how can they help?
- How can investments in solving wicked problems be economically valued?
- How can investment decision-making be approached as a portfolio?

This chapter presents an overall approach to addressing transformation and innovation in public-private ecosystems. I begin by characterizing the complex nature of these ecosystems and central challenges in addressing this complexity, including how to represent the phenomena that underlie this complexity.

The notion of "wicked problems" is reviewed in terms of how the characteristics of such problems are manifested in the four ecosystems. This leads to presentation of an overall approach to addressing such problems. This approach is strongly based on the concept of "human-centered design." I discuss how interactive visualizations can enable explorations by stakeholders.

I then review approaches to economic valuation of alternative innovations that possibly could contribute to transformation. Not surprisingly, how one attaches value to investments, operating costs, and returns on investments can have an enormous impact on the relative value of alternatives.

Economic valuations directly affect decision-making related to if and how to proceed. I employ a multi-level investment rubric to move beyond simple yes or no decisions to designing portfolios of investments. In this way, transformation is no longer "betting the organization" or not, but creating a portfolio of investments with each individual investment contributing in differing ways.

Transforming Public-Private Ecosystems. William B. Rouse, Oxford University Press.
© William B. Rouse (2022). DOI: 10.1093/oso/9780192866530.003.0002

Multi-Level Ecosystems

The nature of human and social phenomena within our four ecosystems is a central consideration. Systems where such phenomena play substantial roles are often considered to belong to a class of systems termed complex adaptive systems (Rouse, 2000, 2008). Systems of this type have the following characteristics:

- They tend to be **nonlinear, dynamic** and do not inherently reach fixed equilibrium points. The resulting system behaviors may appear to be random or chaotic.
- They are composed of **independent agents** whose behaviors can be described as based on physical, psychological, or social rules, rather than being completely dictated by the physical dynamics of the system.
- Agents' needs or desires, reflected in their rules, are not homogeneous and, therefore, their **goals and behaviors are likely to differ or even conflict**—these conflicts or competitions tend to lead agents to adapt to each other's behaviors.
- Agents are **intelligent and learn** as they experiment and gain experience, perhaps via "meta" rules, and consequently change behaviors. Thus, overall system properties inherently change over time.
- Adaptation and learning tends to result in **self-organization** and patterns of behavior that emerge rather than being designed into the system. The nature of such emergent behaviors may range from valuable innovations to unfortunate accidents.
- There is **no single point(s) of control**—system behaviors are often unpredictable and uncontrollable, and no one is "in charge." Consequently, the behaviors of complex adaptive systems usually can be influenced more than they can be controlled.

As might be expected, understanding and influencing systems having these characteristics creates significant complications. For example, the use of simulations to represent such systems often does not yield the same results each time they are run. Random variation may lead to varying "tipping points" among stakeholders for different simulation runs. Simulation models can be useful in the exploration of leading indicators of the different tipping points and in assessing potential mitigations for undesirable outcomes.

Underlying Phenomena

There are a variety of challenges in addressing complex adaptive systems. The first challenge is to understand the central phenomena that underlie an ecosystem. What are the "physics" of the ecosystem and the rules of the game? Subject matter experts are usually essential to make sure central phenomena are considered and understood.

Second, one needs to understand the stakeholders associated with each of these phenomena. Who are the economic, technical, and user influences? Are there social and political influences? How are influences empowered and resourced? What are their values, concerns, and perceptions?

Third, one needs to understand how to impact the central phenomena. Typically, impacts are through stakeholders or agents. One needs to also understand stakeholders' likely responses to your attempts to impact them. You need to understand how to cultivate positive responses to your initiatives.

Relationships Among Phenomena

I have found it to be quite useful to think of ecosystems as having multiple levels that typically vary in terms of levels of abstraction. In April 2008, I co-chaired a Workshop on Engineering the Learning Healthcare Delivery System hosted by the National Academy of Engineering and the Institute of Medicine (now National Academy of Medicine). On the morning of the second day of the workshop, my task was to summarize the findings of the first day. The speakers on the first day had included clinicians, informaticists, engineers, and computer scientists. It was clear to me that these various experts were talking about different levels of the system.

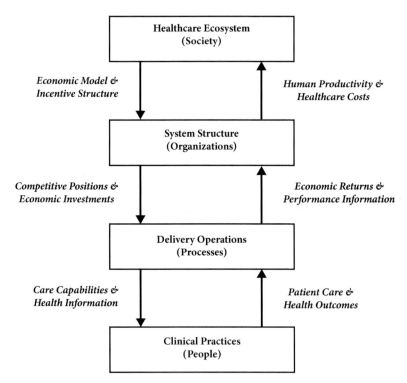

Fig. 2.1 Architecture of Healthcare Delivery Enterprise

Figure 2.1 was the essence of my report that morning (Rouse, 2009; Rouse & Cortese, 2010). The efficiencies that can be gained at the lowest level (clinical practices) are limited by nature of the next level (delivery operations). For example, functionally organized practices are much less efficient than delivery organized around processes.

Similarly, the level above (system structure) limits efficiencies that can be gained in operations. Functional operations are driven by organizations structured around specialties, e.g., anesthesiology and radiology. And, of course, efficiencies in system structure are limited by the healthcare ecosystem in which organizations operate. Differing experiences of other countries provide ample evidence of this.

The fee-for-service model central to healthcare in the United States assures that provider income is linked to activities rather than outcomes. The focus on disease and restoration of health rather than wellness and productivity assures that healthcare expenditures will be viewed as costs rather than investments. That morning, I argued that recasting of "the problem" in terms of outcomes characterized by wellness and productivity may enable identification and pursuit of efficiencies that could not be imagined within our current frame of reference.

Figure 2.1 provided a framework for analysis of healthcare delivery that enabled multi-level explanations across people, processes, organizations, and society.

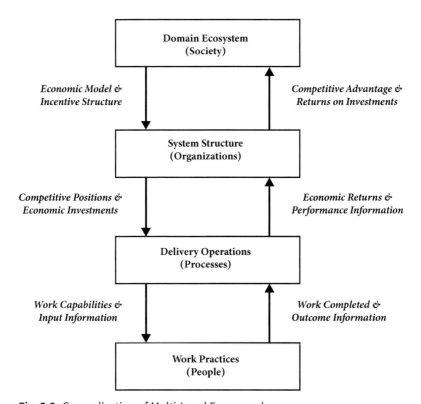

Fig. 2.2 Generalization of Multi-Level Framework

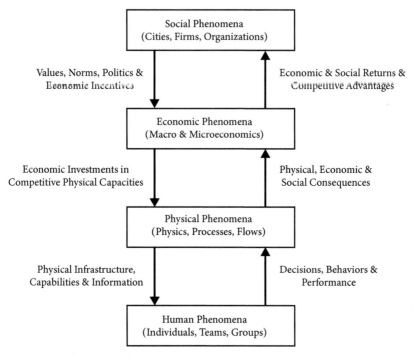

Fig. 2.3 Further Generalized Multi-Level Framework

Figure 2.2 provides a generalization of the framework applicable to many domains. Humans interact with processes that are enabled by economic investments that are made within the context of society's values, norms, and incentives.

Experiences with a wide range of applications led to the development of an overall methodology for modeling and visualization of complex systems and enterprises (Rouse, 2015). The overall framework was further generalized as shown in Figure 2.3, in part to better align with the guidance provided by this methodology.

The generalization of Figure 2.3 has to be tailored to each context and the questions of interest. For example, the physical level may enable human activity, e.g., in cities, or human activity may affect the physical environment, e.g., in climate change. Consequently, the generalized framework is simply the starting point for a problem solving process that always results in morphing the representation to fit the problem. In Chapters 3–6, the multi-level framework is tailored to the ecosystem addressed in each chapter.

Wicked Problems

Transforming a complex adaptive ecosystem easily qualifies as a "wicked problem." Horst Rittel, almost five decades ago, characterized addressing such systems

Table 2.1 Characteristics of Wicked Problems in Four Ecosystems.

Problem Attributes	Public–Private Ecosystem			
	National Security	Healthcare Delivery	Higher Education	Energy & Climate
No definitive problem formulation	Symptoms not uniquely attributable to problems	Symptoms not uniquely attributable to problems	Symptoms not uniquely attributable to problems	Symptoms not uniquely attributable to problems
Difficult to measure success	Difficult to attribute consequences to interventions	Difficult to attribute consequences to interventions	Difficult to attribute consequences to interventions	Difficult to attribute consequences to interventions
Solutions not correct or incorrect	Cannot "solve" national security	Cannot "solve" healthcare delivery	Cannot "solve" higher education	Cannot "solve" energy & climate
No solution best practices	Hindered by lack of repeated experiences	Hindered by lack of repeated experiences	Hindered by lack of repeated experiences	Hindered by lack of repeated experiences
Multiple problem explanations	Stakeholders have varying explanations	Stakeholders have varying explanations	Stakeholders have varying explanations	Stakeholders have varying explanations
Multiple interrelated problems	Cannot isolate unique national security problem	Cannot isolate unique healthcare delivery problem	Cannot isolate unique higher education problem	Cannot isolate unique energy & climate problem
Lack of definitive validity tests	Cannot know when national security is solved	Cannot know when healthcare delivery is solved	Cannot know when higher education is solved	Cannot know when energy & climate are solved
Change inhibits learning	Constantly evolving problems inhibit learning	Constantly evolving problems inhibit learning	Constantly evolving problems inhibit learning	Constantly evolving problems inhibit learning
Every problem is unique	Difficult to employ past solutions	Difficult to employ past solutions	Difficult to employ past solutions	Difficult to employ past solutions
Responsible decision makers	Humans responsible for successful transformation	Humans responsible for successful transformation	Humans responsible for successful transformation	Humans responsible for successful transformation

as wicked problems. A wicked problem is a social or cultural problem laced with incomplete or contradictory knowledge, large numbers of people and opinions involved, substantial economic burdens, and the interconnected nature of these problems with other problems. Problems such as poverty, sustainability, equality, health and wellness, and climate change challenge our nation and our world.

Consider Rittel's ten characteristics of wicked problems (Rittel & Webber, 1973). Wicked problems have no definitive formulation, i.e., they are not exemplars of any standard taxonomy of problems. It is difficult to measure or claim success in solving wicked problems, in part because solutions can be only better or worse, but not correct or incorrect.

Given the uniqueness of each wicked problem, there are no best practices that can be adopted from previous problem solving. This is due, in part, to every problem being a symptom of other problems. This is aggravated by there always being multiple explanations for problems, especially when there are many stakeholders.

Solutions to problems involve single chances of success because one is trying to address a moving target driven by the complex adaptive nature of the ecosystem. Consequently, solution strategies have no definitive validity tests. Dealing with such situations requires that policy decision-makers be empowered and responsible, keeping in mind that rarely is there one decision authority.

Table 2.1 summarizes how these ten characteristics are manifested in our four ecosystems. I elaborate each of these assessments in Chapters 3–6.

Perspectives on Social Systems

The approach I have adopted in this book is based on systems science and engineering. Thus, public-private ecosystems are characterized as complex networks of stakeholders and relationships that need to be understood and then incentivized and motivated to engage in transformation. There are other approaches to characterizing these ecosystems. In this section, I review several of these approaches.

Three perspectives account for much of sociology.

- **Structural Functionalism** is concerned with relationships between the parts of society. Functionalists argue that society is created and sustained by social consensus in which members of society agree upon, and work together to achieve, what is best for society as a whole.
- **Symbolic Interactionism** is focused on the use of symbols, with particular emphasis on face to face interactions. Proponents of this perspective are concerned with symbols and details of everyday life, what these symbols mean, and how people interact with each other.
- The **Conflict Perspective** emphasizes competition for scarce resources and how the elite control the poor and weak. Proponents of this perspective attribute

humanitarian efforts, altruism, democracy, civil rights, and other positive aspects of society to designs to control the masses, rather than preserving society and social order.

Polanyi's classic book (1944) deals with transformation in terms of the social and political upheavals associated with the rise of the market economy. He argues that this has resulted in humanity's economic mentality changing. Prior to this transformation, people based their economies on reciprocity and redistribution across personal and communal relationships. Industrialization and increasing state influence led to competitive markets that undermined these previous social tendencies, replacing them with formal institutions that aimed to promote a self-regulating market economy.

This encouraged the myth of humans' propensity toward rational free trade. However, he asserts instead that "man's economy, as a rule, is submerged in his social relationships." He proposes an alternative ethnographic economic approach called "substantivism", in opposition to "formalism" —he coined both terms. He argues that markets cannot solely be understood through economic theory, as they are embedded in social and political logics, which makes it necessary to take into account politics.

Polanyi argues that the term "*economics*" has two meanings: the formal meaning refers to economics as the logic of rational action and decision-making, as a rational choice between the alternative uses of limited means. The second, substantive meaning, however, presupposes neither rational decision-making nor conditions of scarcity. It simply refers to the study of how humans make a living from their social and natural environment, which may or may not involve utility maximization. Anthropologists have embraced the substantive position as it does not impose western cultural assumptions on other societies.

Giddens (1979) provides a broad view both historically and culturally. He argues that there is a duality of structure by which social practice, his principal unit of investigation, has both a structural and an agency component. The structural environment constrains individual behavior, but it also makes it possible. Social actors are reflexive and monitor the ongoing flow of activities and structural conditions to adapt their actions to their evolving understandings.

Giddens calls this two-tiered, interpretive and dialectical relationship between social scientific knowledge and human practices the double hermeneutic. He also stresses the importance of power, which provides means to ends, and hence is directly involved in the actions of every person. He emphasizes the transformative capacity of people to change the social and material world.

Habermas (1988) addresses legitimation and communication in his studies of the origins, nature, and evolution of public opinion in democratic societies. Feudal societies were transformed into bourgeois liberal constitutional entities that distinguished between the public and private realms, including a public sphere for rational-critical political debate leading to a new phenomenon called public opinion. Spearheading this shift was the growth of a literary public sphere in which the bourgeoisie learned to critically reflect upon itself and its role in society.

Habermas then traces the transition from the liberal bourgeois public sphere to the modern mass society of the social welfare state. The result was the rise of mass societies characterized by consumer capitalism in the twentieth century. Holub (1991) elaborates the centrality of Habermas' perspective on communication and understanding. Kellner (2000) elaborates Habermas' notion of structural transformation and necessary conditions for a genuine democracy.

The scope of Habermas' approach to transformation considers society over centuries. This book is not so ambitious in that the focus is on particular ecosystems, e.g., health and education, rather than all of society. Further, the time frame is decades at most, rather than centuries.

Luhmann (1995) focuses on a general theory of systems, with emphasis on understanding meaning and communication. He is interested in cybernetic models that no longer require the assumption of the external observer. The cybernetic view of people, organizations, and society as composed of various levels of feedback control systems is consistent with the approach elaborated and applied in this book.

Castells (1996) provides a contemporary view of technology-mediated society. Based on research across many global regions, a systematic theory of the information society is formulated which reflects the fundamental effects of information technology on the contemporary world. He argues that "A network society is a society where the key social structures and activities are organized around electronically processed information networks."

Wright (2010) explores alternatives to unbridled capitalism. He observes that liberal capitalism is seen as the only viable choice. He explores alternatives to capitalism. While interesting, none of the cases discussed in this book address the scope of the whole economic-social-political system. Indeed, the aspirations in these cases are much less grand than "fixing capitalism."

This brief summary provides a perspective for how sociology addresses social systems. The goal is to explain social trends and events, often over long periods of time. This is very interesting, but the approach is this book needs to go further. Beyond explanation, we need to predict what stakeholders are likely to do, influence their choices and behaviors, and design interventions and incentives for their engagement in change.

Kidd and Holtz-Bacha (2008) define three key constructs that help to put these aspirations in context. "*Polity* is used in the sense of "community." The term comes from the Greek word "polis" and includes not only the city state, but also other forms of politically organized societies such as the nation-state and the empire. *Politics* describes the theory and practice of the power struggle between the players inside the polity. It constitutes the core of the political system. *Policy* aims at the planned formation of social domains such as economy, environment, or education through collectively binding decisions ("policy making")."

The focus in this book is primarily on policy—either government policy or private sector management policy. To successfully pursue this goal, we need to understand the politics of the ecosystem of interest. This, in turn, requires that we understand the polity stakeholders and their values, concerns, and perceptions.

Overall Approach

In this section, I provide several qualitative guidelines for approaching transformation of complex adaptive organizational ecosystems. In subsequent sections, I will discuss the quantitative analytic framework for addressing the details of pursuing change.

Characterize the Nature of the Wicked Problem

What makes the problem at hand wicked? Are there large numbers of different types of stakeholders? Are there inherent conflicts among stakeholder groups? Are there reasons to expect any groups will try to stymie or undermine solutions to the problem? In general, be very honest and clear about likely difficulties.

Identify Anticipated or Experienced Value Deficiencies

What are the value deficiencies and how are they manifested? Typical examples include performance that is poor, slow, and expensive. Diminished competitive advantage is another, perhaps due to under-investment in new capabilities. Determine whether deficiencies are widely recognized or known only to a few people.

Determine What Processes Need to Be Redesigned or Designed

What organizational processes underlie the value deficiencies? How are these processes contributing to the value deficiencies? Do these processes need to be substantially improved or completely replaced? Identify the stakeholders most aligned with sustaining the status quo.

Engage Stakeholders in How They Would Proceed With Changes

It is essential to involve those stakeholders who will be central to enabling and living with any changes. Seek their insights into the sources of value deficiencies. Solicit their ideas for redesigns or new designs. Make sure that a representative subset of these people is on the team.

Synthesize an Integrated Approach Across Contexts and Time

Consider how alternative solutions will dovetail with contexts, e.g., finance, personnel, operations. Develop staged plans to implement changes over time. Be realistic about the number of stages and time likely needed. Make sure that the whole team understands the staging and timing.

Involve Stakeholders to Support These Changes, Likely Incrementally

Carefully manage stakeholders' expectations of the current stage of implementation so that they do not see this as overwhelming. Inform them that the downstream stages of implementation will be reconsidered and adapted as necessary once the current stage is done.

Secure and Sustain Resources to Accomplish Changes

Make sure that human and financial resources are sufficiently budgeted to be successful. Insufficient budgets will diminish the likelihood of success. Lack of success will undermine stakeholder support. This can easily change the cultural mood from optimism to pessimism.

Execute Changes, Learning Along the Way and Adapting

Execute plans, keeping an eye on lessons learned about hindrances, i.e., things more difficult than expected, and affordances, i.e., things easier than expected. Solicit comments and suggestions on the compilation of lessons learned, including implications for the next stage. Be on the lookout for people with leadership proclivities and leverage their talents for subsequent stages (Rouse, 2011).

Overarching Principles

- Think long term but act short term, creating relatively quick wins
- Leverage support of quick wins to enable planning for next wins
- Learn from early wins to rethink plans for next wins

Possible quick wins addressed in later chapters include decreasing the compliance culture in national security, increasing reliance on telemedicine in health, increasing high quality online instruction in education, and incentivizing adoption of renewables in energy. All of these are happening already and can be leveraged, as well as enhanced

Human-Centered Design

The overall approach outlined above requires deciding whose preferences should influence decisions? In some situations, there may be one ultimate decision-maker, although this is very rare in public-private ecosystems. Success usually depends an understanding all stakeholders.

Human-centered design addresses the concerns, values, and perceptions of all stakeholders in designing, developing, deploying, and employing policies, products, and services. The basic idea is to delight primary stakeholders and gain the support of the secondary stakeholders.

This notion first occurred to me at a workshop in the late 1980s at the NASA Langley Research Center near Hampton, Virginia. Many participants were discussing pilot-centered design that focused on enhancing aircraft pilots' abilities, overcoming pilots' limitations, and fostering pilots' acceptance. I suggested that we should do this for all the human stakeholders involved in the success of an aircraft program. People asked what I specifically meant.

I responded, "Pilots may fly 'em, but they don't build 'em or buy 'em!"

In other words, pilots being supportive of design choices may be necessary for success, but it is not sufficient. The airlines have to want to buy the airplanes, the aerospace companies have to be willing to produce them, and regulatory bodies have to certify the use of the planes. The buyers, builders, and regulators have criteria beyond those important to pilots.

I have elaborated the human-centered design construct and an associated methodology in a book, **Design for Success** (Rouse, 1991). Two other books soon followed (Rouse, 1992, 1993), addressing innovation and organizational change. The human-centered design methodology has been applied many times and continually refined (Rouse, 2007, 2015, 2019).

The premise of human-centered design is that the major stakeholders need to perceive policies, products, and services to be valid, acceptable, and viable. Valid policies, products, and services demonstrably help solve the problems for which they are intended. Acceptable policies, products, and services solve problems in ways that stakeholders prefer. Viable policies, products, and services provide benefits that are worth the costs of use. Costs here include the efforts needed to learn and use policies, products and services, not just the purchase price.

The overall approach presented in this chapter is intended to increase validity, acceptability, and viability beyond that usually experienced with the ways in which problems of the scope addressed in this book are usually pursued. This begs the question of what shortcomings plague existing approaches.

First and foremost are viability issues. Sponsors of transformation efforts complain that they take too long and are too expensive. This is due in part to the business processes of sponsors. However, more fundamentally, much time and money goes into developing aspects of policies that, at least in retrospect, were not needed to address the questions of primary interest.

Second are acceptability issues. Many key stakeholders of the types of problems addressed in this book are not educated in analytic methods and tools. Nevertheless, they are often highly talented, have considerable influence, and will not accept that the optimal policy, somehow magically produced, is X equals 12. We need methods and tools that are more engaging for these types of stakeholders (Rouse, 1998, 2014).

Third are validity issues. There is often concern that overall analyses are of questionable validity (Rouse, 2015, 2019). This concern is due in part to the possibility that assumptions are inconsistent across component analyses. There is also the issue of incompatible definitions of organizational states across component analyses, which can lead to misleading or incorrect results. This is particularly plaguing when one is unaware of these incompatibilities.

The overall approach outlined earlier overcomes these issues in several ways. The early steps of the methodology focus on problem formulation, with particular emphasis on interactive pruning of the problem space prior to any in-depth explorations. In-depth analyses tend to be expensive, so it is important to be sure they are warranted.

Second, we have found that key stakeholders value being immersed in interactive visualizations of the phenomena, and relationships among phenomena associated with their domain and the questions of interest. This enables them to manipulate controls and explore responses. This is typically done in a group setting with much discussion and debate.

Third, the overall approach explicitly addresses agreeing on a consistent set of assumptions across analyses. This prompts delving into the underpinnings of each type of analysis. The overarching question is whether connecting multiple types of analysis will yield results that are valid in the context of the questions at hand.

Table 2.2 Stakeholders Versus Ecosystems.

Stakeholder	Ecosystem			
	National Security	Healthcare Delivery	Higher Education	Climate & Energy
Constituencies	Congress, Warfighters, Public	Congress, Patients, Families, Employers	Congress, Students, Parents, Employers	Congress, Public
Government Agencies	DOD, DHS, Intelligence, States	HHS, MHS, VHA, States, Cities	DOE, States, Cities	DOE, EPA, NOAA, FEMA, States, Cities
Agencies Workforce	Employees, unions	Employees, unions	Employees, unions	Employees, unions
Industry & Institutions	A/D Contractors, Suppliers, Tech Companies	Providers, Payers, Suppliers	Institutions, Publishers, Suppliers	Coal, Oil, Gas Companies & Related Services
Industry Workforce	Employees, unions	Employees, unions	Employees, unions	Employees, unions
Oversight Organizations	DCMA, DCAA, GAO	Accreditation & Licensing Organizations, AHA, et al.	Accreditation & Licensing Organizations, AHEE	FERC, AEOA, GAO
Advocacy Groups	American Legion, Disabled American Veterans, USO, et al.	NAHAC, Cancer Society, Heart Assoc., et al.	Learning Disabilities, Education Trust, Stand for Children, et al.	Nature Conservancy, World Wide Fund for Nature, et al.

Stakeholders

Who are the stakeholders in the four ecosystems? Table 2.2 provides a good sampling, although it is inevitable that key players are missing. The central point, however, is that transformation affects an enormous range of stakeholders whose values, concerns, and perceptions have to be understood and addressed if transformation is to be successful. I have found that even a single key stakeholder who is dead set against the changes being considered can stymie an initiative.

Attributes

What do stakeholders care about? In other words, what are the attributes they will use to assess the utility of each alternative? Table 2.3 provides a high level definition of attributes for each ecosystem. These high-level definitions become much more specific in Chapters 3–6.

Table 2.3 Ecosystems Versus Attributes.

Ecosystem	Attributes		
	Validity	Acceptability	Viability
National Security	Proposed interven tions are supported by key stakeholders	Proposed interven tions are aligned with security values and norms	Security & economic benefits of change outweigh costs of change
Healthcare Delivery	Proposed in- terventions are evidence-based and supported by key stakeholders	Proposed interven- tions are aligned with healthcare values and norms	Educational & eco- nomic benefits of change outweigh costs of change
Higher Education	Proposed inter- ventions will have desired educational impacts	Proposed interven- tions are aligned with educational values and norms	Educational benefits of change outweigh costs of change
Energy & Climate	Impacts of proposed interventions are clear and believed	Proposed interven- tions are aligned with domain values and norms	Climate benefits outweigh costs of change

Analytic Framework

Figure 2.4 shows how we bring all the human-centered design concepts together. This representation embodies the principles of human-centered design, built around Set-Based Design (Sobek, Ward & Liker, 1999), Quality Function Deployment (Hauser & Clausing, 1988), and Design Structure Matrices (Eppinger & Browning, 2012). As later discussed, multi-stakeholder, multi-attribute utility theory (Keeney & Raiffa, 1993) is used to project the value of alternatives. Note that validity, acceptability, and viability in Figure 2.4 are defined in the above discussion of human-centered design.

Sobek, Ward and Liker (1999) contrast Set-Based Design (SBD) with Point-Based Design. Developed by Toyota, SBD considers a broader range of possible designs and delays certain decisions longer. They argue that, "Taking time up front to explore and document feasible solutions from design and manufacturing perspectives leads to tremendous gains in efficiency and product integration later in the process and for subsequent development cycles." Al-Ashaab and colleagues (2013) and Singer and colleagues (2017) report on interesting applications of SBD to helicopter engines and surface combatant ships, respectively.

SBD is reflected in Figure 2.4 in terms of defining and elaborating multiple solu-tions, including those of competitors or adversaries. Quality Function Deployment (Hauser & Clausing, 1988) translates the "voice of the customer" into engineering characteristics. For Figure 2.4, this translates into "voices of the stakeholders." Design

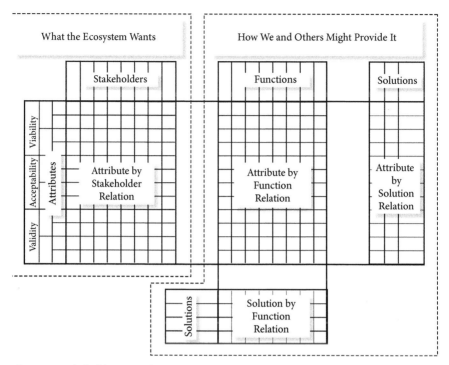

Fig. 2.4 Stakeholders, Attributes, Functions and Solutions

Structure Matrices (Eppinger & Browning, 2012) are used to model the structure of complex systems or processes. In Figure 2.4, multiple models are maintained to represent alternative offerings as well as current and anticipated competitors' offerings

The "What the Ecosystem Wants" section of Figure 2.4 characterizes the stakeholders in the solution, e.g., a policy or regulation, and their utility functions associated with context-specific attributes clustered in terms of validity, acceptability, and viability. The section of Figure 2.4 labeled "How We and Others Might Provide It" specifies, on the right, the attribute values associated with each solution. The functions associated with each solution are defined on the left of this section. Functions are things like steering, accelerating, and braking, as well as functions that may not be available in all solutions, e.g., backup camera. For policy analyses, functions might involve, for example, fuel efficiency targets, penalties for missing targets, and communications and educational offerings.

Attributes to function relationships in Figure 2.4 are expressed on a somewhat arbitrary scale from −3 to +3. Positive numbers indicate that improving a function increases the attribute. Negative numbers indicate that improving a function decreases an attribute. For example, a rear backup camera may increase the price of the vehicle but decrease insurance costs. The penalty levels in a policy may increases compliance, unless the economic costs of compliance are not sustainable. These relationships are of use for projecting where improvements are most likely to pay off.

Solutions at the bottom of Figure 2.4 are composed of functions, which are related to attributes of interest to stakeholders. In keeping with the principles of Set-Based Design, multiple solutions are pursued in parallel, including potential offerings by adversaries or competitors. While it is typical for one solution to be selected for major investment—while others may secure lessor investments—the representations of all solutions are retained, quite often being reused for subsequent opportunities.

There are additional considerations beyond SBD, QFD, and DSM. Uncertain or volatile requirements can be due to evolving performance targets, e.g., (Ferreira et al., 2009), or surprises by competitors or adversaries, e.g., the Ford Taurus or iPhone. Both causes tend to result in expensive rework, unless investments have been made in anticipation of such contingencies.

Decision making may involve more than one epoch (Ross & Rhodes, 2008) including both near-term and later decisions. For example, at GM, Epoch 1 involved creating an Escalade as a rebadged GMC in 1999. Epoch 2 involved offering an Escalade as a unique upscale SUV in 2002 that took market share from the Lincoln Navigator.

Another issue is the costs of switching from one solution to another (Silver & de Weck, 2007). A surveillance and reconnaissance mission adopted an initial solution of a manned aircraft with an option to replace this solution with an Unmanned Air Vehicle (UAV) several years later (Rouse, 2010). A deterrent to switching was the very expensive manned aircraft, which would no longer be needed. This problem was resolved by negotiating, in advance, the sale of the aircraft to another agency, effectively taking it "off the books." Thus, there can be significant value in flexibility. "A system is flexible to the extent that it can be cost-effectively modified to meet new needs or to capitalize on new opportunities" (Deshmukh, et al., 2010).

Identifying options can be difficult (Mikaelian et al., 2012). What can you do, when, and what will it cost? Rouse and colleagues (2000) discuss case studies from the semiconductor industry. Rouse and Boff (2004) summarize 14 case studies from automotive, computing, defense, materials, and semiconductor industries.

Expected Utilities of Alternative Solutions

Using the framework provided by Figure 2.4, and principles from SBD, QFD, DSM, etc., one can create multi-attribute models of how alternatives address the concerns, values, and perceptions of all the stakeholders in designing, developing, manufacturing, buying, and using policies, products, and services. The next issue of importance is the likely uncertainties associated with the attributes of the alternatives. These uncertainties involve what the market or mission needs—or will need—and how well solutions, in terms of functions and underlying technologies, will be able to meet these needs.

The expected value of an alternative can be defined as the value of the outcomes a solution provides times the probability that these outcomes will result. The probability may be discrete or it may be represented as a probability density function. For the former, the calculation involves multiplication and summation; for the latter, the calculation involves integration.

Following Keeney and Raiffa (1993), we will approach this problem using multi-stakeholder, multi-attribute utility theory. We can define the utility function of stakeholder i across the N attributes by

$$u_i = u\left(x_{1i}, x_{2i}, \ldots, x_{Ni}\right) = u\left(x_i\right) \tag{2.1}$$

where the bold **x** denotes the vector of attributes. The utility of an alternative across all M stakeholders is given by

$$U = U\left[u\left(x_1\right), u\left(x_2\right), \ldots, u\left(x_M\right)\right] \tag{2.2}$$

The appropriate forms of these functions vary by the assumptions one is willing to make. Figure 2.5 summarizes typical forms. There is also a question of how individual utility functions are combined. Keeney and Raiffa (1993) discuss a variety of approaches.

However, when there are many attributes, a weighted linear form is usually the most practical. The weights in equation (1) reflect how much a particular stakeholder cares about the attribute being weighted. It is quite common for most stakeholders to only care about a small subset of the overall set of attributes. Those for which they do not care receive weights of zero.

The weights in equation (2) reflect the extent to which the overall decision-maker or decision process cares about particular stakeholders. For example, is the customer

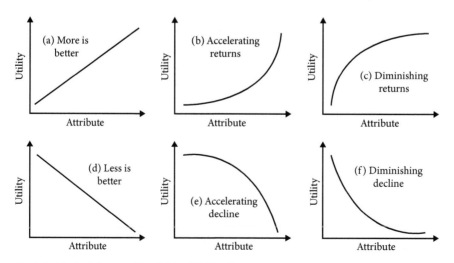

Fig. 2.5 Typical Forms of Individual Utility Functions

the most important stakeholder or do corporate finances drive the decision? These weights are usually subject to considerable sensitivity analyses.

Exploring Alternative Solutions

We can employ equations 2.1 and 2.2, along with probability distribution functions representing the likelihoods of attribute levels associated with possible outcomes of alternative solutions, to calculate expected utilities of alternatives. One can then choose the alternative with the highest expected utility.

My experience is that this seldom happens. While one or more alternatives may seem to predominate, decision-makers want to understand how alternative assumptions affect this dominance. For example, they may see that alternative X prevails with particular assumptions, while alternative Y may seem stronger with another set of assumptions. I have found that insightful decision-makers will then turn to the group and ask, "What creative changes could we make so that these two outcomes are not so different?'

The analytic platform then becomes a means for exploring various "what if?" scenarios. What if agency A provided agency B a subsidy for enabling particular outcomes? But, that's illegal. OK, but we can address that later. Could that make the difference in this impasse? The abilities to mutually and creatively explore "what if?" questions are often the key to new futures.

Employment in Four Ecosystems

Transformation is likely to affect employment in the four ecosystems as summarized in Table 2.4. The most disruptive changes will be in energy and climate. Perhaps one million fossil fuel related jobs will disappear over time. Fortunately, this ecosystem is likely to generate the most new jobs, as projected by the U.S. Bureau of Labor Statistics.

Total U.S. employment is 156 million, so the four ecosystems account for roughly 25 percent of U.S. employment.

Impacts on Ecosystems

How will transformation likely impact the assets of each ecosystem?

- Defense—increased efficiency and agility will increase asset values
- Health—increased health needs will require greater assets
- Education—asset values of less bricks and mortar will likely decline
- Energy—governments may have to buy fossil fuel assets

Table 2.4 Transformation & Employment.

Ecosystem	Employment	Prospects
National Security	5 million	Persists despite decreased defense contractor employment
Healthcare Delivery	16 million	Grows via new practices and technologies, while others become becoming obsolete
Higher Education	4 million in higher ed 11 million in K-12	Persists despite practices changing and institutions regularly disappearing
Energy & Climate	7 million 1 million threatened 1+ million new jobs	Persists despite the mix of energy sources changing

The likely implications include:

- Losses will have to be dovetailed with new opportunities
- Opportunities will need to include workforce training for new jobs
- Investors in new directions will have to be incentivized
- Investments needed will require government augmentation

What will likely be the biggest impediments to change? The workforce's fear and experience of losing jobs and incomes will clearly dominate. Demonstrable reassurance will be needed. Investors will react to losing asset values. Many people will be skeptical of the future envisioned.

The resources required will be substantial, but broad economic valuations will show that the likely changes will pay off. Nevertheless, there are risks of subversion of resources by key stakeholders, e.g., U.S. Congress. Greater transparency will lessen the chances of funds ending up in the wrong places for the wrong purposes.

Interactive Visualizations

How should all of the above information be presented to stakeholders? Traditionally, professional analysts perform the types of analyses described in the last section. They then prepare a report or, more likely, a PowerPoint presentation for decision-makers, recommending courses of action. I have found that this can be rather sterile.

In contrast, we have developed the notion of policy flight simulators (Rouse, 2014). These simulators are computational instantiations of the analysis framework describer earlier, with interactive visualizations that enable the decision-makers to take the controls and explore the complexity of their ecosystem. Typically, they do this as a team, as shown in Figure 2.6. This leads to considerable discovery, discussion, and debate. Consequently teams develop "shared mental models" of the phenomena of interest, differing perspectives, and creative ways forward.

Fig. 2.6 Policy Flight Simulator for New York City. (Yu, Rouse, Serban & Veral, 2016)

Of particular importance, when key stakeholders take the controls and adjust various assumptions, they often have suggestions for elaboration of the simulator. Once these changes are implemented, usually for the next meeting, those suggesting these changes typically articulate great "buy in" when they see that the simulator now reflects their ideas.

Economic Valuation

The relevant attributes vary significantly across the four public-private ecosystems. However, they all have one very important attribute in common—money. Thus, economic valuation is central to all ecosystems.

A key to useful economic valuation is careful assessment of the time series of costs and benefits, especially when considering ambitious and cross-cutting initiatives (Sage & Rouse, 2011). Broader views are better than narrower views, particularly when investing in people (Rouse, 2010). In this section, I define the central phenomena to be modeled and alternative assessment metrics.

Cash Flows

There are several cash flows of interest:

- Investments over time
- Revenues over time, r_i, i = 0, 1, ... N
- Costs over time, c_i, i = 0, 1, ... N
- Net of revenues minus costs

In public-private ecosystems, a proxy for revenues can be cost savings or increased income tax cash flows. For example, upstream investments in preventive health-care can result in downstream savings of the costs of healthcare due to, for in-stance, reduced incidence of chronic diseases. Increased investments in education can lead to higher paying jobs with greater incomes and hence larger income tax revenues.

Money received in the future is not as valuable as money received today, for example, because one has to borrow money to sustain waiting for future monies. For this reason, future cash flows are discounted by the interest or discount rate to calculate a Net Present Value (NPV). This is often referred to as discounted cash flow analysis.

Equations 2.3–2.5 summarize the basic calculations of the discounted cash flow model for time series over N time periods. Given projections of costs, c_i, i = 0, 1, ... N, and revenues, r_i, i = 0, 1, ... N, the calculations of Net Present Value (NPV), Internal Rate of Return (IRR), or Cost/Benefit Ratio (CBR) are quite straightforward elements of financial management (Brigham & Gapenski, 1988). The only subtlety is choosing a discount rate, DR, to reflect the current value of future returns decreasing as the time until those returns will be realized increases.

$$\text{NPV} = \sum_{i=0}^{N} (r_i - c_i)/(1 + \text{DR})^i \qquad (2.3)$$

$$\text{IRR} = \text{DR such that} \sum_{i=0}^{N} (r_i - c_i)/(1 + \text{DR})^i = 0 \qquad (2.4)$$

$$\text{CBR} = [\sum_{i=0}^{N} c_i/(1 + \text{DR})^i]/[\sum_{i=0}^{N} r_i/(1 + \text{DR})^i] \qquad (2.5)$$

It is quite possible for DR to change with time; possibly reflecting expected increases in interest rates in the future. Equation 2.3–2.5 must be modified appropriately for time-varying discount rates.

The metrics in Equation 2.3–2.5 are interpreted as follows:

- NPV reflects the amount one should be willing to pay now for benefits received in the future. These future benefits are discounted by the interest paid now to enable waiting for these later benefits.
- IRR, in contrast, is the value of DR if NPV is zero. This metric enables comparing alternative investments by forcing the NPV of each investment to zero. Note that this assumes a fixed interest rate and reinvestment of intermediate returns at the internal rate of return.

- CBR simply reflects the discounted cash outflows divided by the discounted cash inflows, or benefits.

Real Options

NPV assumes that the projected costs and revenues occur regardless of intervening circumstances. Hence, the above three metrics tend to be very conservative due to the underlying fundamental assumption that one will stay the course regardless of intervening outcomes.

In many situations, however, the results for the first year or two may cause reconsidering the investment, perhaps even exiting the investment. In such situations, one should consider the first year or two of investment as having purchased an "option" on the subsequent years. In this situation, one should calculate a Net Option Value (NOV).

The models employed for option-based valuations were initially developed for valuation of financial instruments (Black & Scholes, 1973; Merton, 1973). For example, an option might provide the right to buy shares of stock at a predetermined price sometime in the future. Valuation concerns what such an option is worth. This depends, obviously, on the likelihood that the stock price will be greater than the predetermined exercise price associated with the option.

More specifically, the value of the option equals the discounted expected value of the stock at maturity, conditional on the stock price at maturity exceeding the exercise price, minus the discounted exercise price, all times the probability that, at maturity, the stock price is greater than the exercise price (Smithson, 1998). Net Option Value equals the option value calculated in this manner minus the cost of purchasing the option as shown in equation 2.6.

$$\text{NOV} = [\text{AAM}|\text{Value} > \text{OEP}) - \text{OEP}]\text{xProb.}\,(\text{Value} > \text{OEP}) - \text{OPP} \qquad (2.6)$$

where AAM is the NPV of the asset at maturity, OPP is the option purchase price and OEP is the option exercise price.

Thus, there are Net Present Values embedded in the determination of Net Option Values. However, in addition, there is explicit representation of the fact that one will not exercise an option at maturity if the current market share price is less than or equal to the exercise price. As mentioned earlier, sources such as Amram and Kulatilaka (1999), Boer (1998, 1999), Luehrman (1998), Luenberger (1997), and Smithson (1998) provide a wealth of illustrations of how option values are calculated for a range of models.

It is important to note that the options addressed here are usually termed "real" options in the sense that the investments associated with these options are usually intended to create tangible assets rather than purely financial assets. Application of financially derived models to non-financial investments often raises the issue of the extent to which assumptions from financial markets are valid in the domains of non-financial investments. This concern is usually addressed with sensitivity analysis.

The assumptions underlying the option-pricing model and the estimates used as input data for the model are usually subject to much uncertainty. This uncertainty should be reflected in option valuations calculated. Therefore, what is needed is a probability distribution of valuations rather than solely a point estimate. This probability distribution can be generated using Monte Carlo simulation to systematically vary model and input variables using assumed distributions of parameter/data variations.

These analyses enable consideration of options in terms of both returns and risks. Interesting "What if?" scenarios can be explored. A question that we have frequently encountered when performing these analyses is, "How bad can it get and have this decision still make sense?" This question reflects a desire to thoroughly understand the decision being entertained, not just get better numbers.

The option value resulting from the above formulation is totally premised on the assumption that waiting does not preempt deciding later. In other words, the assumption is that the decision to exercise an option cannot be preempted by somebody else deciding earlier. In typical situations where other actors (e.g., competitors or adversaries) can affect possible returns, it is common to represent their impact in terms of changes of projected cash flows (Amram & Kulatilaka, 1999). In many cases, competitors acting first will decrease potential cash flows that will decrease the option value. It is often possible to construct alternative competitive scenarios and determine an optimal exercise date.

A central attraction of this model is the explicit recognition that the purpose of an investment now (i.e., purchasing an option) is to assure the option to make a subsequent and usually larger investment later (i.e., exercising the option). Thus, for example, one invests in creating new technologies for the option of later incorporating these technologies in product and service lines. The significance of the contingent nature of this decision makes an option-pricing model a much better fit than a traditional discounted cash flow model.

Rouse (2010) includes several examples of human systems integration investments that were framed as real options and shown to have substantial economic value. In several cases, the cash flow estimates needed for the option pricing models reflected savings of downstream operating costs once systems were deployed.

However, not all long-term investment decisions have substantial contingent elements. For example, one may invest in training and development to later have the option of selecting among talented managers for elevation to executive positions. There are minimal investments associated with exercising such options—almost all of the investment occurs up front. Thus, option-pricing models are not useful for such decisions.

NPV Versus NOV

How does options-based thinking change the way an organization operates? Investment decision criteria change, as elaborated below. Beyond this direct change, there are broader organizational implications of adopting options-based thinking that I outline in later discussions.

An enterprise simulation, **R&D World**, was used to assess the merits of alternative decision criteria for R&D investments (Bodner & Rouse, 2007). This case study focused on R&D investments by a large forest products company. This simulation was used to compare criteria of NPV, NOV, and this company's other stage-gate-criteria, e.g., strategic fit.

The **R&D World** simulation was unveiled as a meeting of CTO's of leading forest products companies. Only one of the CTOs knew that the company being simulated was his. Each CTO was asked to propose what he or she would use for decision criteria. The 15 proposals were simulated for 10 replications of 25-year periods. The resulting average profits ranged from a loss of $250 million to profits of $1.55 billion.

The CTOs were shocked. One commented, "I had no idea these criteria could make so much difference." A key distinction emerged. Emphasis on NPV preserves the R&D budget. Indeed, often the R&D budget was not fully expended due to lack of positive NPV proposals.

In contrast, emphasis on NOV results in all, or nearly all, of the budget being expended. More projects are funded—modestly at first, as they are options. The company has more options that may (or may not) be exercised. Rather than preserving the R&D budget, emphasis on NOV maximizes earnings per share. It seems reasonable to assume that this is the primary purpose of the R&D budget.

Strategic Value

An investment portfolio may include some investments characterized by NPV, some characterized by NOV, and some with both NPV and NOV. Boer (2009) suggests how to value a portfolio that includes some investments characterized by both metrics. He argues for Strategic Value (SV), which is given by

$$SV = NPV + NOV \tag{2.7}$$

The NPV component represents the value associated with commitments already made, while the NOV component represents contingent opportunities for further investments, should the options be "in the money" at a later time. I elaborate the distinctions between the two types of investments in examples in later chapters.

A very significant issue in these types of analyses is the distinction between who bears the costs of investments and who realizes the returns on these investments. If it is the same entity, interpretation of the results is fairly straightforward. In contrast, if one entity invests and a different entity realizes the returns, the investing entity will tend to see expenditures as costs and try to minimize them (Rouse, 2010). This is a common problem in public-private ecosystems.

Decision-Making

At this point, one has identified alternative innovations that potentially can contribute to transformation. One will have projections of stakeholders' expected utility for each alternative, as well as economic valuations of each alternative. Of course, these economic projections will be important attributes to some stakeholders, but likely not all stakeholders. The next concern is **not** whether to invest in each alternative, but how to invest in a portfolio of alternatives.

There are several strategies an enterprise might adopt to make these investment decisions. The choice depends on enterprises' abilities to predict their futures, as well as their abilities to respond to these futures. What strategies might enterprise decision-makers adopt to address alternative futures? As shown in Figure 2.7, we have found that there are four basic strategies that decision makers can use: optimize; adapt; hedge; and accept.

If the phenomena of interest are highly predictable, then there is little chance that the enterprise will be pushed into unanticipated territory. Consequently, it is in the best interest of the enterprise to optimize its policies, products and services to be as efficient as possible. In other words, if the unexpected cannot happen, then there is no reason to expend resources beyond process refinement and improvement.

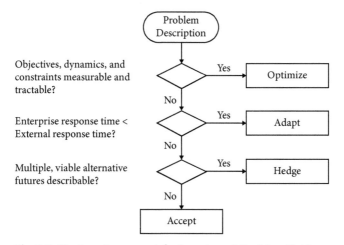

Fig. 2.7 Strategy Framework for Investment Decision-Making (Pennock & Rouse, 2016)

If the phenomena of interest are not highly predictable, but policies, products, and services can be appropriately adapted when necessary, it may be in the best interest for the enterprise to plan to adapt. For example, agile capacities can be designed to enable their use in multiple ways to adapt to changing demands, e.g., the way Honda did but other automakers could not in response to the Great Recession. In this case, some efficiency has been traded for the ability to adapt.

For this approach to work, the enterprise must be able to identify and respond to potential issues faster than the ecosystem changes. For example, consider unexpected increased customer demands that tax capacities beyond their designed limits. Design and building of new or expanded facilities can take considerable time. On the other hand, reconfiguration of agile capacities should be much faster, as the Honda example illustrates.

If the phenomena of interest are not very predictable and the enterprise has a limited ability to respond, it may be in the best interest of the enterprise to hedge its position. In this case, it can explore scenarios where the enterprise may not be able to handle sudden changes without prior investment. For example, an enterprise concerned about potential obsolescence of existing policies, products, and services may choose to invest in multiple, potential new offerings. Such investments might be pilot projects that enable learning how to deploy policies or deliver products and services differently, or perhaps deploy different policies, or deliver different products and services.

Over time, it will become clear which of these options make most sense and the enterprise can exercise the best option by scaling up these offerings based on what they have learned during the pilot projects. In contrast, if the enterprise were to take a wait and see approach, it might not be able to respond quickly enough, and it might lose out to its competitors or adversaries.

If the phenomena of interest are totally unpredictable and there is no viable way to respond, then the enterprise has no choice but to accept the risk. Accept is not so much a strategy as a default condition. If one is attempting to address a strategic challenge where there is little ability to optimize the efficacy of offerings, limited ability to adapt offerings, and no viable hedges against the uncertainties associated with these offerings, the enterprise must accept the conditions that emerge.

There is another possibility that deserves mention—stay with the status quo. Yu, Rouse and Serban (2013) developed a computational theory of enterprise transformation, elaborating on the qualitative theory presented earlier (Rouse, 2005, 2006). They employed this computational theory to assess when investing in change is attractive and unattractive. Investing in transformation is likely to be attractive when one is currently underperforming and the circumstances are such that investments will likely improve enterprise performance. In contrast, if one is already performing well, investments in change will be difficult to justify. Similarly, if performance cannot be predictably improved—due to noisy markets and/or highly discriminating constituencies—then investments may not be warranted despite current underperformance.

Conclusions

The approach presented in this chapter is intended to be rather comprehensive. However, it need not be overwhelming. Consider the various steps, models, and equations to be guidelines rather than procedures that should be strictly followed. As will be seen in Chapters 3–6, many of the case studies discussed only employed a subset of these guidelines. A key point is that methods and tools have to be tailored to contexts and the questions of interest.

References

Al-Ashaab, A., et al. (2013). The transformation of the product development process into lean environment using set-based concurrent engineering. *International Journal of Concurrent Engineering: Research and Applications*. 18 (1), 41–53

Amram, M. and Kulatilaka, N. (1999). *Real Options: Managing Strategic Investment in an Uncertain World*. Boston: Harvard Business School Press

Black, F. and Scholes, M. (1973). The pricing of options and corporate liabilities. *Journal of Political Economy*, 81, 637–659

Bodner, D. and Rouse, W.B. (2007). Understanding R&D value creation with organizational simulation, *Systems Engineering*, 10 (1), 64–82

Boer, F.P. (1998). Traps, pitfalls, and snares in the valuation of technology. *Research Technology Management*, September-October, 45–54

Boer, F.P. (2009). *The Valuation of Technology: Business and Financial Issues in R&D*. New York: Wiley

Brigham, E.F. and Gapenski, L.C. (1988). *Financial Management: Theory and Practice*. Chicago, IL: Dryden

Castells, M. (1996). *Rise of the Network Society*, Malden, MA: Blackwell

Deshmukh, A. et al. (2010). Valuing flexibility. *Proceedings of the 2nd Annual SERC Research Review Conference*, November 9–10, College Park, MD

Eppinger, S.D. and Browning, T.R. (2012). **Design Structure Matrix Methods and Applications**. Cambridge, MA: MIT Press

Ferreira, S., Collofello, J., Shunk, D, and Mackulak, G. (2009). Understanding the effects of requirements volatility in software engineering by using analytical modeling and software process simulation. *Journal of Systems and Software*, 82, (10), 1568–1577

Giddens, A. (1979). *Central Problems in Social Theory: Action, Structure and Contradictions in Social Analysis*, Berkeley: University of California Press

Habermas, J. (1988). *Structural Transformation of the Public Sphere*, Cambridge: MIT-Press

Hauser, J.R. and Clausing, D. (1988, May-June). The house of quality. *Harvard Business Review*, 63–73

Holub, R. C. (1991). *Jürgen Habermas: Critic in the Public Sphere*. London: Routledge.

Keeney, R.L. and Raiffa, H. (1993). *Decisions with Multiple Objectives: Preference and Value Tradeoffs*. Cambridge, UK: Cambridge University Press

Kellner, D. (2000). Habermas, The Public Sphere and Democracy. In Hahn, L. E. (eds) *Perspectives on Habermas* (pp. 259–287). Chicago: Open Court

Kidd, L.L. and Holtz-Bacha, C. (eds) (2008). *Encyclopedia of Political Communication*. Thousand Oaks, CA: Sage Publications

Luehrman, T.A. (1998). Investment opportunities as real options. *Harvard Business Review*, July-August, 51–67

Luenberger, D.G. (1997). *Investment Science*. Oxford, UK: Oxford University Press.

Luhmann, N. (1995). *Social Systems*, Stanford: Stanford University Press

Merton, R.C. (1973). Theory of rational option pricing. *Bell Journal of Economics and Management Science*, 4 (1),141–183

Mikaelian, T., Rhodes, D.H., Nightingale, D.J. and Hastings, D.E. (2012). A logical approach to real options identification with application to UAV systems. *IEEE Transactions on Systems, Man, and Cybernetics – Part A. Systems and Humans*. 42 (1), 32–47

Pennock, M.J. and Rouse, W.B. (2016). The epistemology of enterprises. *Systems Engineering*, 19 (1), 24–43

Polanyi, K. (1944). *The Great Transformation—The Political and Economic Origins of Our Time*. New York: Farrar & Rinehart

Rittel, H.W. J., and Webber, M.M. (1973). Dilemmas in a General Theory of Planning. *Policy Sciences*, 4 (2), 155–169

Ross, A.M. and Rhodes, D.H. (2008), Using natural value-centric time scales for conceptualizing system timelines through Epoch-Era Analysis. Proceedings of INCOSE International Symposium, 18 (1), 1186–1201

Rouse, W.B. (1991). *Design or Success: A Human-Centered Approach to Designing Successful Products and Systems*. New York: Wiley

Rouse, W.B. (1992). *Strategies for Innovation: Creating Successful Products, Systems, and Organizations*. New York: Wiley

Rouse, W.B. (1993). *Catalysts for Change: Concepts and Principles for Enabling Innovation*. New York: Wiley

Rouse, W.B. (1998). Computer support of collaborative planning. *Journal of the American Society for Information Science*, 49 (9), 832–839

Rouse, W.B. (2000). Managing complexity: Disease control as a complex adaptive system. *Information · Knowledge · Systems Management*, 2 (2), 143–165

Rouse, W.B. (2005). A theory of enterprise transformation, *Systems Engineering*, 8 (4), 279–295

Rouse, W.B. (ed.) (2006). *Enterprise Transformation: Understanding and Enabling Fundamental Change*. New York: Wiley

Rouse, W.B. (2007). *People and Organizations: Explorations of Human-Centered Design*. New York: Wiley

Rouse, W.B. (2008). Healthcare as a complex adaptive system: Implications for design and management. *The Bridge*, 38 (1), 17–25

Rouse, W.B. (2009). Engineering perspectives on healthcare delivery: Can we afford technological innovation in healthcare? *Journal of Systems Research and Behavioral Science*, 26, 1–10. Reprinted in Grossman, C., Goolsby, A., Olsen, L.A. and McGinnis, J.M. (eds) (2011). *Engineering a Learning Healthcare System: A Look at the Future* (pp. 65–75). Washington, DC: National Academies Press

Rouse, W.B. (ed). (2010). *The Economics of Human Systems Integration: Valuation of Investments in People's Training and Education, Safety and Health, and Work Productivity*. New York: John Wiley

Rouse, W.B. (2011). Necessary competencies for transforming an enterprise, *Journal of Enterprise Transformation*, 1 (1), 71–92

Rouse, W.B. (2014). Human interaction with policy flight simulators. *Journal of Applied Ergonomics*, 45 (1), 72–77

Rouse, W.B. (2015). *Modeling and Visualization of Complex Systems and Enterprises: Explorations of Physical, Human, Economic, and Social Phenomena*. Hoboken, NJ: John Wiley.

Rouse, W.B. (2019). *Computing Possible Futures: Model Based Explorations of "What if?"* Oxford, UK: Oxford University Press

Rouse, W.B. and Boff, K.R. (2004). Value-centered R&D organizations: Ten principles for characterizing, assessing and managing value. *Journal of Systems Engineering*, 7 (2), 167–185

Rouse, W.B. and Cortese, D.A. (eds) (2010). *Engineering the System of Healthcare Delivery*. Amsterdam: IOS Press

Rouse, W.B., Howard, C.W., Carns, W.E. and Prendergast, E.J. (2000). Technology investment advisor: An options-based approach to technology strategy. *Information • Knowledge • Systems Management*, 2 (1), 63–81

Sage, A.P. and Rouse, W.B. (2011). *Economic System Analysis and Assessment*. New York: Wiley

Silver, M.R. and de Weck, O.L. (2007). Time-expanded decision networks: A framework for designing evolvable complex systems. *Journal of Systems Engineering*, 10, (2),167–188

Singer, D., Strickland, J., Doerry, N., McKenney, T. and Whitcomb, C. (2017). *Set-Based Design*. Alexandria, VA: Society of Naval Architects and Marine Engineers, Technical and Research Bulletin 7–12

Smithson, C.W. (1998). *Managing Financial Risk: A Guide to Derivative Products, Financial Engineering, and Value Maximization*. New York: McGraw-Hill, New York

Sobek, D.K., Ward, A.C. and Lifer, J.K. (1999). Toyota's principles of set-based concurrent engineering. *Sloan Management Review*, 40 (2), 67–83

Wright, E. O. (2010). *Envisioning Real Utopias*. London: Verso.

Yu, X., Rouse, W.B. and Serban, N. (2011). A computational theory of enterprise transformation. *Systems Engineering*, 14 (4), 441–454

Yu, X., Serban, N., and Rouse, W.B. (2013). The demographics of change: Enterprise characteristics and behaviors that influence enterprise transformation. *Journal of Enterprise Transformation*, 3 (4), 285–306

Yu, Z., Rouse, W.B., Serban, N. and Veral, E. (2016). A data-rich agent-based decision support model for hospital consolidation. *Journal of Enterprise Transformation*, 6 (3/4), 136–161

3

National Security

This chapter addresses the following questions:

- What is the national security ecosystem?
- What types of innovation are needed?
- How might these innovations be enabled?
- How might enterprise transformation facilitate these innovations?
- How can such investments be economically justified?

The Ecosystem

Figure 3.1 Provides a multi-level depiction of the national security ecosystem. At the level of work practices, systems are engineered and developed, military engagements are conducted and, in general, delivery operations are accessed and utilized.

At the level of delivery operations, processes for acquisition, supply, finance, human resources, etc. provide capabilities and information to support work practices. The system structure level includes government agencies such as the Departments of Defense (DoD) and Homeland Security (DHS), as well as the intelligence agencies. Private sector OEMs (original equipment manufacturers) and their suppliers are also at this level. These entities invest in delivery operations and deliver national security.

The level of the defense ecosystem includes the public, Congress and the Executive and Judicial branches of government. They provide laws, regulations, and funding. In return, they expect competitive advantages, economic growth, jobs, and growth.

Figure 3.1 does not include allies, e.g., NATO, or adversaries. These entities are very much relevant, but not central to the case studies considered in this chapter. for this and other reasons, Figure 3.1 is very much a simplification.

Stakeholders

Table 3.1 lists stakeholders and examples initially discussed in Chapter 2. Expanding just government stakeholders, the number of stakeholders becomes substantially larger.

At the policy level, there is the overall Congress, the House and Senate Armed Services Committees, and the House and Senate Appropriations Committees. The

Transforming Public-Private Ecosystems. William B. Rouse, Oxford University Press.
© William B. Rouse (2022). DOI: 10.1093/oso/9780192866530.003.0003

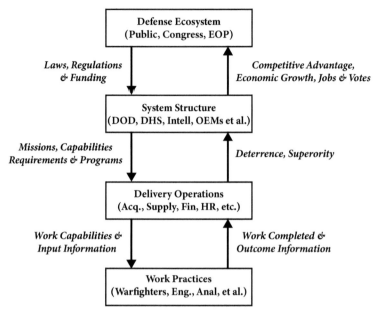

Fig. 3.1 National Security Ecosystem

Office of the Secretary of Defense includes functions for policy, acquisition and sustainment, research and engineering, information technology, and cost assessment and program evaluation.

Considering requirements, stakeholders include the Joint Staff, the Army Futures Command, the Air Force Warfare Integration Center, and the Navy Warfare Systems. For programs, there are Service Acquisition Executives and Program Executive Officers. Evaluation functions include Operational Test and Evaluation and Component Test Centers. Finally, there are a plethora of Contracting Offices.

Table 3.1 Stakeholders in National Security.

Stakeholders	Examples
Constituencies	Congress, Warfighters, Public
Government Agencies	DOD, DHS, Intelligence, States
Agencies Workforce	Employees, Unions
Industry & Institutions	Aero/Defense & Tech Companies, Suppliers
Industry Workforce	Employees, unions
Oversight Organizations	DCMA, DCAA, GAO
Advocacy Groups	American Legion, Disabled American Veterans, et al.

DOD = Dept. of Defense; DHS = Dept. of Homeland Security; DCMA = Defense Contract Management Agency; DCAA = Defense Contract Audit Agency; GAO = Government Accountability Office

Industry stakeholders include the CEOs and CTOs of the "Big 5" defense contractors—Boeing, General Dynamics, Lockheed Martin, Northrop Grumman, and Raytheon—as well as their major suppliers and a range of high technology smaller businesses. There are also advocates for small businesses owned by women and under-represented minorities.

Yet another set of stakeholders includes thoughts leaders such as Defense Advanced Research Projects Agency (DARPA), Defense Innovation Unit, Defense Innovation Board, Defense Universities, Service Academies, Defense Acquisition University, National Defense University, Federally Funded Research and Development Centers, University Affiliated Research Centers, and Joint Artificial Intelligence Center.

Obviously, the complexity of the networks of stakeholders in national security is an enormous challenge. Past efforts to manage this complexity are discussed in the next section. Nevertheless, innovation does happen, as the following five case studies clearly illustrate.

Past Innovations

Defense Act (1920)

Representative Julius Kahn, Republican of California, sponsored the National Defense Act of 1920. This legislation reorganized the U.S. Army and decentralized procurement and acquisition processes for equipment, weapons, supplies and vehicles.

The Act required the Army to conduct studies and planning for wartime mobilization, rather than waiting for war to be declared to begin planning. This shift to contingency planning and a long-range outlook led to decentralization of the contracting and procurement process, and increased coordination between military leaders and leaders of business and industry.

One result was diminished roles of government arsenals and increased reliance on defense contractors. The combined military and civilian workforce at arsenals continued to shrink over the next several years (Else, 2011).

UARCs (1942)

A University Affiliated Research Center (UARC) is a strategic United States Department of Defense (DoD) research center associated with a university. UARCs were developed to ensure that essential engineering and technology capabilities of particular importance to the DoD are maintained (AcqNotes, 2020). Johns Hopkins' Applied Physics Lab became the first UARC in 1942. There are currently 17 UARCs.

These nonprofit organizations maintain essential research, development and engineering "core" capabilities; maintain long-term strategic relationships with their DoD sponsors; and operate in the public interest, free from real or perceived conflicts of interest. Collaboration with the educational and research resources available at their universities enhances each UARC's ability to meet the needs of their sponsors (AcqNotes, 2020).

UARCs do not compete for contracts against industry; they only perform research, development, and prototyping. For example, a UARC built a prototype spacecraft for satellite navigation, but not the constellation of five. Because UARCs must only do work they are chartered for, they generally do not use subcontracts (Waugh, 2020).

The UARCs play a key role in supporting the Services and other agencies on highly technical issues. They have outstanding access to advanced technology at leading universities and have the potential to play a greater role in DoD's outreach to companies and organizations not traditionally affiliated with DoD (DBB, 2017).

Armed Services Procurement Act (1947)

Each of the military services had created their own procurement regulations. There was not one unified procurement regulation, which created significant difficulties when contractors worked for more than one service. Specifically, there was a need to consolidate all of the diverse service-specific procurement rules and regulations into a single set of rules and regulations.

The Armed Services Procurement Act, signed into law in 1947, consolidated all the various contract laws that had proliferated over the years; one for defense agencies and one for civilian agencies. The Act continued the sealed bid as the preferred method of procurement, with specific exceptions.

The law led to the formation of two sets of regulations: The Armed Services Procurement Regulation (for defense procurement) and the Federal Procurement Regulation (for civilian procurement) (Pregnato, 2018). The Act also attempted to place procurement rules in one location under the Armed Services Procurement Regulation (ASPR).

As important as this consolidation was, it did not result in a streamlined set of rules and regulations. Thus, bidding on and executing government contracts remained rather complicated. Later discussion of the Packard Commission elaborates this point.

DARPA (1958)

The Soviet Union (USSR) launched the first satellite ever on October 4, 1957. This event triggered the creation of the Advanced Research Projects Agency (ARPA) on

February 7, 1958 by President Dwight D. Eisenhower. The stated intention was to collaborate with academic, industry, and government partners to formulate and execute research and development projects to expand the frontiers of technology and science, with abilities to reach beyond immediate U.S. military requirements.

ARPA—later renamed DARPA—investments led to time-shared computing, the ARPANET (forerunner of the Internet), the artificial intelligence fields of speech recognition and signal processing, hypermedia, and virtual reality. Successful investments in foundational technologies in automatic target recognition, space-based sensing, propulsion, and materials were transferred to the military services.

The Strategic Computing Program enabled DARPA to exploit advanced processing and networking technologies and, in the process, rebuild and strengthen relationships with universities after the Vietnam War. One component of this program was the Pilot's Associate. We were subcontractors to Lockheed Martin with responsibility for designing and developing a pilot-vehicle interface that could literally understood the pilot's intentions—at the moment—and then reconfigure the interface to support those intentions.

Our pilot-vehicle interface concept integrated results of research we had been conducting for many years for the Air Force, Army, Navy and NASA. Every function of the interface was justified based on evidence published in scholarly journals. All the pieces were evidence-based but the integration was speculative. Could all these pieces work together and enhance pilot-vehicle performance? DARPA was willing to accept the risks associated with this speculation. The pieces played together quite nicely.

My association with DARPA led to my being invited to facilitate the strategic planning for one of the DARPA research offices. I had served in this role many times for various companies and agencies. Nevertheless, I found it difficult to keep the planning team on the task of planning. For example, one team member mentioned a possible need, then another team member suggested how a special integrated circuit could meet this need, then before I knew what was happening the whole team was working on designing the integrated circuit. I asked the office director what I should do. He responded that these diversions happened all the time. It was part of the DARPA culture.

Packard Commission (1986)

The President's Blue Ribbon Commission on Defense Management, informally known as the Packard Commission, was a federal government commission by President Ronald Reagan in 1986. The Commission Report was issued later that year (Packard, 1986).

The acquisition process is highly multi-faceted. It is infused with disparate goals and objectives: to have the highest performing technology at the lowest price possible in the fastest amount of time; to ensure the defense industry and related economies remain solvent; and to encourage small business, minority contractors, and women-owned businesses (Cancian, 1995).

Historically, reforms have been enacted for primarily two reasons: increasing complexity of the technologies involved and individual corruption and abuse for monetary gain. Excesses in time and cost, or deficits in performance, are some of the more obvious outward signs that reform is warranted. But these are just symptoms, and it is instructive to elucidate the contributing factors. First, is the government acquiring the right systems to meet its needs, and second, is it acquiring those systems well?

The first question addresses the agility of the acquisition enterprise. With an ever-changing world, the actions of both adversaries and allies can alter the efficacy of military systems both deployed and under development with little warning. Consequently, a program could be run with perfect efficiency and achieve all of its performance objectives, yet the resulting systems could be useless upon completion. While this does not constitute a failure in the traditional sense, a lack of agility in the acquisition system means that resources continue to be expended on a program even after it is recognized that it is no longer viable.

The second question addresses the efficiency of the acquisition process. That is, assuming that the mission is sound, does the acquisition enterprise deliver systems in the most cost effective way possible? This category includes most of the issues one typically associates with acquisition failings including excessive oversight, lack of competition, political interference, requirements creep, and the inclusion of immature technologies. Issues with acquisition efficiency are linked to the structure of the acquisition process as well as the discipline with which the process is implemented.

With acquisition, it is sometimes difficult to define a failure since even troubled programs often result in the acquisition of something. However, in hindsight at least, it is not always the case that the right weapon was acquired to address the right threat. Further, the costs of acquired systems often far exceed original projections, and the desired capability is often provided much later than originally planned. These are the factors that determine the effectiveness of acquisition. History has shown that not all acquisition efforts are successful with regard to these factors. These phenomena can be better illustrated by providing some examples.

Loss of Mission occurs when the threat that was to have been addressed by the system is no longer viable, or a new type of threat emerges. One such example is the B-70 Valkyrie. The Valkyrie was intended to be a high-altitude, Mach 3+ strategic bomber. However, concerns over the aircraft's vulnerability to surface-to-air missiles as well as the increasing dominance of ICBMs in the nuclear strike role lead both the Eisenhower and Kennedy administrations to question its military viability. Eventually, the program was transformed into a research program, the XB-70. Another example of loss of mission is the Drone Anti-Submarine Helicopter (DASH). It was originally developed as an expendable anti-submarine platform. However, since submarines were not a significant threat during the Vietnam War, the DASH program was canceled in 1969. Both of these examples illustrate a lack of agility in the acquisition process in that resources were redeployed long after the changing threat had been identified.

Process Failure can cause the cancellation of programs as well. For example, the M247 Sergeant York DIVAD (Division Air Defense gun) was born of the Army's need for a replacement for the ageing M163 20mm Vulcan A/A gun and M48 Chaparral missile system. Despite the fact that the system utilized as much off the shelf technology as possible, when the first production vehicles were delivered in late 1983 there were many performance deficits, including issues with the fire control system, clutter handling, turret traverse rate, and ECCM suite. Consequently, in December 1986 after about 50 vehicles had been produced, the entire program was terminated. Of course, most acquisition process problems do not lead to cancellation. Many acquisition programs deliver highly capable systems, but only after delays and cost overruns. An example of such is the F-22 Raptor. Considered one of the most technologically advanced aircraft in the world, it is also one of the most expensive. The program began with the award of the Advanced Tactical Fighter Demonstration/Validation contract in 1986 and achieved Initial Operational Capability in 2005. The inclusion of many advanced technologies such as advanced avionics and low-observable materials helped contribute to the long duration and high cost of the program.

These and many other instances have driven desires for acquisition reform. However, past reform efforts have been less than fully successful, as shown by Drezner and colleagues (1993). Drezner reported that reform initiatives from 1960 to 1990 did not reduce cost growth on 197 defense programs. In fact, the average cost growth on these programs was 20 percent and did not change significantly for 30 years. Christensen and colleagues (1999) reaffirmed this conclusion and also found that initiatives based on the specific recommendations of the Packard Commission did not reduce the average cost overrun experienced (as a percent of costs) on 269 completed defense acquisition contracts evaluated over an eight-year period (1988–1995). Actually, cost performance experienced on development contracts and on contracts managed by the Air Force worsened significantly.

Roughly ten years after the Packard Commission Report was published, the Secretary of Defense, William J. Perry, ordered the DoD to adopt many of the commercial practices recommended by the Commission. This is a good illustration of the roles that top leadership and champions play in advocating fundamental change.

The lack of reform success can, in part, be attributed to one or more of the causes discussed above. Since the 1980's, the military threat has changed from full-scale thermonuclear war to domestic terrorism, information warfare, and asymmetric warfare. Not only are weapons programs designed for a Cold War threat not always appropriate, but the entire system of acquisition has become too slow to adapt to emerging threats. The rate of technological change has advanced so rapidly that weapon systems can become obsolete before they leave the design stage. In response, the Department of Defense has attempted large scale, fundamental change in all facets of its operation.

The DoD has begun transforming its acquisition process to create more efficient and effective ways to acquire goods and services faster, better, and cheaper

(DAU, 2005). The exponential rate of technological advance combined with the availability of new technologies on the commercial market has added a sense of urgency to the acquisition environment. DoD would like to access these advances before adversaries can use them against the U.S.

A good example of the types of changes sought is the pursuit of evolutionary acquisition strategies that rely on spiral development processes. This approach focuses on providing the warfighter with an initial capability (that may not be the final capability) as a tradeoff for earlier delivery, flexibility, affordability, and risk reduction. The capabilities delivered are provided over a shorter period of time, followed by subsequent increments of capability over time that incorporate the latest technology and flexibility to reach the full capability of the system (Apte, 2005).

In a Defense Science Board summer study on transformation (DSB, 2006), it was recommended that the Undersecretary of Defense (AT&L) "should renew efforts to remove barriers that prevent the entry of non-traditional companies to the Defense business and Defense access to commercial technology, attacking the myriad rules, regulations, and practices that limit the use of OTA, Part 12, and other programs to reach beyond traditional defense companies." The study goes on to recommend intense integration with global and commercial supply chains, as well as transforming the export license process.

Potential Innovations

I was an officer in the U.S. Air Force from 1991–2003. My active duty stint was a research assignment at Air Force Cambridge Labs at Hanscom Field in Bedford, Massachusetts focused on interactive analytics for atmosphere research. Most of my service was subsequently in the inactive reserves. I achieved the rank of Captain (O-3).

Much later, I served two terms on the Air Force Scientific Advisory Board, 1996–2000, with a protocol rank of Lieutenant General (O-9). I served as a consultant to the Air Force CIO, in the early 2000s, helping to develop the Air Force information strategy, and to the Air Force Acquisition Organization (SAF/AQ), also in the early 2000s, facilitating the deliberations of the Work Culture Transformation Board.

From the 1970s through the 2000s, I received decades of research sponsorship from the Air Force, Army, and Navy as well as NASA. I addressed training and aiding of operators and maintainers of complex platforms for military and space missions, as well as decision support for the design, development, and deployment of these platforms.

Case Studies

We undertook several major studies of how defense investments, acquisition processes, and deployment operations might be both more innovative and economically attractive. The four case studies summarized here addressed the following:

- Science and technology investment options, supported by the U.S. Air Force
- Value-centered R&D management, supported by the U.S. Air Force
- Acquisition of military ships, supported by the U.S. Navy
- Operations of airborne surveillance and reconnaissance operations, supported by the Singapore Ministry of Defense

Each of these case studies of potential innovations is rather substantial. Consequently, a full section of this chapter is devoted to each case.

S&T Options for Human Effectiveness

Human effectiveness concerns enhancing people's direct performance (aiding), improving their potential to perform (training), and assuring their availability to perform (health and safety). These are central issues in human systems integration. Investments in human effectiveness also have the potential of increasing returns on other investments by, for example, enabling people to take full advantage of new technologies.

This case study addresses three examples of science and technology (S&T) aiding, training, and health and safety investments—VCATS (aiding), DMT (training), and PTOX (health and safety). These examples focus on enhancing human effectiveness and human systems integration in military systems—particularly, Air Force systems. The applicability of these technologies, and the relevance of the following analysis of the impacts of these technologies, to other military services and to non-military problems should also be readily apparent (Rouse & Boff, 2012).

Visually Coupled Targeting and Acquisition System

The Visually Coupled Targeting and Acquisition System (VCATS) provides aiding to military aircraft pilots. VCATS includes a helmet-mounted tracker and display (HMT/D), associated signal processing sensor/transducer hardware, interchangeable panoramic night vision goggle with head-up display (PNVG-HUD), and extensive upgrades to the aircraft's operational flight program software. VCATS enables the pilot to cue and be cued by on-board and off-board systems, sensors, and weapons, as well as be spatially and temporally coupled with the control processes implemented with the HMT/D and PNVG-HUD. The system is particularly effective in helping pilots to cue weapons and sensors to targets, maintain "ownship" formation situation awareness, and avoid threats via provision of a real-time, three-dimensional portrayal of the pilots' tactical and global battlefield status. In general, VCATS enables pilots to acquire targets and threats faster. This results in improvements in terms of: 1) how far, 2) how quickly and, 3) how long—for both initial contacts and countermeasures.

To a great extent, the case for advanced development had already been made for VCATS and current support was substantial. However, the transition from advanced development to production involves assuring that the options created by VCATS and validated by combat pilots are exercised. The case has also been argued for ongoing investments in basic research and exploratory development to assure that VCATS has future technology options, particularly for migration to multi-role fighter aircraft. The maturity of the program should help in making this case in terms of benefits already demonstrated. However, in the budget climate at that time, there was also substantial risk that VCATS research would be viewed as essentially "done." This raised the potential for negative decisions regarding further investments.

Distributed Mission Training

Distributed mission training (DMT) involves aircraft, virtual simulators, and constructive models that, collectively, provide opportunities for military pilots to gain experiences deemed important to their performance proficiency relative to anticipated mission requirements. The desired training experiences were determined from competencies identified as needed to fulfill mission requirements. These competency requirements were translated to training requirements stated in terms of types and durations of experiences deemed sufficient to gain competency.

The case to be made for DMT involved investments to address research issues and technology upgrades of near-term capabilities. The primary options-oriented argument was that investments in R&D in DMT would create contingent possibilities for cost savings in training due to reduced use of actual aircraft. More specifically, DMT options, if exercised, would provide cash flows of savings that justify the investments needed to field this family of technologies.

A much more subtle options-oriented argument concerns the training experiences provided by DMT that could not otherwise be obtained. Clearly, the opportunity to have relevant training experiences must be better than not having these experiences. The option, therefore, related to proficiency vs. possible lack of proficiency.

As straightforward as this may seem, it quickly encountered the difficulty of projecting mission impacts—and the value of these impacts—of not having proficient personnel. One possible approach to quantifying these benefits is to project the costs of using real aircraft to gain the desired proficiencies. While these costs are likely to be prohibitive—and thus never would be seriously considered—they nevertheless characterize the benefits of DMT.

Predictive Toxicology

Predictive toxicology (PTOX) is concerned with projecting the impacts on humans from exposure to operational chemicals (individual and mixtures). The impact can be characterized in terms of the possibility of performance decrement and consequent loss of force effectiveness, possible military and civilian casualties, and potential long-term health impacts. Also of concern were the impacts of countermeasures relative to sustaining immediate performance and minimizing long-term health impacts.

The case to be made involved investment in basic research and exploratory development programs, with longer-term investment in an advanced development program to create deployable predictive toxicology capabilities. The requisite R&D involved developing and evaluating models for predicting performance and health impacts of operational chemicals. Advanced development would focus on field sensing and prediction—termed deployment toxicology. The nature of the necessary models was strongly affected by the real time requirements imposed by deployment.

Stakeholders

This involved identifying people—usually types of people—and organizations that had a stake in these technologies. All three of the examples involve three classes of stakeholders—warfighters, developers, and the public. A key issue concerns the relative importance of these three types of stakeholders. Some would argue that warfighter preferences should dominate decisions. Others recognize the strong role that developers, and their constituencies, play in procurement decisions. Yet another argument is that the dominating factor is value to the public, with the other stakeholders being secondary in importance.

Warfighters as stakeholders include military personnel in general, especially for PTOX. Warfighters of particular importance include aircraft pilots, personnel who support flight operations, and military commanders. Developers as stakeholders include companies and their constituencies, e.g., stockholders, employees, and communities. Several agents including Congress, the executive functions within the military services, and the military procurement establishment represent the public's interests. Pilots and other military personnel are users of the technologies of interest, developers are the providers, and the public's agents are the customers for these technologies. There are obvious tradeoffs across the interests of users, providers, and customers.

Attributes

Attributes tend to fall into general classes. Example attributes that benefit military organizations and contractors include:

- Enhanced Impact: ➔ Increased lethality, survivability, and availability
- Enhanced Operability ➔ Decreased response time and increased throughput
- Enhanced Design ➔ New techniques and larger pool of experienced people
- Increased Opportunities ➔ New tactics and countermeasures

Example attributes that represent costs to military procurement include:

- Investment Costs ➔ Capital investments and R&D costs
- Recurring Costs ➔ Operating and G&A costs
- Time Costs ➔ Time from development to fielding to competent use
- Opportunity Costs ➔ Other cost/benefits foregone

These general classes of attributes can be translated into specific benefit and cost attributes for the three classes of stakeholders in VCATS, DMT, and PTOX. Benefits for warfighters (users) include enhanced performance (e.g., response time), confidence in performance, and health and safety—in varying combinations for the three examples. Costs for these stakeholders include learning time and changing their ways of doing things to assure compatibility between new and legacy technologies.

Benefits for companies and their constituencies (providers) include R&D funds received, subsequent intellectual property created, and competitive advantages that result. Also important are jobs, and economic impacts in the community. Direct costs include bid and proposal costs as well as opportunity costs. Less direct costs include, for instance, economic development resources and incentives provided to the companies by their communities.

The primary benefit sought by the public's agents (customer) is mission performance/dollar. It can easily be argued for all three examples that mission performance is increased. Unfortunately, it is difficult to attach a value to this increase. For example, what is the value of being able to generate 5 percent more sorties per time period? The answer depends on whether more sorties are needed.

Few would argue with the importance of successfully meeting mission requirements. However, if the types of innovations represented by these examples enable exceeding mission requirements, what are such increases worth? This is a politically sensitive question. If better performance is of substantive value, why wasn't this level of performance specified in the original requirements?

A good way to avoid this difficulty is to take mission requirements as a given and determine how much money could be saved in meeting these requirements by adopting the technologies in question. For example, could requirements be met with fewer aircraft, pilots, and support personnel? As shown in Table 3.2, the cost savings due to these decreases can be viewed as benefits of the technologies. It also might be possible for VCATS, DMT, or PTOX to enable meeting mission requirements with less-capable systems, rather than just fewer systems. This possibility provides substantial opportunities for increased benefits due to these technologies.

The rationale for the benefits indicated in Table 3.2 for each of the three examples include:

- VCATS enables pilots to compete with threats, increase the number of wins vs. losses, and counter threats (e.g., missiles) in ways that they could not do otherwise. Consequently, it must be possible to meet fixed mission requirements with

Table 3.2 Benefits and Costs for Three Examples.

	VCATS	DMT	PTOX
Benefits	Fewer aircraft and associated personnel to meet mission requirements due to better performance and fewer aircraft losses	Fewer aircraft and associated personnel to meet mission requirements due to better performance, fewer aircraft losses, and fewer aircraft for training	Fewer personnel to meet mission requirements and decreased medical costs due to fewer people affected by toxic materials, fewer people lost to toxic effects, fewer people to care for people affected, and decreased downstream medical costs
Costs	Initial investment (option price) for proposed R&D costs and later, contingent investment (exercise price) for subsequent fielding of technology	Initial investment (option price) for proposed R&D costs and later, contingent investment (exercise price) for subsequent fielding of technology	Initial investment (option price) for proposed R&D costs and later, contingent investment (exercise price) for subsequent fielding of technology

Note that this philosophy amounts to trying to provide a given level of defense for the least investment. Another approach might be to attempt to provide the most defense per investment dollar. However, this immediately begs the question of how much defense is enough. Unlike the business world where value is defined by the market place and, hence, can provide a basis for optimization, there is no widely agreed-upon approach to measuring military value and optimizing accordingly.

fewer aircraft and associated infrastructure. These benefits can be translated into financial returns in terms of cost avoidance
- DMT provides opportunities to practice behaviors that would not otherwise be practiced, for the most part due to the costs of practice. This decreases the probability of not performing acceptably given inadequate training. DMT also provides training experiences that would not otherwise be possible. For example, in the DMT environment, pilot "kills" actually disappear. In contrast, field exercises often "reuse" kills because of the costs of getting adversaries into the exercise in the first place
- PTOX enables larger proportions of deployed forces to be fully functional, less dependent on medical surveillance or medication, and earlier intervention, before the onset of problems. In principle, this should enable reducing the size of deployed force, which is critical for increasingly likely expeditionary military missions (Fuchs, et al., 1997)
- PTOX also provides cost avoidance due to downstream health impacts. The ability to predict the "body burden" of toxicity during deployment should enable personnel to be removed from risk once the burden is approaching predetermined limits. These capabilities are likely to also be very important for non-military operations such as disaster clean-up

It is **not** essential that the savings indicated in Table 3.2 actually occur. For example, it may be that the number of aircraft is not decreased, perhaps due to factors far beyond the scope of these analyses. However, one can nevertheless attribute to these technologies the benefits of having provided opportunities to meet mission requirements in less costly manners. Technologies that provide such opportunities are valuable—the extent of this value is the extent of the opportunities for savings.

This argument puts all three examples on common ground. The benefits of all alternative technologies can be expressed as reduced costs to meet requirements. From an options pricing perspective, these savings can be viewed as free cash flow returned on investments in these technologies. The "option price" is the R&D costs. The "exercise price" is the subsequent costs of fielding the technologies. Thus, assuming costs savings can be projected (albeit with substantial volatility), the option values of investing in these technologies can be calculated.

Stakeholders' Utility Functions

Different stakeholders' preferences over the benefit and cost attributes will vary substantially with specific situations. However, as discussed in Chapter 2, there is a small family of functional relationships that captures most, if not all, expressed preferences. Thus, while context-specific tailoring is needed, it can be performed within a prescribed set of functions, both within and across stakeholders. Similarly, alternative parameter choices can be prescribed in terms of choices of weightings.

An important aspect of this analysis is the likely nonlinear nature of utility functions. In particular, diminishing returns and aspiration levels tend to be central to stakeholders' "preference spaces." In other words, while linear functions imply that incremental increases (or decreases) of attributes always yield the same incremental changes in utility, nonlinear functions lead to shifting preferences as attributes increase (or decrease). Figure 2.5 in Chapter 2 summarized a range of example utility functions.

To illustrate how these types of relationships can be employed to represent the preferences of users, providers, and customers, the general forms of each type of stakeholder's utility function are shown in equations 3.1–3.3:

$$U_{user} = U\left[u\left(performance\right), u\left(confidence\right), u\left(cost\ of\ change\right)\right] \quad (3.1)$$

$$U_{provider} = U\left[u\left(resources\right), u\left(advantage\right), u\left(cost\ of\ pursuit\right)\right] \quad (3.2)$$

$$U_{customer} = u\left(option\ value\right) \quad (3.3)$$

As noted earlier, users are primarily concerned with the impact of investments on their performance, their confidence in their performance, and the costs of changing their ways of performing. Providers are concerned with the investment resources supplied to develop the technologies in question, the competitive advantages created by the intellectual property created, and the costs of pursuing the investment opportunities. Finally, customers are focused on the financial attractiveness of the investments as reflected in the option values of the alternatives, which are based on projected cash flows (i.e., costs savings), volatility of cash flows, magnitudes of investments required, and time periods until returns are realized.

Considering the elements of equations 3.1–3.3, the appropriate functional forms from Figure 2.5 are likely to be as follows:

- u(performance) is an accelerating returns function:
  - ○ VCATS is least concave since relatively modest performance improvements are of substantial utility
  - ○ DMT is moderately concave since training on otherwise untrained tasks must produce substantial improvements to yield high utility
  - ○ PTOX is most concave since major decreases in performance risk are needed to assure high utility increases of personnel availability
- u(confidence) is a linear function since greater confidence is always better, but there are unlikely to be significant thresholds
- u(cost of change) is an accelerating decline function since low to moderate costs are easily sustained while larger costs present difficulties
- u(resources) is an accelerating returns function since moderate to large resources are needed to make opportunities attractive
- u(advantage) is a linear function since greater advantage is always better, but there are unlikely to be significant thresholds
- u(cost of pursuit) is an accelerating decline since low to moderate costs are easily sustained while larger costs present difficulties
- u(option value) is a linear function since customers will inherently gain the expected value across a large number of investments

It is important to note the importance of this last assumption. If customers'—that is, the public's—utility function were not linear, it would be necessary to entertain assessing the specific form of their function. Unlike users and providers, the public is not so easily identified and interviewed.

With the identification of the stakeholders, and determination of the attributes, the process of deciding on the form of stakeholders' utility functions can draw upon considerable standard "machinery" of decision analysis. The specific versions of the functional forms discussed above are likely to vary with VCATS, DMT, and PTOX. However, the overall formulation chosen is quite general.

Utility Functions Across Stakeholders

Another important aspect of the utility functions is their typical lack of alignment across stakeholders. Specifically, either different stakeholders care about different things, or possibly they care about the same things in different ways. For example, customers may be very price-sensitive while users, who seldom pay prices themselves, are usually much more concerned with impacts on their job performance.

For the types of investment problems considered in this case study, preferences typically differ across time horizons and across people with vested interests in different investment opportunities. Thus far in the formulation of the three examples, the stakeholders do not have attributes in common. However, they are nevertheless likely to have competing preferences since, for example, the alternative providing the greatest performance impact may not have the largest option value.

Differing preferences across stakeholders are often driving forces in pursuing cost/benefit analyses. These differing preferences can be aggregated, and traded off, by formulating a composite utility function such as

$$U = U \left[U_{user}, U_{provider}, U_{customer} \right] \qquad (3.4)$$

Often equation 3.4 will be linear in form with weights assigned to component utility functions to reflect the relative importance of stakeholders. Slightly more complicated are multi-linear forms which include products of component functions, e.g., $U_{user} \times U_{customer}$. Multi-linear formulations tend to assure that all stakeholders gain non-zero utility because, otherwise, zero in either term in a product yields zero overall.

Considering tradeoffs across stakeholders, it is important to note that the formulation of the analysis can often be usefully expanded to include a broader set of stakeholders. These additional stakeholders may include other entities that will benefit by advances in the technologies in question, although they may have little or no stake in the immediate application for the technology. It is also quite possible that stakeholders such as "the public" have multiple interests, e.g., military effectiveness and public safety from toxic risks.

Broadening the analysis in this way is likely to have differing impacts on the assessment for the three examples due to the natures of the technologies and issues being pursued. The three examples differ in this regard in the following ways:

- VCATS addresses a rather esoteric set of issues from the public's perspective
- DMT addresses an issue with broad general support from the public, but narrower specific constituencies
- PTOX addresses strong cross-cutting health and safety issues of substantial concern to the public

These differences suggest that PTOX would gain a larger ΔU than DMT, and DMT would in turn gain a larger ΔU than VCATS, by broadening the number of stakeholders and issues. Quite simply, the "spin-off" benefits of PTOX are likely to be perceived as much greater by a larger number of stakeholders.

However, if the formulation is further broadened to consider the likelihood that the desired technologies will emerge elsewhere if investments are not made in these efforts, the ΔU impacts are likely be the opposite. PTOX research and development are being pursued by several agencies. DMT has broad applicability for both military and non-military applications and consequently is being pursued by other parties. VCATS, in contrast, is highly specialized and is unlikely to emerge from other sources.

These two possibilities for broadening the formulation—in terms of stakeholders and issues—clearly illustrate the substantial impact of the way in which assessments are framed. If the framing is too focused, important spin-off benefits may not be included. On the other hand, framing the analysis too broadly may raise issues that are difficult to quantify—even roughly—and include stakeholders whose preferences are difficult to assess.

Overall Expected Utility

The remaining steps of the overall approach involve assessing parameters of utility functions, forecasting levels of attributes, and calculating expected utilities. Performing these steps obviously depends on having data on stakeholders' preferences and projected/targeted attribute levels. Consideration of such data is well beyond the scope of this discussion—and, in light of the nature of the examples, it would be difficult to publish the requisite data.

The needed data can, in many instances, be quite difficult to compile. It can be particularly difficult to relate returns on human effectiveness investments to organizational impacts. Relationships between human and organizational performance are needed. These relationships should answer the following types of questions:

- How do improvements in human performance (e.g., via aiding) translate to increased organizational impacts? Specifically, how does a two-second improvement in pilot response time due to VCATS affect mission performance?
- How do improvements in human potential to perform (e.g., via training) translate to actual performance and consequent increased organizational impacts? Specifically, how does increased practice via DMT impact subsequent performance and, in turn, translate to improved mission performance?
- How do improvements in human availability to perform (e.g., via health and safety) translate to actual performance and consequent increased organizational impacts? Specifically, how does prevention of toxic exposure, due to PTOX, affect immediate unit performance and thereby affect mission performance?

These can be difficult questions. For the VCATS, DMT, and PTOX examples, it may be possible to translate human performance improvements to organizational impacts via mission models. Such models are typically used to determine, for example, the "logistics footprint" needed to support a targeted sortie generation rate or, as another illustration, the combat wins and losses likely with competing defensive measures and countermeasures. Such models can be applied, perhaps with extensions, to project the impacts of faster responses due to VCATS, improved task performance due to DMT, and increased personnel availability due to PTOX.

It is important to note, however, that even if such projections are not available, the multi-attribute methodology presented here can still be employed. However, the validity of assessments and predictions will then depend upon subjective perceptions of attribute levels and the relative importance of attributes. Any limitations of this more subjective approach reflect underlying limitations of knowledge rather than inherent limitations of the methodology.

Once $U[U_{user}, U_{provider}, U_{customer}]$ is fully specified, both functionally and in terms of parameters of these functions, one is in position to project attribute levels (e.g., option values), calculate the expected utility of the alternative investments, e.g., VCATS, DMT, and PTOX, and perform sensitivity analyses. This provides the basis for making investment decisions. There are several ways that these cost/benefit assessments can be used to inform decision making.

The most common way of using expected utility cost/benefit assessments is to rank order alternative investments in terms of decreasing $U[U_{user}, U_{provider}, U_{customer}]$ and then allocate investment resources from highest ranked to lowest ranked until resources are exhausted. This approach allows the possibility of alternatives with mediocre $U_{customer}$ making the cut by having substantial U_{user} and $U_{provider}$. To avoid this possibility, one can rank order by $U[U_{user}, U_{provider}, U_{customer}]$ all alternatives with $U_{customer} > U_{co}$, which implies a minimum acceptable option value.

If resources are relatively unconstrained, one can, invest in all alternatives for which $U_{user} > U_{uo}$, $U_{provider} > U_{po}$, and $U_{customer} > U_{co}$. This reflects situations where all stakeholders prefer investment to no investment. Of course, one can also rank order these alternatives by $U[U_{user}, U_{provider}, U_{customer}]$ to determine priorities for investment. However, if resources are truly unconstrained, this rank ordering will not change the resulting investment decisions.

Summary

The three examples discussed in this case study have portrayed a cross-section of human effectiveness investments to enhance human systems integration, ranging from aiding to training to health and safety investments. The discussion has shown how this range of investment alternatives can be fully addressed with an overarching multi-stakeholder, multi-attribute utility formulation. The stakeholder classes of user, provider, and customer are broadly applicable. The classes of attributes discussed also have broad applicability.

These examples have also served to illustrate the merits of a hybrid approach. In particular, option value theory has been used to define the issue of primary interest to customers—assuring that investments make financial sense—and this issue has then been incorporated into the overall multi-attribute formulation. This enabled including in the formulation a substantial degree of objective rigor as well as important subjective attributes and perceptions. As a result, rigor is not sacrificed, but instead balanced with broader, less quantifiable considerations.

Value-Centered Organizations

Options-based thinking as outlined in Chapter 2, and illustrated with the case study just discussed, evolved to formulation of a framework for creating value-centered organizations (Rouse & Boff, 2004). Value is concerned with organizational outcomes or outputs, not inputs like budgets and staff. The focus should be on creating valuable outcomes despite facing considerable uncertainties.

The first concern is *characterizing value*. Value is created in R&D organizations by providing "technology options" for meeting contingent needs of the enterprise. In this way, R&D organizations provide a primary means for enterprises to manage uncertainty by generating options for addressing contingent needs. A central challenge for R&D organizations is to create a portfolio of viable options. Whether or not options are exercised is an enterprise challenge. Figure 3.2 summarizes the overall idea of multi-stage contingent investments.

The next concern is *assessing value*. Value streams, or value networks, provide a means for representing value flow and assessing the value of options created.

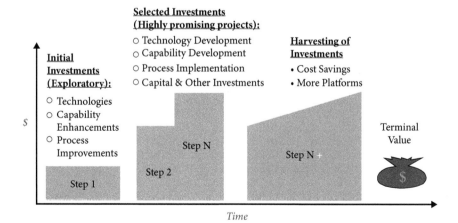

Fig. 3.2 Multi-Stage Approach to Contingent Investments

Valuation of R&D investments can be addressed by assessing the value of the options created in the value network. The options-based approach outlined in Chapter 2, and the case studies in this chapter, provides the means for this assessment.

A third and crucial concern is *managing value*. Decision making processes—governance—are central to managing the flow of value. Specifically, if NOV is communicated as a key metric, then this metric should affect decisions. If other factors dominate, e.g., who knows whom, then emphases on NOV will be quickly and cynically dismissed.

Organizational structure affects value flow, with significant differences between hierarchical vs. heterarchical structures. In two studies of R&D organizations, one in industry and one in government, we found that projects where appeal to the hierarchy for permission or resources was necessary, resulted in delays of execution for months and sometimes years.

Individual and team affiliations and identities affect value flow; dovetailing processes with disciplines is essential. People need to be affiliated with value streams *and* their disciplinary base. Without the former, recognitions of contributions are likely diminished. Without the latter, disciplinary expertise can whither.

Champions play important, yet subtle, roles in value flow. Supporting champions is necessary but not sufficient for success. In one study, we encountered a situation where deployment of R&D outcomes only occurred when champions found ways to circumvent processes intended to help them. This is not a sustainable approach to value.

Incentives and rewards affect value flow. Aligning these systems with value maximization is critical. If the incentive and reward system remains aligned to outdated value propositions, people in the organization will continue to march to the old drummer. A good example is academia where multi-disciplinary research is extolled but incentives and rewards remain tightly tied to individual accomplishments.

Successful technology adoption depends on good ideas, adequate resources, and hard work, but that is not enough. Value needs to be characterized and assessed appropriately. Value needs to be managed to align behavioral and social phenomena with the value proposition being pursued. Misalignment can undermine ideas, resources, and work.

I have applied this value-centered thinking in over 30 engagements with industry and government agencies. Rouse and Boff (2004) summarizes 14 of these case studies. Many billions of dollars of value were unearthed, both for companies and government agencies. One CEO wrote, "I am much more comfortable with the financial projections resulting from this approach. Much more important than the numbers, however, was the realization that we need to formulate and manage a rich portfolio of options."

Acquisition of Military Ships

Figure 3.3 depicts the Defense Acquisition Management Framework provided in the Defense Directive 5000.1. This process provides both the context for transformation of acquisition and an opportunity, in itself, for transformation. In fact, the ways in which the many stakeholders in the acquisition enterprise exercise this process strongly affect the time, costs, and uncertainties associated with the acquisition of complex systems. In light of recent Secretary of Defenses' stated transformation priorities, this process would seem to be a good candidate for fundamental change.

Military Shipbuilding

Consider the enterprise of military shipbuilding. This enterprise is facing serious cost challenges. Shipbuilding costs have increased enormously in the past several decades, far beyond inflation during this period. It certainly can reasonably be argued that these more expensive ships are much more capable than earlier ships. Thus, you may need fewer ships. It is quite possible, however, that increased costs will cause the number of ships you can buy to decrease faster than new capabilities reduce the number of ships needed. Thus, these cost challenges cannot be dismissed. This situation raises the question of where investments in shipbuilding should be focused. In this case study, I describe a method for assessing the economic value of transforming acquisition processes and use the example of the shipbuilding enterprise to illustrate this method (Pennock, Rouse & Kollar, 2007)

As indicated in Figure 3.4, the enterprise of interest includes a set of stakeholders and issues much broader than those directly associated with the ships of interest. Congress, the armed services, defense contractors, and workforce organizations have

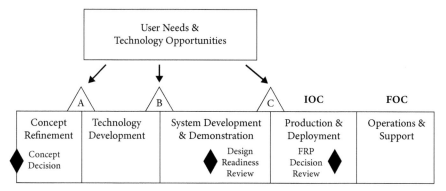

Fig. 3.3 Defense Acquisition Management Framework

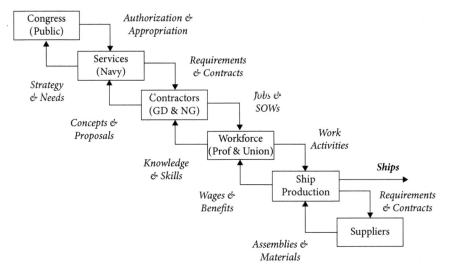

Fig. 3.4 The Overall Shipbuilding Enterprise

significant impact on the returns and risks associated with alternative investments. These stakeholders affect the shipbuilding enterprise in a variety of ways:

- Congressional interests and mandates, e.g., jobs and other economic interests
- Service interests and oversights, e.g., procedures, documentation and reviews
- Incentives and rewards forcontractors, e.g., cost-plus vs. firm fixed price
- Lack of market-based competition, e.g., hiring and retention problems
- Aging workforce and lack of attraction of jobs, e.g., outsourcing limitations, underutilization of capacity

In discussion with senior U.S. Navy executives, we learned that the Navy would like to transform the way it acquires ships and, therefore, would like to consider several changes that will streamline the development and design process and reduce rework. Thus, the Navy would like the option to transform its ship acquisition enterprise. More specifically, they want to entertain streamlining the development and design process and reduce rework, which affects the Technology Development and System Development and Demonstration phases in Figure 3.3

In order to determine whether or not the Navy should initiate transformation, an option model was developed. First, we developed a method to value a successful transformation, with transformation analogous to the underlying asset they wish to acquire. Next, we structured a multistage option to acquire this asset. The multiple stages served to mitigate both the market and technical risks inherent in transformation. Finally, we used the binomial method, advanced compared to that discussed in Chapter 2, to determine the value of the option to transform as well as the optimal exercise policy.

Ship Production

First, we needed to value a successful transformation. Transformation means that we exchange the current cost stream for a new cost stream. One could simply consider the cost savings (i.e., the difference between the two cost streams) as the value of the transformation, but this would be neglecting some of the benefits. The cost of a ship is related to the production rate. More specifically, military shipbuilding exhibits increasing returns to scale. That is the higher the rate of production, the lower the cost per unit. Consequently, if we use the cost savings to produce more ships, the increase in production rate will actually decrease the price per ship further resulting in an even greater gain.

The first feature of this problem that we must consider is the ship production process. To keep the model simple, we made several assumptions that will facilitate interpretation of the results within the context of this case study. These are summarized in Table 3.3. Of course, if one were to use this method to evaluate any particular proposed transformation project, these assumptions would be adjusted as appropriate. First, we will assume that the model is continuous. While in reality ships are discrete items, and budgets are set annually, we are considering the long-term trends, and consequently, the discontinuities diminish in importance as we increase our time horizon.

With our production model, we can determine the impact of transformation in terms of number of ships produced. Parameters were set in accordance with the above assumptions. The current production rate was set to one ship per year, but costs were growing faster than the budget. The production rate was declining 3.5 percent per year. That meant that if current conditions continued, we would only be able to produce 14 ships over the next twenty years.

This may be surprising since cost growth is only outpacing budget growth by 3 percent, but this model is exhibiting increasing returns to scale, i.e., equivalent to

Table 3.3 Modeling Assumptions.

Assumption	Justification
Shipbuilding budget grows exponentially	Allows us to consider the impact of growing or declining budgets.
Ship construction input costs follow geometric Brownian motion	Models the exponential growth in ship cost while accounting for economic noise in prices.
Ship production process is governed by a Cobb-Douglas production function	Allows us to consider the impact of economies of scale on the quantity of ships produced.
Ship production is continuous	Allows us to focus on the long-term trends in ship production sustainability.

an 85 percent learning curve. The non-linearity of the production function means that as the production level drops, the per-unit cost of production rises. This is the feedback effect that the Navy was experiencing in its shipbuilding program. As ship costs rise, the Navy can afford fewer ships thus lowering the production rate. As the production rate falls, more inefficient means of production are used and the cost per ship rises even more. Thus, the production rate declines even faster than apparent from the budget shortfall.

Thus, we can see how the compounding effect from increasing returns to scale hurts production when costs are rising. If we look at cost savings, on the other hand, the opposite is true. Let us assume that our transformation instantaneously drops input costs 20 percent. With increasing returns to scale the production rate increases 34 percent, while under constant returns to scale the increase is only 25 percent. Over the next 20 years, the Navy will produce 19 ships under increasing returns to scale and only 18 ships under constant returns to scale.

While the production levels are certainly of interest, it would be easier to value the investment if we could convert it into monetary terms. Since we indicated earlier that simple cost savings are under-representing the return, we need a means to capture both the initial effect of the savings and the secondary effect of reduced production costs. As stated earlier, we can accomplish this by measuring the increase in the buying power of the budget. If a cost reduction decreases the cost per ship, this effectively increases the buying power of the budget since it can be used to purchase more ships.

Transformation Stages

There are technical risks to implementing the transformation. To mitigate these risks we will assume that there is a three-stage process. The first is for concept development and feasibility analysis. This stage is relatively short and inexpensive. If the transformation idea proves to be infeasible at this stage, the Navy can terminate the project at no additional cost. The second stage pilot tests the changes on the acquisition of a single ship. If the project fails at this stage, rework costs will be required to rectify the situation and complete the acquisition of the ship. Finally, the third stage involves implementing the transformation across the whole shipbuilding enterprise. If the transformation fails in this stage, a substantial cost in rework is incurred. Table 3.4 contains the staging parameter values for this example.

The "Stage Cost" column lists the costs required to execute each stage, and the "Rework Cost" column lists the cost incurred if a particular stage fails. The "P(Success)" column lists the probability that each stage will succeed. Finally, the "Duration" column lists the length of each stage. We assume in this example that all costs are deterministic, and are funded from outside the ship construction budget.

The parameters in Table 3.4, in conjunction with the model outlined above, resulted in NPV equaled to $-453 million and NOV equaled to $309 million. The NPV approach inherently assumes that one executes all three stages—even if the first or

Table 3.4 Stage Parameter Values.

Stage	Stage Cost ($ billions)	P(Success)	Rework Cost ($ billions)	Duration (years)
1	0.001	0.4	0	0.5
2	0.01	0.6	1	3
3	0.1	0.8	10	N/A

second stages fail. Given that the overall probability of success is 0.2 (0.4 × 0.6×0.8), we would expect to incur a substantial loss by initiating this project.

Here we can see the discrepancy between the NOV and the NPV. The NPV is too conservative because it fails to account for the risk mitigation inherent in staging. So, in this example, a decision-maker using NPV as the decision criterion would reject a potentially beneficial program.

This illustrates the importance of properly considering the staged nature of most risky projects. NPV fails as a decision criterion in this respect and can result in overly conservative decision-making because it undervalues high-risk, high-return investments. An options approach accounts for the risk mitigation inherent in staged projects with well-defined "off ramps" and provides a more realistic assessment of a project's worth.

The Navy executives that prompted this study originally asked, "What level of return on investment might we expect from investing in ship production?" We reported our findings, which addressed the process for acquiring ships rather than the nature of the ships themselves. The bottom line was, "If you want ships faster and cheaper, you have to change the way you buy them." After much discussion, the Navy executives agreed with our findings. Then they added, "What you have found makes great sense, but unfortunately it would be illegal!"

The Navy manages the process of acquiring ships, but cannot unilaterally decide how to proceed. They need approval from the Armed Services and Appropriations Committees of the House and Senate of the U.S. Congress. Key members of these committees include Representatives and Senators from Connecticut, Maine, Mississippi, Rhode Island, and Virginia. Bath Iron Works in Maine and Huntington-Ingalls in Mississippi mainly build destroyers and amphibious assault ships. Electric Boat in Connecticut and Rhode Island builds submarines. Newport News in Virginia builds aircraft carriers and submarines. These companies employ more than 70,000 people in shipbuilding. It is clearly a public-private ecosystem.

Options for Surveillance and Reconnaissance

This case study emerged from a keen interest in "the value of defense" or, put differently, the question, "What is defense worth?" Of course, considerable attention has been paid to the cost of defense. Ideally, one would like the cost to be significantly less than the value. That makes defense a good investment.

I have applied this approach to a large number of case studies in the private sector in industries ranging from aerospace, automotive and electronics, to semiconductors, computers, and pharmaceuticals. In all these applications, an upfront investment secured the possibility of future free cash flow. The difficulty with defense investments is identifying the free cash flow.

It would appear that money always flows from taxpayers through Congress to the Department of Defense and then to defense contractors. Cash does not seem to flow the other way. However, reduced expenditures in the future, relative to what they would have been without investment, can be characterized as cash flows. Thus, we should, in principle at least, be able to estimate the cash flow returns from defense investments.

There is one significant difficulty, however. What is the value of the performance impacts of the systems acquired through defense expenditures? This leads to questions of the relative value of an aircraft sortie compared to a ship patrol. One quickly gets to the point of having to compare the value of things that serve completely different purposes.

We finessed this difficulty by taking performance requirements as a given. Thus, all alternatives are characterized in ways that they meet performance requirements. As this case study illustrates, assuring parity in this way can take some creativity. However, once this is accomplished, all comparisons are primarily economic. We can, for example, view current investments in R&D as providing options for future reductions in operating costs (Rouse, 2010).

This case study was conducted for the Singapore Ministry of Defense (MINDEF). I first address framing the investment decisions of interest. Alternative investments are then considered. Investment valuations are then discussed, from both Net Present Value and Net Option Value perspectives. The economic valuation results are then integrated with a broader multi-stakeholder, multi-attribute analysis. Finally, the investment strategy I recommended is summarized and the resulting decisions discussed.

Framing the Investment

Investment analyses should always begin with consideration of the goals of the investment. It is certainly the case that all investors desire "returns" on their investments. In many cases, the returns sought are purely financial. However, for public sector investments, "returns" can be much more multi-dimensional.

Effects and Capabilities. For defense investments, the goal is national defense. Much thinking has emphasized characterizing the goals of defense investments in terms of the effects sought, rather than platforms acquired (Rouse & Boff, 2001). In this study, the effects sought were characterized as deterrence and superiority.

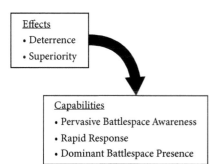

Fig. 3.5 Desired Effects and Capabilities

The first goal concerns inhibiting aggression. The second goal involves competitive advantage in the face of aggression.

Effects are achieved by capabilities that may be provided in various ways. Three capabilities were sought from the investment under consideration:

- Pervasive battlespace awareness
- Rapid response
- Dominant battlespace presence

Succinctly, as shown in Figure 3.5, MINDEF wanted to be fully aware of the current and emerging states of the environment of interest, be able to respond to these states quickly, and be dominant in their response. There are many alternative platforms that have the potential to provide these capabilities. The objective of this case study was to assess the economic value of these alternatives.

Mission Scenarios. It is helpful to think about effects and capabilities in the contexts of specific missions. Three scenarios were developed to help define more specific capabilities

- Battlefield
  - o Detect, identify, and monitor forces and their movements
  - o Recognize and classify patterns of movements, intent etc.
- Period of Tension
  - o Detect (anticipate) transition to conflict
  - o Demonstrate presence to deter transition
- Terrorist
  - o Detect violation of geographical boundaries
  - o Monitor ongoing status of activities
  - o Search and identify targets with known characteristics
  - o Monitor transactions (financial, supply chains)

As l later discuss, these three scenarios served as surrogates for the public's interests in the investments being considered. This is a useful approach to answering the question, "What does the taxpayer want?" The answer is that the public wants the military to be able to successfully perform the missions for which it is responsible.

Sensing Requirements. Analysis of the scenarios led to determination of sensing requirements for the capabilities sought from the investment of interest. The quantitative nature of these requirements cannot be reported here.

- Physical location
- Physical size and shape
- Physical dispersion
- Physical weight and density
- Physical movement
- Communications
- Electrical activity
- Temperature
- Light
- Rates of change

Alternative Investments

The framing of the investment decision led to consideration of alternative means for providing the desired capabilities. Seven alternatives were defined:

- Manned Aircraft
- GEO Satellite
- LEO Satellite
- Micro Satellite (MICRO)
- Predator
- Global Hawk
- LALEE

MICRO and LALEE were the alternatives being pursued by internal R&D at MIN-DEF. MICRO is a very small satellite. LALEE is a very large unmanned air vehicle. An overarching question was which of these two should be pursued further, or whether both should be abandoned for capabilities procured externally.

Manned aircraft provide a traditional approach to surveillance and reconnaissance. Geosynchronous and low earth orbiting satellites can be almost purchased off the shelf. Predator and Global Hawk are U.S. unmanned air vehicles, at that time not available to Singapore, but nevertheless interesting alternatives.

Substantial discussion was devoted to determining how each of these alternatives could provide the desired capabilities. A central question was how many units would be needed to satisfy sensing requirements and support typical duty cycles. For example, it was determined that they would need one GEO or many LEOs. Numbers for all the alternatives cannot be reported here.

It was very important that all of the alternatives be capable of the same sensing performance. As noted earlier, this eliminated the need to address cost vs. performance tradeoffs. Since the payloads of the alternatives varied significantly, this strongly affected the number of units needed to achieve performance parity. While the parity achieved was not perfect, the key stakeholders in this case study felt that it was close enough to focus solely on economic valuation, at least initially.

System Schedules. The study team then shifted its attention to the timelines for development, acquisition, and deployment of the alternatives. MICRO and LALEE were the only alternatives needing development. The other five alternatives could, in principle, be acquired and deployed. Consequently, the timelines of the seven alternatives varied greatly.

Table 3.5 shows the format developed for compiling the timeline information. The contents of this table cannot be provided here. However, the most important point is that considerable effort was invested in reaching agreement on the contents of this table.

System Costs. One of the most time-consuming aspects of this case study was compiling cost information in the format shown in Table 3.6. While Table 3.5 defined the starting year in each row of Table 3.6 for each alternative, developing the cost estimates for subsequent cells required some sleuthing.

Table 3.5 Development, Acquisition, and Deployment Schedules.

System	Development Duration	Acquisition Duration	Deployment Date	Comments
Aircraft				
GEO				
LEO				
Micro				
Predator				
Hawk				
LALEE				

Table 3.6 Cost Projections Developed for Each System Alternative.

Costs	Year 1	Year 2	Year 3	...	Year 20
Development					
Acquisition					
Operating					
Total					

The data compilation process employed involved having representatives of all key stakeholders around a large table in a conference room. Each person's laptop was connected to the MNDEF network. Each person also had a cell phone. Over the course of a couple of days, many "data calls" were made via either email or cell phone. Of particular importance was the estimation of operating costs for each alternative. Acquisition costs were more readily available. Development costs came from internal proposals for MICRO and LALEE.

The cost estimates developed in this way were vetted following these intense meetings. Interestingly, very few changes resulted. It is, of course, very important to have realistic and credible cost estimates. Such estimates can also include uncertainties that can be employed in Monte Carlo simulations to yield probability distributions of economic values rather than just point values. Such distributions can also provide the means for estimating risks as well as returns, perhaps expressed as the probability that the return exceeds zero.

Investment Valuations

The data from Table 3.6 was first used to calculate the Net Present Value for each alternative—see Chapter 2 for how this calculation is done. Figure 3.6 shows the results, stated in terms of Net Present Cost so the numbers are positive. Note that

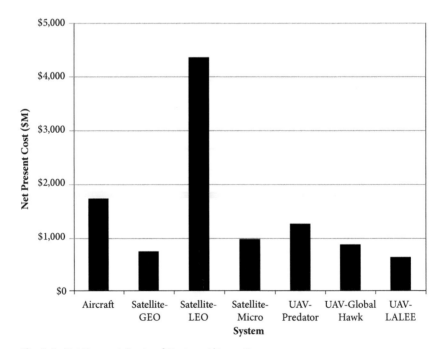

Fig. 3.6 Net Present Costs of System Alternatives

the cost of the aircraft is dominated by operating costs, while the cost of LEO is dominated by the number of units that must be deployed to satisfy sensing requirements.

At this point, LALEE looked most attractive, followed by GEO and then Global Hawk. This might suggest that MINDEF should select LALEE and move on. However, this choice would result in not having the desirable capabilities for many years. The only way to gain these capabilities relatively quickly was to employ manned aircraft. (Recall that Predator and Global Hawk were not really available to Singapore.)

Investment Options

Discussion of this situation led to framing of two options. Both involve purchasing and deploying the aircraft as soon as possible. The options were defined as follows:

- Replace Aircraft with MICRO ➔ Deploy aircraft in Year X, replace with MICRO in Year Y, with operating costs reduced $A per year.
- Replace Aircraft With LALEE ➔ Deploy aircraft in Year X, replace with LALEE in Year Z, with operating costs reduced $B per year.

Note that the years and amounts indicated above cannot be provided in this exposition.

Using the real options model introduced in Chapter 2, the Net Option Value was calculated for each of these options. The results are shown in Figure 3.7. The black bars on the left represent the initial results. Both MICRO and LALEE are very unattractive. This is due to the acquisition costs of the aircraft. In other words, the purchase price of the option—that is, the costs of the aircraft plus the costs of R&D for MICRO or LALEE—are too high considering the likely downstream returns.

This led to an intense discussion of what to do with the aircraft. Selling it on the open market was a possibility. However, it was decided that it could be "sold" to a different mission. An equivalent "purchase price" was determined and represented as a positive cash flow in the year of its "sale." The bar to the right of the black bars in Figure 3.7 shows the result.

Therefore, at this point, both MICRO and LALEE looked economically attractive. The decision-makers had two concerns at this point, both of which involved possible variability in actual costs vs. those projected in Table 3.6.

- What if R&D costs exceed projections?
- What if operating savings are overestimated?

The impact of these possibilities was assessed using Monte Carlo analysis assuming the mean R&D costs were 110 percent of projections, with a 10 percent standard deviation. Mean operating savings were assumed to be 90 percent of projections, also

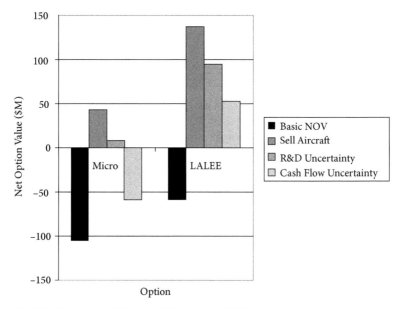

Fig. 3.7 Net Option Values of Micro and LALEE

with a 10 percent standard deviation. The two rightmost bars in Figure 3.7 show the results of this analysis. The attractiveness of MICRO is at risk with these new assumptions, while LALEE remains attractive despite these possibilities.

Multi-Attribute Analysis

Attention now shifted to non-economic attributes of these investments. The team developed a list of 22 attributes, five of which were economic. The types of attributes are shown below:

- Sensor Coverage
  - Geographical
  - Spectral
  - Temporal
- Benefits & Costs
  - Opportunity Benefits
  - Development Costs
  - Acquisition Costs
  - Operating Costs
- Other Factors
  - Intrusiveness
  - Development Time
  - Development Risks

Table 3.7 Relative Strengths of Alternatives.

	Aircraft	GEO	Micro	LALEE
Sensor Coverage				
Benefits & Costs				
Other Factors				

The attribute "intrusiveness" merits discussion. MINDEF decision-makers were concerned with the public's perception of the alternatives. How would people feel about a large unmanned aircraft circling the city? Possible negative perceptions were carefully considered and included in the multi-attribute analysis.

Another consideration was how to represent the public's interest in the capabilities provided by the alternatives. As indicated earlier, it was concluded, after much discussion, that the public is primarily interested that the capabilities being procured can successfully perform the missions for which they were intended. Thus, the public as a stakeholder entered the multi-attribute analysis via preferences for mission success.

A multi-stakeholder, multi-attribute analysis, as described in Chapter 2, was performed. A qualitative summary of the results is shown in Table 3.7. Dark grey indicates areas where alternatives are strong, while light grey indicates potential weaknesses.

The overall analysis showed that LALEE had the greatest expected utility across stakeholders and attributes. The manned aircraft had strengths but was hurt by high operating costs, which far exceed acquisition costs. In fact, the manned aircraft would be unattractive even if the acquisition costs were zero!

The analysis also addressed where increased investment would best pay off. Not surprisingly, the technologists associated with MICRO and LALEE had many ideas for increased functionality. However, this analysis unequivocally showed that the most attractive incremental investments should focus on decreasing time until deployment and decreasing development risks, not increasing system functionality.

The importance of executing faster and managing risks is often underestimated. Economic analyses that address the time value of money and explicitly consider the impacts of uncertainties can enable attaching value to these process-oriented investments.

Investment Strategy

The results of the investment analyses provided the foundation for a recommended investment strategy

- Proceed with Aircraft
- Replace with MICRO <u>or</u> LALEE
- Invest in options for MICRO <u>and</u> LALEE
  - Invest in R&D for these development efforts
  - Consider other means to gain options in the future
- Use R&D to deploy faster as well as reduce risks and uncertainties

This proposed strategy, along with the supporting analyses, was presented to the Singapore Secretary of Defense, along with heads of other ministries who were interested in the overall approach to investment analysis. The outcome of this presentation was an immediate decision to pursue the recommended strategy.

It is useful to reflect on what was decided. Quite simply, the Secretary of Defense committed to the R&D funding for MICRO and LALEE for the next year. In each subsequent year, this decision would be revisited. Considering the time value of money, these investments should become more attractive, unless something changes. This possibility motivated the "consider other means" phrase included in the strategy.

Options-based valuations and, more importantly, options-based thinking provide important management flexibility to commit incrementally, and only continue commitments that still make economic sense. In this way, investments are buying options that may or may not be exercised, but nonetheless have value as hedges against future contingencies.

It is also useful to contrast the decision-making by the Singapore Ministry of Defense and that of the U.S. Air Force and U.S. Navy in the earlier case studies. The Singapore Secretary of Defense immediately committed to the recommended strategy. In contrast, the senior executives of the US military services faced a series of hurdles before they could seriously consider pursuing the recommendations. Clearly, not all public-private ecosystems are similar.

Summary

This case study has demonstrated the ability to assess the economic value of defense investments. We can go beyond the question, "What will it cost?" to address the question, "What will it be worth?" This is critical for investment decision-making. It does require, however, for those considering funding initiatives of interest to see themselves as investors, not just as "bill payers."

Unfortunately, the common view of defense expenditures tends to not be willing to spend significantly more now to substantially decrease costs later—to invest now for future returns. Consequently, out-year life cycle costs are greatly increased and future taxpayers find more of their resources committed to yesterday's lack of perspective. This case study has, hopefully, shown that there is a better way to think about defense investments.

Approach to Transformation

What can be learned from the four transformation case studies just reviewed? The first case study focused on new economic metrics for assessing investments in science and technology. The second case study generalized this approach. This led to 20+ transformative investments in automobiles, computing, electronics, and semiconductors, but only one in the defense ecosystem, by a non-U.S. defense enterprise.

The third case study addressed transforming the acquisition of military ships. Using new economic metrics, it was found that transforming the process of acquiring ships, rather than changing the ships themselves could create substantial value. The fourth case study addressed formulating options to decrease the costs of airborne operations. The Ministry of Defense of Singapore immediately implemented the findings of this case study.

It seems to me that the U.S. Department of Defense readily invests in innovative new approaches to strategic decision-making, but other enterprises more quickly reap the benefits of these approaches. The public-private ecosystem of national security has great difficulty taking advantage of the fruits of its investments. The large numbers of stakeholders, the competition among vested interests, and distributed and often dysfunctional governance processes makes fundamental transformation extremely difficult.

Economic Valuation

NPV is very conservative because it assumes economic commitments will be sustained regardless of intermediate outcomes. This may be a reasonable assumption as production contracts often lead to producing platforms that are no longer relevant to current military missions. The U.S. Congress zealously defends jobs created by these contracts.

NOV results in a much richer portfolio of options that, depending on future contingencies, may not be exercised and deployed. Options-based thinking has seen very significant adoption by the U.S. non-defense industries such as automobiles, computing, electronics, pharmaceuticals, and semiconductors. As elaborated in Chapter 2, this approach is much better in terms of maximizing companies' earnings per share rather than trying to conserve R&D budgets.

The U.S. national security culture is very risk averse and compliance oriented. The emphasis is on not taking risks and making sure all procedures and processes are followed. Preserving the status quo is the dominant objective. Significant transformation of this ecosystem may depend on the U.S. adopting practices more like those of Singapore.

Conclusions

What have we learned from 100+ years of attempts to transform national security? To use just one example, the Bath Iron Works in Bath, Maine was founded in 1884. The stakeholders associated with this enterprise, both private and public sector, are committed to keeping the many thousands of people employed by Bath Iron Works productively employed. This aspiration is only marginally related to national security objectives. The unstated assumption is that the ships produced will be critical to national security, not to mention critical to the local economy.

Transforming the ecosystem of national security is not just about improved economic measures of innovation, or measures of defense investments. It is about understanding and improving how investments in national security are directly linked to improved competitiveness and smarter investments in technologies. It is not just about how we spend our money, but why. In Chapter 7, I discuss how transformation efforts can pay off across ecosystems. Technology investments by DOD, for example, can provide great value to energy and healthcare.

References

AcqNotes (2020). *Defense Acquisitions Notes*. http://acqnotes.com/acqnote/industry/uarc

Apte, A. (2005). *Spiral Development: A Perspective*. Monterey, CA: Naval Postgraduate School, Graduate School of Business and Public Policy.

Cancian, M. (1995). Acquisition reform: It's not as easy as it seems. *Acquisition Review Quarterly*. Summer, 190–192.

Christensen, D. S., Searle, D. A., and Vickery, C. (1999). The impact of the Packard Commission's recommendations on reducing cost overruns on defense acquisition contracts. *Acquisition Review Quarterly*. Summer, 252–256

DAU, (2005). *Introduction to Defense Acquisition Management*, (7th ed.). Washington, DC: Department of Defense, Defense Acquisition University Press.

DBB (2017). *Future Models for Federally Funded Research and Development Center Contracts*. Washington, DC: Defense Business Board.

Drezner, J.A., Jarvaise, J., Hess, R., Hough, P., and Norton, D. (1993). *An Analysis of Weapon System Cost Growth* (MR-291-AF). Santa Monica, CA: RAND Corporation

DSB (2006). *Transformation: A Progress Assessment* (Vol. 1). Washington, DC: Defense Science Board.

Else, D.H. (2011). *The Arsenal Act: Context and Legislative History*. Washington, DC: Congressional Research Service.

Fuchs, R., McCarthy, J., Corder, J., Rankine, R., Miller, W., & Gawron, V., (1997). *United States Air Force Expeditionary Forces*. Washington, DC: Air Force Scientific Advisory Board.

Packard, D. (1986). *A Quest for Excellence: Final Report to the President by the President's Blue Ribbon Commission on Defense Management*. Washington, DC: The Commission.

Pennock, M.J., Rouse, W.B., and Kollar, D.L. (2007). Transforming the acquisition enterprise: A framework for analysis and a case study of ship acquisition. *Journal of Systems Engineering*, 10 (2), 99–117.

Pregnato, J. (2018). *Federal Procurement Reform: A Mixed Record at Best*. Washington, DC: U.S. Government Accountability Office.

Rouse, W.B. (2010). Options for surveillance and reconnaissance. In W.B. Rouse, ed., *The Economics of Human Systems Integration: Valuation of Investments in People's Training and Education, Safety and Health, and Work Productivity* (Chap. 15). New Work: Wiley.

Rouse, W.B. and Boff, K.R. (2001). Impacts of next-generation concepts of military operations on human effectiveness. *Information Knowledge Systems Management*, 2 (4), 347–357.

Rouse, W.B. and Boff, K.R. (2004). Value-centered R&D organizations: Ten principles for characterizing, assessing & managing value. *Journal of Systems Engineering*, 7 (2), 167–185.

Rouse, W.B. and Boff, K.R., (2012). Cost/benefit analysis for human systems investments: Assessing and trading off economic and non-economic impacts of human factors and ergonomics. In G. Salvendy, ed., *Handbook of Human Factors and Ergonomics* (4th Edition, Chapter 40). New York: Wiley.

Waugh, S. (2020). *University Affiliated Research Centers: Revolutionizing Acquisitions*. Defense Acquisition University, July 01, https://www.dau.edu/library/defense-atl/blog/

4

Healthcare Delivery

This chapter addresses the following questions:

- What is the healthcare delivery ecosystem?
- What types of innovation are needed?
- How might these innovations be enabled?
- How might enterprise transformation facilitate these innovations?
- How can such investments be economically justified?

The Ecosystem

Steadily increasing costs, long waiting times, aging population, declining reimbursements and a fragmented system are how many people characterize healthcare in the U.S. In addition, the Affordable Care Act (ACA) is causing a transformation of the healthcare industry. This industry also involves complicated relationships among patients, physicians, hospitals, health plans, pharmaceutical companies, healthcare equipment companies and government.

Figure 4.1 depicts the intricacy of the U.S. health care system, with immense numbers of complex interconnections. It suggests that stakeholders' strategic decisions—for example, healthcare providers' plans, health insurance's reimbursement schemes, and preventive healthcare initiatives—will experience both positive and negative—and often, unforeseen—consequences. Because of this complexity, even proactive decision-makers who thoroughly game out what might happen can easily fail to anticipate how various actors or competitors will respond. Methods drawing upon significant insights into decision-making processes are needed (Rouse & Cortese, 2010; Rouse & Serban, 2014).

Among the stakeholders in the complex U.S. healthcare system, hospitals are dominant players, with significant contributions to the overall economy. Because of the uncertainties associated with the U.S. healthcare system, it is quite understandable that hospitals are uncertain about how they should best respond to pressures and opportunities. This is particularly relevant for hospitals located in competitive metropolitan areas such as New York City, where more than 50 hospital corporations are competing, among which many are the nation's best. Questions that arise in this uncertain environment include:

Transforming Public-Private Ecosystems. William B. Rouse, Oxford University Press.
© William B. Rouse (2022). DOI: 10.1093/oso/9780192866530.003.0004

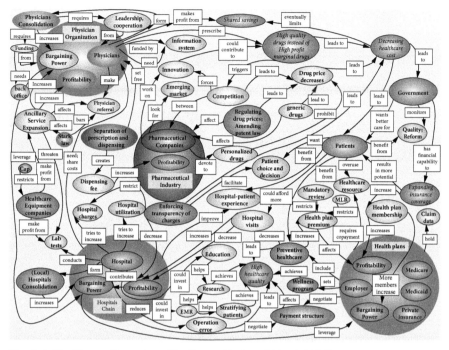

Fig. 4.1 Healthcare Ecosystem (Yu, Rouse, Serban & Veral, 2016)

- What if we wait until the healthcare market stabilizes and, in the near term, only invest in operational efficiency?
- Should we merge with competing hospitals to decrease competition and increase negotiating power with payers and suppliers?
- Should we mainly focus on acquiring physician practices in highly reimbursed diagnostic groups?

Aggregated decisions from numerous hospitals could change the future hospital market, potentially affecting cost and quality of delivered services. The diagram in Figure 4.1 was the starting point for developing an agent-based model of the New York City healthcare delivery ecosystem to explore likely merger and acquisition scenarios (Yu, Rouse, Serban & Veral, 2016)

Figure 4.2 shows the healthcare delivery ecosystem, as introduced in Chapter 2. Patients and clinicians interact at the People level. The Process level provides capabilities and information that enable care and outcomes. The Organization level includes entities that invest in capabilities and compete for economic returns. Society defines the rules of the game and expects a healthy and productive population, within acceptable costs. My later expansion of this depiction to include population health will significantly increase complexity.

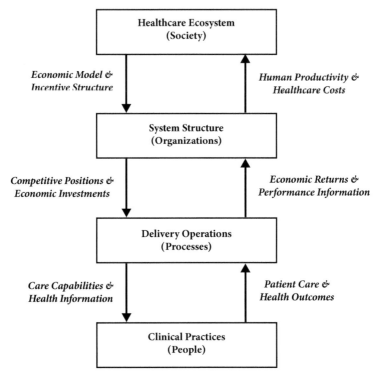

Fig. 4.2 Healthcare Delivery Ecosystem

Stakeholders

Table 4.1 lists stakeholders and examples initially discussed in Chapter 2. Expanding a few of these categories of stakeholders, the number of stakeholders becomes substantially larger.

Table 4.1 Stakeholders in Healthcare Delivery.

Stakeholders	Examples
Constituencies	Congress, Patients, Families, Employers
Government Agencies	HHS, MHS, VHA, States, Cities
Agencies Workforce	Employees, unions
Industry & Institutions	Providers, Payers, Suppliers
Industry Workforce	Employees, unions
Oversight Organizations	Accreditation & Licensing Orgs., AHA, et al.
Advocacy Groups	NAHAC, Cancer Society, Heart Assoc., et al.

HHS = Dept. of Health & Human Serv.; MHS = Military Health System; VHA = Veterans Health Admin.; AHA = American Hospital Assoc.; NAHAC = National Assoc. of Healthcare Advocacy

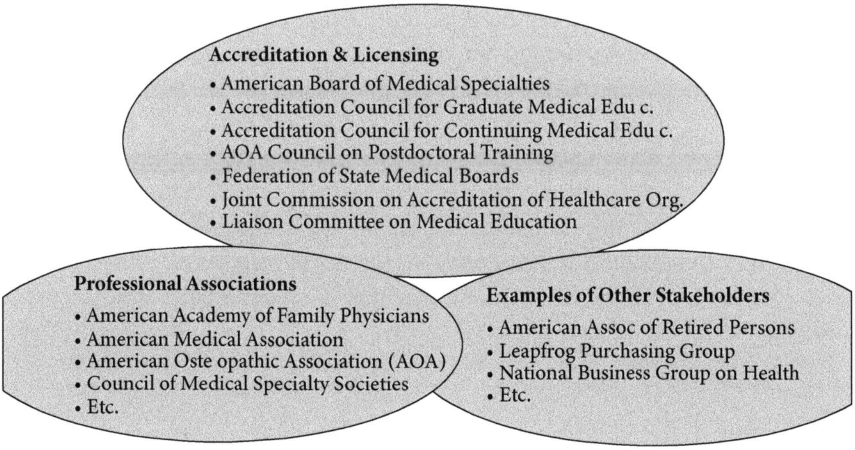

Fig. 4.3 Key Stakeholders in the Medical Community

Figure 4.3 lists representative stakeholders in the processes of accreditation and licensing, professional associations, advocacy groups, and business groups. Two observations are of particular note. First, each U.S. state addresses clinician licensing in its own way—there is no national clinician license. Second, there are over 1,200 recognized patient advocacy groups in the U.S.

Clearly, the healthcare delivery ecosystem in the U.S. is very complex. I have often characterized it as a federation of millions of entrepreneurs with no one in charge. I have found that every audience relates to this characterization.

Past Innovations

Flexner Report (1910)

The American Medical Association formed the Council on Medical Education with a goal of restructuring American medical education. They contracted with the Carnegie Foundation for the Advancement of Teaching to survey American medical education. Carnegie chose Abraham Flexner to conduct the survey. Flexner was not a physician, a scientist, or a medical educator.

He visited every one of the 150 medical schools then in operation in North America. His findings were highly critical of contemporary education practices. Using Johns Hopkins as the model for quality medical education, he recommended reducing the number of medical schools, increasing the prerequisites to enter medical education, training physicians to practice in a scientific manner and engaging medical faculty in research, giving medical schools control of clinical instruction in hospitals, and strengthening state regulations of medical licensure (Flexner, 1910).

Many current aspects of the medical profession in North America are conse-quences of the Flexner Report. Many of its recommendations remain relevant—particularly those concerning the physician as a "social instrument whose function is fast becoming social and preventive, rather than individual and curative." This seminal report led to the science-based professionalization of medicine.

This is the only case study in this section that was not directly influenced by federal or state governments. However, it had enormous implications for governmental in-volvement in accreditation and licensing. In this way, the private sector led the public sector, but the support of the latter was essential to the eventual transformation of medicine.

Social Security (1935)

The New Deal was a series of programs initiated during the Great Depression by President Franklin D. Roosevelt with the goal of restoring prosperity to Americans. When Roosevelt took office in 1933, he acted swiftly to stabilize the economy and provide jobs and relief to people who were suffering the economic consequences of the Depression.

The New Deal's social welfare programs included the Resettlement Administra-tion (RA), the Rural Electrification Administration (REA), rural welfare projects sponsored by the Works Progress Administration (WPA), the National Youth Ad-ministration (NYA), the Forest Service and the Civilian Conservation Corps (CCC). The centerpiece of the New Deal was the Social Security Act that Roosevelt signed into law on August 14, 1935. The Act created a social insurance program that paid retired workers age 65 or older a continuing income after retirement.

A primary goal of Social Security was to protect aged and disabled people from the expenses of illnesses that might deplete their savings. One of the motivations for the act was a tendency for elderly people to avoid medical care that they felt they could not afford. Social Security expenditures have grown to roughly 25 perent of the federal budget.

Medicare & Medicaid (1965)

Roosevelt tried to include national health insurance in the Social Security Act of 1935 but could not bring together enough support. The American Medical Association (AMA) attacked the idea. The National Health Care Acts of 1939 and 1943 failed as well.

President Harry Truman included universal health care in his Fair Deal in 1945 and 1949 but strong opposition stopped it. The AMA, the American Hospital As-sociation, the American Bar Association, and most of the nation's press detested the plan, labeling it "socialized medicine," which was associated with the idea with communism.

By the 1960s, public opinion had shifted towards the problem of the uninsured, especially the elderly. This would, of course, likely affect everyone eventually. According to the Department of Health, Education, and Welfare, the problem of elderly Americans lacking health care was substantial. Older Americans required much more hospital care than younger people. Social Security benefits were not sufficient to cover the costs of hospitalization, which were already rising rapidly due to medical advances.

Senator John Kennedy announced his support for what was now called Medicare during his 1960 Presidential campaign. As President, Kennedy authorized a substantial public-relations effort in support of Medicare. The AMA launched an aggressive campaign in opposition to this initiative. The insurance lobby worked in the background to undermine the bill.

Democratic Representative Wilbur Mills of Arkansas, chair of the House Ways and Means Committee, stood in the way of the legislation. Kennedy sent the proposal to Congress, but Mills would not bring the Medicare bill up for a vote.

When Lyndon Johnson became President, he was determined to pass Medicare. His overriding goal was to pass a second New Deal. Medicare was at the top of his list, as well as civil rights. With the 1964 landslide election, the Democrats controlled everything. Outnumbered, Mills had no choice but to go along.

In crafting the legislation, Mills argued for adding what would become Medicaid. He was also creative in defining how the costs of Medicare and Medicaid would be paid. President Lyndon Johnson signed the Social Security Amendments of 1965 into law on July 30, 1965. These programs now consume 25 percent of the federal budget.

Affordable Care Act (2010)

The Affordable Care Act (ACA), formally known as the Patient Protection and Affordable Care Act, and commonly known as Obamacare, was enacted by the United States Congress and signed into law by President Barack Obama on March 23, 2010. The bill passed in the House by 220-215 and in the Senate by 60-40. Only one Republican in the House and none in the Senate voted for the bill. The lone Republican vote came after the vote total was already sufficient to pass the bill.

The act largely retained the existing structure of Medicare, Medicaid and the employer market, but individual markets were substantially changed. Insurers had to accept all applicants and prices could not be based on pre-existing conditions or demographic status, other than age. To combat the problem of low-risk patients avoiding buying insurance, it was mandated that individuals buy insurance or pay a fine, and that insurers cover a list of "essential health benefits".

The case for change was compelling. There were 50 million people without health care coverage. There was evidence that the health care system was not always delivering at the highest quality. For example, if you had diabetes, you only got recommended care about half of the time. It was very difficult to get such major legislation passed through the House and Senate and signed by the President, particularly because this legislation was complicated and had vast impacts. Fortunately, the example of Massachusetts showed that it could be done. Nevertheless, presidential leadership was absolutely critical (Seervai, 2020).

This is an excellent example of innovation in a complex public-private ecosystem. Key stakeholders included the public, of course, but also providers, payers, and suppliers of drugs and devices. The "story" had to explain how this would work for everyone, what compromises were necessary, and how it would be economically feasible. Nevertheless, many Members of Congress opposed the bill.

Telemedicine (2020)

The Institute of Medicine, now the National Academy of Medicine, defined telemedicine in 1996 as "the use of electronic information and communications technologies to provide and support health care when distance separates participants" (NAP, 2012). A wide range of telemedicine practices has been in use for many decades.

A primary impediment to adoption has been reimbursement practices that limit payments to face-to-face visits at clinicians' offices, clinics and hospitals. Another impediment has been state licensing laws that limit clinicians' abilities to practice across state lines. Thus, technological capabilities and effectiveness have not been significant hurdles.

The first break in this deadlock occurred relatively recently. In 2018, the U.S. Department of Veterans Affairs (VA) announced "a new federal rule that will allow VA doctors, nurses and other health-care providers to administer care to Veterans using telehealth, or virtual technology, regardless of where in the United States the provider or veteran is located" (VA, 2018).

The coronavirus pandemic of 2020 has, at least temporarily, eliminated the impediments (CMS, 2020). Use of telemedicine for outpatient care has grown from 1 percent to roughly 70 percent. Estimates of increased usage have ranged from 11,000 percent to 20,000 percent (Licurse, et al., 2020). Such extremes are unlikely to be sustained after the pandemic. However, necessity has been the mother of invention and this innovation will likely be sustained, particularly for providers who are also payers, e.g., Kaiser Permanente and Veterans Health.

Potential Innovations

My first exposure to the healthcare delivery ecosystem, other than as a patient, was when I held a visiting faculty position in 1973 at Tufts University. This included participation in a research project at the New England Medical Center. The project focused on automated control for positioning radiotherapy equipment. With my freshly minted PhD from MIT, I did not like being treated as technician by the MDs.

I avoided involvement in the ecosystem after that until the mid 1990s when the American Cancer Society retained me to assist the executive team in addressing a variety of strategy issues. The MDs treated me as a peer and it was a rather creative time, for example, characterizing healthcare delivery as a complex adaptive system as discussed in Chapter 2. I had a similar engagement with the Cystic Fibrosis Foundation.

Around the same period, the National Academy of Engineering, of which I had become an elected member, and the Institute of Medicine (now the National Academy of Medicine) began a series of collaborations which persist to this day. My later discussion of the cancer control study is a recent example of this collaboration.

The workshop mentioned in Chapter 2 led Denis Cortese, then CEO of Mayo Clinic, and me to organize an edited collection *Engineering the System of Health Delivery* (Rouse & Cortese, 2010) featuring numerous thought leaders in the healthcare ecosystem. A few years later, Nicoleta Serban, a statistician, and I wrote *Understanding and Managing the Complexity of Health*care (Rouse & Serban, 2014). All told, I have been increasingly immersed in healthcare for two decades.

Case Studies

The four case studies discussed in this chapter address transformation in several ways. First, I consider the challenge of scaling successful trial results to widespread adoption. Next, the use of computational models to assess likely impacts of policies is discussed. The notion of "population health" is then introduced and innovations necessary to enabling it outlined. Finally, I discuss assistive technologies for disabled and older adults. These are the four case studies:

- Scaling successful trials, one at Emory Health and another at Indiana Health
- Computational policy analysis, illustrated for a Medicare policy
- Population health for substance abuse and cancer control
- Assistive technologies for disabled and older adults

Each of these case studies of potential innovations is rather substantial. Consequently, a full section of this chapter is devoted to each case.

Scaling Successful Trials

I have served on several National Academy committees associated with potential innovations in healthcare. We often began by considering existing success stories where typically provider organizations had implemented and evaluated new practices or procedures. The two examples in this section are good illustrations.

We almost always discovered that local successes were not scaled to broader application. One reason was that the passion of the team that created local success was difficult to duplicate. Another, perhaps more practical reason was that the implications of scaling from 1,000 patients to 100,000 patients were not well understood. That was the case for the following two examples

Emory Prevention and Wellness

This case study addressed the employee prevention and wellness program of Emory University (Park, et al., 2012). The application of the multi-level model focused on the roughly 700 people in this cohort and their risks of diabetes mellitus (DM) and coronary heart disease (CHD). Each person's risk of each disease was calculated using DM and CHD risk models from the medical literature, using initial individual assessments of blood pressure, fasting glucose level, etc. Subsequent assessment data were used to estimate annual risk changes as a function of initial risks of each disease.

The model of this healthcare delivery enterprise included the four levels of Figure 4.2—Ecosystem, Organization, Process, and People. Each level provided a corresponding conceptual set of issues and decisions for both the payer and provider. In this case, the Human Resources Department of Emory University (HR) was the payer responsible for health care costs for university employees, while the Predictive Health Institute (PHI) was the provider focused on prevention and maintenance of employee health.

The Ecosystem level allowed decision-makers to test different combinations of policies from the perspective of HR. For instance, this level determined the allocation of payments to PHI based on a hybrid capitated and pay-for-outcome formula. It also involved choices of parameters such as projected healthcare inflation rate, general economy inflation rate, and discount rate that affect the economic valuation of the prevention and wellness program. One of the greatest concerns of HR was achieving a satisfactory return on investment (ROI) on any investments in prevention and wellness.

The concerns at the Organization level included the economic sustainability of PHI—their revenue must be equal to or greater than their costs. To achieve sustainability, PHI must appropriately design its operational processes and rules. Two issues are central. What risk levels should be used to stratify the participant population? What assessment and coaching processes should be employed for each strata of the population? Other Organization level considerations include the growth rate of the participant population, the age ranges targeted for growth, and the program duration before participants are moved to "maintenance."

The Process level represents the daily operations of PHI. Participants visit PHI every six to twelve months. Seven health partners employed by PHI perform assessments, work with participants to set health goals, and perform follow-up calls or emails to monitor participants and encourage them to follow their plan.

All of these activities are captured in the Process level. The costs of these activities are aggregated and reflected in the Organization level as the costs of running PHI.

The People level is the replication of the actual population of PHI participants. Over a three-year period, roughly 700 participants joined this prevention and wellness program. Each of them had various assessment measurements recorded, such as blood pressure, fasting glucose level, etc. Each participant was instantiated in the model as an agent. Based on the assessment measurements, the risk of developing DM or CHD was computed for each agent. Then, total healthcare costs were estimated for their remaining life based on their risk level for each disease. The reduced amount of aggregated total healthcare cost achieved by PHI is an Ecosystem level benefit to the HR organization.

Runs of the multi-level simulation were set up using an interactive dashboard. Beyond the decision variables discussed above, decision-makers could decide what data source to employ to parameterize the models—either data from the American Diabetes Association (ADA) and American Heart Association (AHA), or data specific to Emory employees. Decision-makers could choose to only count savings until age 65 or also project post-retirement savings.

The dashboard also enabled inputs from Organization level decision-makers, namely PHI. Beyond the variables mentioned above, these decision-makers had to choose how to stratify the participant population into low and high-risk groups for each disease. Once they chose a level on the risk threshold slider, a set point appeared on the percent risk reduction slider that represented what PHI was actually achieving based on analysis of their ongoing assessment data. Decision makers could choose to operate at the set point by moving the slider to this point, or they could explore the consequences of larger or smaller risk reductions.

Evaluating PHI as it was currently operating resulted in several conclusions. If Emory scaled up its current prevention and wellness program it would yield an annual (delete this dash) −minus 96 percent ROI—about as bad as you can get. Yet, they were achieving dramatic improvements for people with high risks of diabetes and heart disease. When we radically reorganized this program (computationally), we could achieve a 7 percent ROI for Emory and sustain the program. Those were the results through age 65.

If we extended the analysis to age 80, we achieved a 30 percent ROI. This difference is all to the benefit of the U.S. Centers for Medicare and Medicaid Services (CMS). Thus, in principle at least, CMS should incentivize Emory to provide prevention and wellness to its employees. In general, CMS should incentivize all employers to keep people healthy so that when they enter Medicare at age 65, they are much healthier and less expensive to CMS.

To achieve this impressive ROI and stay in business, PHI had to change its business model, stratifying the population by risk levels and tailoring processes to each stratum. This included an initial low-cost, streamlined assessment and subsequently

PHI "Lite" for low-risk participants. PHI also needed to develop a low-cost "maintenance" process to sustain reduced risks once they had been achieved. These recommendations significantly influenced the subsequent redesign of PHI.

Indiana Alzheimer's Care

This case study addressed care for patients with memory and emotional problems such as Alzheimer's disease and other related dementia. There is a substantial need to develop new scalable and sustainable brain care services to care for these patients. This care requires extensive psychosocial support, nursing care, and comprehensive patient-centered management, which strains the resources of clinicians, family caregivers and community-based support structures. Indiana University developed such a health management program called the Aging Brain Care Medical Home (ABC) to provide the collaborative care model to 1,500 older adults in central Indiana (LaMantia, et al., 2014).

In order to scale up the ABC collaborative care model to more patients and other geographical areas, it was necessary to understand what factors affect the efficiency and effectiveness of its operations and outcomes. To this end, we developed a multi-level computer simulation model of the ABC program (Boustany, et al., 2016). It was shown that scaling the program without modification would be infeasible. More broadly, the ABC simulation model served as a risk-reduction decision support tool for health care delivery redesign, allowing early identification of operational and redesign issues.

The ABC simulation model included elements from both agent-based and discrete-event modeling, incorporated in the overall multi-level model. The model was used to explore different strategies for scaling up the ABC program. Results showed that as population sizes increase, economies of scale are reached, and thus the contribution of fixed costs to the costs per member or per patient decreases. Another important finding that emerged from this study was that the impact of the ABC program on cost savings reaches a steady state after a period of several years, which is indicated by a decreasing standard error and plateaued ROIs.

In the process of conducting this study we encountered a data set for 70,000 Alzheimer's patients over several years. This allowed is to estimate transition rates among six states of health: normal, mild cognitive impairment, mild Alzheimer's, moderate Alzheimer's, severe Alzheimer's, and death. We also had data on the annual costs of care for each state.

Alzheimer's disease cannot be cured or reversed at this time. However, progression can be delayed via various interventions. We explored the impacts of delays, by varying probabilities of retaining patients in less advanced states of 0 percent, 5 percent or 10 percent. Using simulation, we found that a 5–10 percent increase in retaining patients in less advanced states can yield enormous annual savings of roughly 50 percent by year six. The percent savings increases with age because older patients die before they advance to the severe stage and need nursing home care.

This use of modeling is interesting in that we are predicting the economic value of an unknown intervention. We do not know how to increase the probabilities by 5–10 percent. However, we do know what it would be worth if we could develop this intervention—half the cost of Alzheimer's care in the US. Our goal was to motivate parties who might be able to figure this out.

Computational Policy Analysis

My first involvement in federal policy was as a consultant to the U.S. Air Force CIO. One task involved the roll-out of a policy on server consolidation, i.e., reducing the number of independent installations of computer hardware or software that "serves" other programs or devices called "clients." The policy required all Air Force installations to complete consolidation within 90 days.

During discussions of this policy, I asked, "Why do you think that installations can complete this in 90 days?" There were various technically-oriented answers, but the one that stuck with me was, "Because they are ordered to comply." Ninety days later, the level of compliance was zero. This led me to think about how one could computationally analyze the extent to which it is possible for organizations to comply with policies.

Transition Care Management

The Transitional Care Model (TCM) is a proven care management approach that can contribute to a more person-centered, effective and efficient response to the challenge of chronic illness, including needs to avoid hospital readmissions and associated penalties. Despite TCM's proven value (Naylor, et al., 2012, 2014), it has been challenging to convince decision makers to implement this model.

Success in TCM's spread has been achieved only slowly—one health system or community at a time. Among major barriers to widespread implementation are perceptions that the model has been demonstrated to work in randomized control and comparative effectiveness trials but not in the "real world": it is too complex and costly, requires upfront investment which will largely benefit other providers downstream or is not adaptable to local contextual issues.

While each of these misperceptions have been addressed through successful translation of the TCM in a number of health systems, traditional strategies (e.g., identifying local champions, multiple meetings with decision makers) consume substantial time and are not as efficient as desired in promoting widespread scaling. Such challenges are not limited to the adoption of the TCM and addressing them could

108 Transforming Public-Private Ecosystems

have positive impacts on the widespread adoption of evidence-care throughout the U.S. healthcare system.

To that end, the specific goal of this case study was to determine whether the use of a policy flight simulator could accelerate positive decisions to implement the TCM (Pennock, et al., 2018; Rouse, et al., 2019). As indicated in earlier discussions throughout this book, policy flight simulators fuse aspects of scientific analysis, engineering, social science, and visualization to provide decision-makers with a more comprehensive understanding of the consequences of interventions than that provided by traditional mathematical and computational approaches.

To accomplish this goal, the team conducted two activities in an iterative, adaptive process. First, we elicited barriers and facilitators to adopting evidence-based, highly effective interventions from decision makers representing providers, payers, and purchasers. Second, we developed and continuously refined the TCM policy flight simulator. In the process, several key insights emerged:

- The payment system is central
- Beliefs about evidence vary; peers' actions are important
- Research evidence is not sufficient
- The offering must relate to "my population"

These insights caused us to realize that any investment decision of the magnitude of TCM would likely require the involvement of many stakeholders and organizations in a given healthcare system. Consequently, we elaborated our goal, namely, to determine whether the use of an innovative policy flight simulator would help healthcare decision-makers (providers, payers or purchasers) make better-informed decisions regarding the adoption of TCM, and increase their confidence in a decision to adopt TCM.

Results showed that we had demonstrated the potential value for a policy flight simulator to inform decisions about adopting evidence-based interventions. The TCM simulator enabled providers and payers to project the impact of TCM on their patient populations, using their financial parameters, e.g., local wages. This increased their confidence in how this evidence-based intervention would likely impact them, and decreased the tendency to dismiss evidence that the simulator shows to be well founded.

There is little, if any, doubt that TCM benefits patients across a wide range of patient demographics. Indeed, analysis of benefits by patient demographic characteristics, reported in studies cited earlier, fails to show any variation in effectiveness with these characteristics. The question addressed here was the extent to which TCM would be economically attractive for any and all providers. The answer is that one size does not fit all. Benefits depend on the patient population enrolled in TCM, the extent of readmission penalties, and the nature of the provider, e.g., tertiary versus secondary care and the payment model (capitated vs. fee-for-service).

As the Medicare population grows and new payment models are deployed, providers will have to understand in depth how their practices affect the economics of their enterprise (Goldsmith & Bajner, 2017), and policymakers will want to know how to anticipate those responses. Indeed, CMS will need to understand that not all providers are the same, that policies that work for one subset of the population may not work for other subsets, and which subsets of the providers or populations are most impacted. Policy flight simulators can provide such understanding before policies are deployed.

Population Health

Population health involves integration of health, education, and social services to keep a defined population healthy, to address health challenges holistically, and to assist with the realities of being mortal. Consequently, population health involves a wide range of interventions/services, many of which are not traditionally associated with the healthcare system in Figures 4.1 and 4.2. Figure 4.4 portrays who is involved in providing this wide range of services and the inherent difficulty of accessing these services in the U.S..

Our approach to addressing the complexity of Figures 4.3 is to employ the framework from Figure 4.2 and the analytic approach outlined in Chapter 2. This enables consideration of the physical, human, economic, and social phenomena underlying the complex healthcare delivery ecosystem. The inclusion of health, education, and social services, as shown in Figure 4.3, required the broadening of this framework.

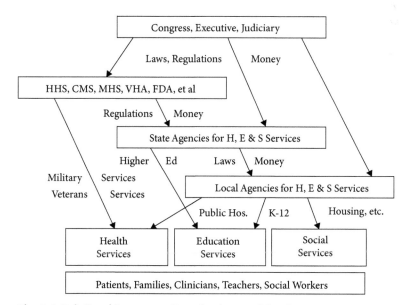

Fig. 4.4 Relationships among Organizations and Services

Phenomena at Each Level

At the People level, central phenomena include establishing a route for people through the many needed services. People may balk (not become patients) or renege (drop out of treatment) along the route, due to delays and other factors.

Process-level phenomena include getting appointments for each service in the route. Delays are highly affected by capacity constraints. Processes also involve the flow of information among service providers. Inefficiencies in the flows of information can disrupt the flow of patients to services.

At the Organization level, capacity constraints are due to investments. Organizations tend to invest in capacities needed to provide services that are highly reimbursed. Thus, for example, cancer, cardio, and ortho services are typically better provisioned than chronic disease management.

On the level of Society, investment policies are related to payer reimbursement policies and how value is defined. Healthy people not only have lower healthcare costs; they also typically work, earn incomes, pay taxes, consume, etc. Thus, society benefits from a healthy population far in excess of the lower healthcare costs. Fragmentation at the highest level undermines accounting for the full benefits of population health.

Integrated Population Health

A primary limitation of many studies of integrated care is the simple fact that most of these studies were conducted in the fragmented U.S. delivery system. How might integration of the overall population health ecosystem be accomplished? Table 4.2 summarizes our suggestions, organized using the framework of Figure 4.2.

The columns for innovations—that is, change in the ecosystem—rely on many well-known ideas and inventions that have not, as yet, pervasively changed the ecosystem. The focus on systems science is in terms of systems thinking, systems engineering (Sage & Rouse, 2009), operations research, and decision analysis (Keeney & Raiffa, 1993). Behavioral economics includes human-centered design (Rouse, 2007, 2015), prospect theory (Kahneman, 2011), and the notion of nudges (Thaler & Sunstein, 2008). Social networks include emergent networks such as analyzed in the Framingham Study (Fowler, 2008), pervasive platforms like Facebook and LinkedIn, and the evolving concept of cyber-social learning systems.

Service Interactions (People). The people level needs decision support, ranging from methods to help clinicians access, organize, and take advantage of the rapidly evolving science base within their specialties, to methods to support patients in understanding and weighing the costs and benefits of the range of services they may need. There are well-known decision theoretic approaches to do this, perhaps amplified with recent developments in artificial intelligence (Rouse & Spohrer, 2018).

Table 4.2 Innovations and Implications for an Integrated Delivery Ecosystem (Rouse, Johns & Pepe, 2019).

Level	Innovations			Implications	
	Systems Science	Behavioral Economics	Social Networks	IT	Governance
Population Ecosystem	Policy flight simulators employed to anticipate likely consequences of policies	Shared understanding of how behavioral and social factors contribute to perceptions of value	Social networks embraced as a complement to typical culture of individual accomplishment	Seamless integration across stakeholders—patients, providers, payers, pharma, et al.	Broad evidence-based view of the "system" of population health across all relevant services
System Structure	Hedging uncertainties of patient demands and payment systems via portfolios of options	Human-centered decision support of humans' bounded rationality and satisficing	Understanding of how networks of networks function across friends, family, employment, affiliations, etc.	Platform orientation, e.g, infrastructure for numerous apps (e.g., cognitive assistants)	Adoption of "public good" values across all players; those undermining such values are penalized
Delivery Operations	Operations research methods to improve process efficiencies and allocation of capacities to processes	Understanding of behavioral and social contributions to process variability enable increasing predictability	Enable access to and use of multiple social networks, including Facebook, LinkedIn, alumni groups, etc.	Seamless integration across processes, including those that cross organizations	Clearly defined and communicated processes for issue identification, development, and decision making
Service Interactions	Decision theoretic approaches to support decision making by clinicians, patients, and families	Use of prospect theory; human-centered understanding of incentives and "nudges"	"People like me" provides pervasive support for patients and caregivers	Consumer friendly and responsive infrastructure; user experience drives all design and development	Mechanisms for feedback from people to enable publicly available benchmarking and learning

These normative approaches need to be augmented by descriptive findings from behavioral economics. Prospect theory provides a basis for understanding human heuristics and biases (Kahneman, 2011) as well as the types of nudges that can influence humans' choices (Thaler & Sunstein, 2008). The notion of nudges, as they affect health related decisions, is receiving increased attention (Patel, et al., 2018).

Variations of "people like me" can provide pervasive support for patients and caregivers. In fact, "clinicians like me" is a target of ongoing AI research. Social networks can be invaluable for helping to negotiate fragmented enterprises. Often the most efficient way to determine how to navigate is to ask someone who has done it before.

The possible impacts of behavioral economic nudges and social networks on health have received considerable attention (Asch, et al., 2012; Patel, et al., 2018). Carroll (2017) reports on several studies aimed at increasing compliance with treatment regimes. Most failed to achieve improvements. Johnson (2018) reviews a 2016 effort by IBM where, despite economic incentives, less than 10 percent of those targeted signed up and fewer actually used the service. Clearly, this area presents a significant challenge.

The IT implications of the needed innovations outlined here include consumer friendly and responsive infrastructure. Desired user experiences should drive all IT design and development. This includes clinician experiences with electronic health records. When user experiences involve tedious use of opaque and confusing user interfaces, people simply avoid using such systems. If use is required, burnout can be a consequence.

From a governance perspective, there need to be mechanisms for feedback from people to enable improvements as well as publicly available benchmarking and learning. The immense frustrations with the fragmented delivery ecosystem need to be made visible. The operators of the various elements of the ecosystem need to be accountable for poor service.

Reducing the complexity of the service network, from users' points of view, combined with well-designed behavioral economics nudges are likely to be important keys to success. Users here refer to clinicians, patients, and families.

Delivery Operations (Processes). Operations research methods have long been employed to improve process efficiencies and allocate capacities to processes (Rouse & Cortese, 2010). These endeavors have mainly happened within delivery organizations rather than across organizations. The only "glue" between siloed organizations tends to be the patients who are often ill prepared to play these roles. More of these types of efforts need to focus at the enterprise level (Rouse, 2015).

We have long known that understanding of behavioral and social contributions to process variability can enable increasing predictability and control, e.g., (Deming, 2000). Within healthcare, such efforts have tended to focus on treatment processes. Attention needs to be paid to the processes whereby patients interact with the whole delivery system, i.e., the processes underlying the phenomena in Figures 4.2 and 4.4.

People often belong to several social groups, e.g., Facebook, LinkedIn, alumni groups, etc. The IT infrastructure needs to enable access to and use of these multiple social networks. This does not imply the actual integration of these platforms, but instead requires integrated access. A user-controlled resource should have seamless access across processes, including those that cross organizations.

From a governance perspective, there need to be clearly defined and communicated processes for issue identification and learning (Rouse, et al., 2017). When things do not work well and especially when they lead to unfortunate consequences, problems need to be identified, solutions developed, and decisions made by involved stakeholders. This is a learning challenge for the ecosystem described by Figure 4.4. Gaps in responsibilities can result in there being no stakeholders who "own" problems. This was identified as a major challenge in the National Academy's study of U.S. abilities to address terrorist threats (NAP, 2002).

System Structure (Organizations). The organizations represented at the Structure level of the ecosystem face considerable uncertainties. The nature and magnitude of patient demands are uncertain as clearly illustrated by the exponential growth of the opioid epidemic and the ongoing pandemic. Payment systems in the U.S. are also highly uncertain with a range of value-based schemes being proposed and evaluated to replace fee-for-service payments.

To hedge against such uncertainties, as discussed in Chapter 2, organizations need to formulate a portfolio of options, i.e., modest investments that enable organizations to respond quickly to whatever eventualities arise (Boer, 1999; Pennock & Rouse, 2016). In this way, rather than being stymied by risks, organizations can see risk management as a core competency. The formulation of portfolios of options tends to be an invaluable learning experience.

Human-centered decision support (Rouse, 2007, 2015) should be central to organizational decision making. Unaided humans inevitably face Simon's (1956, 1957) bounded rationality and satisficing. Appropriate methods and tools are needed to support executives and senior managers in coping with the complexity of the evolving health marketplace. Organizational fragmentation is not a medical problem.

The marketplace increasingly involves networks of networks across organizations, suppliers, etc., but also across patients' friends, family, employment, affiliations, etc. While a source of complexity in itself, these networks of networks are also central to overcoming fragmentation. Clinicians' and patients' experiences can lead them to perceive the ecosystem as integrated if these networks are dovetailed appropriately.

From an IT perspective, a platform orientation is needed (McAfee & Brynjolfsson, 2017). The platform should provide the infrastructure for numerous "apps." For example, the emerging capabilities of "cognitive assistants" (Rouse & Spohrer, 2018) can be deployed on the platform, as apps are currently available on smart phones. This may be challenging for IT vendors but very beneficial for clinicians and patients.

Governance implications include needs to adopt "public good" values across all players. Broad agreement is needed that we are all better off if everyone is healthy, as well as educated. The marketplace should penalize organizations undermining such values.

Population Ecosystem (Society). This level of the enterprise defines the incentive structures that motivate business models intended to result in human productivity and returns on investments. Policies, procedures, regulations, and laws define incentive structures. Ideally, policies should be evidence-based (Haskins & Margolis, 2014).

Policy flight simulators are computational models employed to anticipate likely consequences of policies (Rouse, 2014). These models drive large interactive visualizations that enable stakeholders to explore alternative futures. Thus, they can computationally experiment with policy alternatives to avoid rolling out policies where, for example, compliance does not make sense.

Policy makers need shared understanding of how behavioral and social factors contribute to perceptions of value, or perhaps lack of value. This will enable them to craft policies that foster engagement rather than just compliance. For example, they need to understand how best to communicate the notion of health being a public good.

The roles and benefits of social networks should be embraced. A compelling example is a recent initiative to treat a neighborhood as a patient (Kelleher, et al., 2018). This involved the hospital treating the adjacent neighborhood to address social determinants. Treatment involved a multi-faceted housing intervention that leveraged the social network of the community.

Seamless IT integration across stakeholders—patients, providers, payers, suppliers, et al.—is a key enabler. The Internet, of course, provides an excellent example of such integration. However, sharing consumer information across product and service providers presents privacy and security issues. Blockchain, for instance, may help with these concerns.

Policy makers need broad evidence-based views of the "system" of population health across all relevant services. Health, education, and social services should not be silos. Difficulties accessing services across these silos were elaborated earlier. Payment for services merits some discussion.

Bundled payments for substance abuse treatment might help overcome some of the effects of fragmentation. Payment for outcomes such as sustained abstinence has some intuitive appeal, but might lead providers to avoid very difficult patients. Of course, the impact and unpredictability of payment schemes are pervasive problems across healthcare (Bailey, 2017).

A broad view of payments would consider both expenditures for health and returns in terms of human productivity, salaries and wages, and taxes paid, as well as children raised, educated and subsequently employed. From this perspective, health expenditures are investments that create human assets that provide returns over generations (Rouse, Johns & Cortese, 2010).

Applications

The potential innovations summarized in Table 4.2 have recently influenced two major initiatives with which I have been involved. The first was a National Academy consensus study on cancer control sponsored by the American Cancer Society, the Centers for Disease Control and Prevention, and the National Cancer Institute of the National Institutes of Health. The resulting report is **Guiding Cancer Control: A Path to Transformation** (Johns, et al., 2019). This study adopted the complex adaptive systems framework discussed in Chapter 2, and includes many of the ideas, or equivalent, in Table 4.2.

More recently, we have developed an agent-based simulation model of Washington, DC at the level of each individual citizen (Tolk, et al., 2021). The focus has been on how social interventions, in addition to medical interventions, can deter opioid abuse and enable recovery from addiction. Several of the ideas captured in this model were drawn from the behavioral economics and social networks columns of Table 4.2. We have yet to address the IT and governance implications of these innovations. Addressing these issues computationally at first can help to understand the hurdles that will need to be addressed organizationally and physically.

Assistive Technologies

According to the Pew Research Center (2017), there were 40 million Americans with a disability in 2015, representing almost 13 percent of the civilian non-institutionalized population. Older Americans are more likely to have a disability, 25 percent of those 65–74 and 50 percent of those 75 or older. Pew also reported that disabled Americans are less likely to have home broadband and digital devices.

The number of Americans 65 and older is projected to increase from roughly 50 million today to over 100 million by 2060. This group's share of the total population will rise to nearly 24 percent from 15 percent (PRB, 2018). Thus, the number of disabled and older adults will grow dramatically in the coming decades.

The Assistive Technology Industry Association (2018) indicates that, "Assistive technology (AT) is any item, piece of equipment, software program, or product system that is used to increase, maintain, or improve the functional capabilities of persons with disabilities. Assistive technology helps people who have difficulty speaking, typing, writing, remembering, pointing, seeing, hearing, learning, walking, and many other things. Different disabilities require different assistive technologies."

Market projections for assistive technologies are quite varied, but all predict very substantial growth. McCue (2017) reports that, "The global elderly and disabled assistive devices market was valued at $14 billion in 2015 and is expected to surpass $26 billion by 2024, according to Coherent Market Insights." PRNewswire (2016) reports that "The U.S. market for assistive technologies is projected to grow from $40.6

billion (including eyeglasses and contact lenses) in 2014 to $43.1 billion in 2015 and $58.3 billion in 2020, with a compound annual growth rate of 6.2 percent between 2015 and 2020." Finally, Casey (2012) projects that "The U.S. market for assistive technologies is projected to grow from $39.5 billion in 2010 to $55 billion in 2016. The growth is fueled by an aging population as one in five people are expected to be 65 or older by 2035."

It seems safe to conclude that assistive technologies represent both an enormous societal need and an impressive market opportunity. This section addresses these needs and opportunities by considering the overall delivery ecosystem. The next section provides a brief review of selected technologies and issues. I then consider how to navigate in the ecosystem, how assistive technologies can be integrated into work and a case study of a particular technology. I conclude by considering the economics of assistive technologies.

Cognitive Assistive Technologies

There is a wide range of ways that disabled and older adults can be assisted in their work, be it employed work or daily life work, e.g., (Bartleby, 2018). Physical assistance is, of course, a primary way. The National Academies (NAP, 2017) address the promise of technology for physical assistance. The assistive technologies reviewed included wheeled and seated mobility devices, upper-extremity prostheses, lower-extremity prostheses, hearing aids, and speaking aids. They considered cognitive abilities to use these technologies, but not aids to augment cognitive disabilities.

I have focused on cognitive aids. A calculator is a cognitive aid for those who cannot do arithmetic in their heads. If one included such devices, the market is immense, but this does not really make sense. One could limit inclusion to devices for those with clinical diagnoses of cognitive disabilities, e.g., those with Intellectual and Developmental Disabilities (IDD). More broadly, "clinical diagnoses of cognitive disabilities include autism, Down Syndrome, traumatic brain injury (TBI), and dementia. Less severe cognitive conditions include attention deficit disorder (ADD), dyslexia (difficulty reading), dyscalculia (difficulty with math), and learning disabilities in general." (Mada, 2018)

Jorge (2001) considers adaptive tools for the elderly—devices to cope with age-induced cognitive disabilities. The goal is to develop social assistants that adapt to the needs of their users. He concludes that intelligent devices could be able to nonintrusively monitor people. Another important capability is to support daily routines. Intelligent devices should enhance interpersonal communication. Key elements include machine learning, human-computer interaction, and mobile computing.

Cognitive assistance can include training as well as aiding. Hoffman et al. (2017) report on the effects of technology-assisted therapy for intellectually and visually impaired adults suffering from separation anxiety. The intervention was via iPhone with face-to-face communication through which subjects shared their moods. Results showed significant decreases of separation anxiety and increases of quality of life.

Addressing IDD can be challenging. Boot et al. (2017) provide an overview of the World Health Organization's program on Global Cooperation of Assistive Technology (GATE). They discuss three challenges:

- Communication skills and physical examinations by health care personnel need to be adapted to the intellectual and emotional level of the person with IDD, to get the correct diagnosis and ensure the appropriate assistive product(s) are prescribed
- Awareness needs to be increased among caregivers and health personnel of comorbidities that people with IDD often experience; such as sensory impairment and dementia. These comorbidities may also require the use of assistive products
- People with IDD will experience physical impairments not necessarily associated with IDD, which are equally common in other sectors of the population. Research understanding of these assistive products is derived almost exclusively from users of assistive products without IDD

An important challenge is evaluation of assistive technologies. Bakker, et al. (2016) provides a comprehensive review of mental health smartphone apps. This lengthy and rich review provides 300 references to the relevant literature. Of particular note, they report that mental health apps are rarely subject to evidence-based evaluations. This is of course a very important issue in most regimes of treatment for people with mental health challenges.

Assistive technologies can provide support beyond work performance. Owuor et al. (2018) address the questions of how assistive technology contributes to social inclusion for people with intellectual disabilities. "Social inclusion is the interaction between interpersonal relationships and community participation." The Owuor et al. paper includes a call for participation in a study, but also includes extensive references to relevant literature. They report that as of 2017, only about 10 percent of people with IDD have access to AT.

The National Academies (NAP, 2018) addresses how stereotypes affect the elderly. "Older and wiser" can benefit performance and function. Negative images can undermine performance and function. This is also true for individuals with disabilities. Such stereotypes cause people to be seen as weak, dependent, and incompetent. These phenomena can affect employment opportunities, self-image, and health.

Delivery Ecosystem

A variety of services are needed to support the work of disabled and older adults, both in employment and daily life. As was shown in Figure 4.4, a range of organizations at local, state, and federal levels provides these services. The stakeholders include providers, suppliers, and payers; legislators and regulators; and people and families (Rouse, et al., 2018).

There are five important federal laws that protect individuals with disabilities from discrimination in employment and the job application process (US DOL, 2018):

- The Americans with Disabilities Act
- The Rehabilitation Act
- The Workforce Investment Act
- The Vietnam Era Veterans' Readjustment Assistance Act
- The Civil Service Reform Act

State laws include 33 sets of statutes (NCHS, 2018). Thus, there is an abundance of rules, regulations, and bureaucratic oversight functions, many of which are in conflict with one another

Navigating in the ecosystem of Figure 4.4 is quite complicated for those seeking services. People need to know what services are provided, how to gain access to these services, and how to pay for these services. As indicated earlier, there is an enormous range of cognitive assistive technologies available, most of which have received limited evaluation. There is a need for an organizational entity that can assist in matching resources to people in ways that greatly simplify this complex navigation task. This would constitute an assistive technology in itself, but detailed discussion of such a concept is beyond the scope of this case study.

Wearable Coach

There is a large population of people with various cognitive and intellectual disabilities who are capable of good performance on many work tasks, but lack the executive function to independently complete a workday. Figure 4.5 illustrates the overall functioning of a Wearable Coach (Nishman, 2018). Note that a Beta version of the Job Coach functionality in Figure 4.5 has been completed and evaluated; the Counseling Coach functionality is currently in development.

Using smart phones and tablets, many of the barriers that limit both productivity and independence can be mitigated. Smart phones can be used to prompt employees to redirect them and keep them in context to keep going productively through their day. People with memory issues and learning disabilities benefit from the reminders and repetition that prompting provides. Proper prompting provides an affordable supplement to training.

The design of Wearable Coach enables it to be worn and, for the most part, used without looking at the screen for unobtrusive productive coaching. Users typically provide input to their device using gestures or voice and progress though their day receiving appropriate prompts and reminders. The device branches through varying

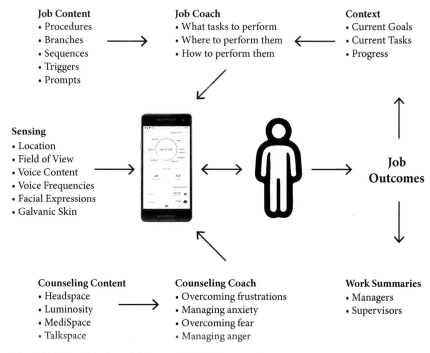

Job Content
- Procedures
- Branches
- Sequences
- Triggers
- Prompts

Job Coach
- What tasks to perform
- Where to perform them
- How to perform them

Context
- Current Goals
- Current Tasks
- Progress

Sensing
- Location
- Field of View
- Voice Content
- Voice Frequencies
- Facial Expressions
- Galvanic Skin

Job Outcomes

Counseling Content
- Headspace
- Luminosity
- MediSpace
- Talkspace

Counseling Coach
- Overcoming frustrations
- Managing anxiety
- Overcoming fear
- Managing anger

Work Summaries
- Managers
- Supervisors

Fig. 4.5 Wearable Coach (Rouse & McBride, 2019)

sequences. Branching is dependent on information within each sequence combined with many things the device can sense like user input, time elapsed, time of day, location, downloaded information about what others may have accomplished and anything else the phone may be able to sense (Nield, 2017).

Information is stored in the cloud, but a copy of relevant information for the user is kept on the user's device. Information about completed work, worker whereabouts or schedule changes are uploaded or downloaded as necessary making real time information accessible to both the worker and management most of the time.

Because the smart phone has the capability of two-way communication it can be an effective management tool, giving supervisors and managers real time information about completed work, real productivity and employee whereabouts. Because it is a valuable tool for management and supervisors, these people have incentives to maintain information and keep this information current.

Typical work sequences and prompts can be maintained in standard libraries. When a specific company has a procedure different from the standard procedure, the company can store their own modified corporate procedure in their corporate library. Custom procedures and prompts can also be stored and can be generated using standard libraries as a base. Simplified creation of work sequences keeps the system easy and inexpensive to maintain.

The sequence for a workday is buildable in a simplified interface that allows one to build, compile, and nest the various sequences to make up a worker's day along with the conditional branching needed to keep the person on track. Schedules can be rearranged in real time during a workday to respond to changing needs. Schedule changes are pushed to user devices whenever these devices have a connection.

The Commissary Helper is a version of the Wearable Coach that has been deployed in Beta test mode at some 30 military commissaries worldwide (SourceAmerica, 2018). Commissary Helper assists employees with disabilities to manage grocery store shelves in terms of scanning expirations, restocking inventory, and retrieving stock from warehouse locations. The use of the Commissary Helper by approximately 50 employees has resulted in substantial increases in productivity and has materially contributed to Source America's ability to retain or extend some dozen commissary support contracts to date.

Economics of Assistive Technologies

It is important to understand the economic value of assistive technologies. Ideally, their value will far exceed their costs. This chapter only includes a brief outline of how to answer this question. Chapter 6 addresses economic assessments in more detail, particularly in terms of driverless cars for disabled and older adults.

There are two overarching economic scenarios:

- People with disabilities, and possibly their caregivers, being employed
- People living in their own homes rather than assistive facilities

For both scenarios, assistive technologies reduce costs of care relative to the baselines without assistance. For those employed, there is increased payment of taxes, fees, etc. Both scenarios yield sustained economic contributions via consumption of goods and services. Thus, there are three cash flows, one due to savings and two due to economic contributions.

These three cash flows can be projected, with inflation, and multiplied by the numbers of people in each class of the population of disabled and older adults in order to project overall cash flows. These projections can then be discounted to estimate net present values. Rather impressive value estimates tend to result, suggesting that significant investments in assistive technologies are warranted.

One difficulty with the fragmented U.S. delivery ecosystem is that these three cash flows do not appear on integrated financial statements. The cash flows accrue to different organizational entities. Thus, for instance, payers may see savings but not economic contributions. Consequently, payers are likely to undervalue expenditures for assistive technologies because their organizational accounting assigns no value to healthy, employed people. Clearly, design and operation of the delivery ecosystem needs to be approached with a view to the whole system.

Summary

It would be transformative to provide support to 100 million disabled and older adults in the U.S. People would be able to perform productive work, including the activities of daily life in their homes. As is elaborated in Chapter 6, the economic value proposition is compelling—if one accounts for revenues, savings, and costs across the ecosystem. Of course, that is a big "if," given that this type of accounting is seldom done now in public-private ecosystems.

The complexity of the ecosystem is likely to be a hindrance to progress. I helped conduct three workshops on this topic in Washington, DC in 2019. Over 200 people participated across the three workshops. Advocacy groups for disabled and older adults were well represented. Their advocacy was forceful, and there were disagreements among these groups. There were also many government participants. I learned that the U.S. Departments of Health and Human Services, Justice, Labor, and Transportation, as well as the Federal Communications Commission, have regulatory oversight of assistive technologies, particularly if used in automobiles. There was strong industry participation, but they focused on listening, not advocating

Fortunately, assistive technologies are evolving rapidly. The pandemic has accelerated adoption, as discussed earlier for telemedicine. Digital devices are already pervasively available, although not everyone can afford them and broadband Internet services are not universally available, particularly in rural areas. Nevertheless, assistive technologies will increasingly support everyone. The complex organizational relationships among the many players in this game will have to catch up.

Approach to Transformation

We have reviewed five historical case studies of innovation and four contemporary case studies of potential innovation. What can we conclude about what works and what challenges transformation initiatives often encounter? Health and well-being are undeniably good outcomes. Why wouldn't everyone endorse this and embrace supporting it?

Consider several challenges. The first is "Not invented here." A frequent assertion is, "Our state, our city, our hospital knows how to best serve our citizens and patients." I was recently in a meeting on cancer control where a participant asserted, "The people in Montana have nothing in common with the people in Mississippi." I asked, "not even biologically?" I was ignored.

Each location is empowered to formulate their own rules of the game. These rules need not be evidence based. In fact, science and data in general can be completely ignored. Change is extremely difficult when the stewards of the status quo ignore any evidence of needs for change. In some situations, those pointing out needs for change are branded traitors.

Additional considerations are Social Determinants of Health (SDOH). Poor health can result from a lack of education, lack of healthy choices, lack of access and inadequate resources. Unhealthy people needing significant healthcare is not simply the result of slovenliness and bad attitudes. These people need the care their circumstances have precipitated. More fundamental, such circumstances need to be remediated.

Attention needs to be paid to the "innovation landscape." Where in the healthcare delivery ecosystem is innovation not happening? Why? It may be that a potential innovation is hindered by a lack of knowledge or supporting technology. Such deficiencies will likely be remediated over time. We will figure out how to address high impact needs.

Another possibility is that innovation is not economically attractive. As noted earlier, cancer, cardio, and ortho interventions are highly compensated. Mental health interventions, in contrast, are poorly reimbursed, if at all. It would be interesting to base compensation on the value of the patient being healthy rather than the costs of the interventions.

Economic Valuation

The economic benefits of a healthy, educated, and productive population that is competitive in the global marketplace are quite clear. However, this obvious objective is not paramount. Providers in the U.S. fee-for-services payment model focus on maximizing the delivery of services. Private sector payers focus on minimizing and perhaps denying services. Investments in decreasing downstream needs for services only make sense if the investor enjoys these savings.

Overall, there are enormous accounting challenges. Who invests to create capabilities? Who pays the operating costs of these capabilities? Who benefits from the revenues, including cost savings, of service innovations? These questions raise enormous accounting challenges. It is very much complicated by the need to balance the benefits to patients and their families and sundry "rice bowls" throughout the ecosystem.

Another perspective is to view healthcare as an investment rather than a cost (Rouse, Johns & Cortese, 2010). The goal is not to minimize the costs of healthcare but to maximize the economic outcomes of a healthy, educated, and productive population. From this perspective, it may make sense to increase investments in healthcare to maximize economic outcomes.

Conclusions

Health and well-being are fundamental societal needs. The US healthcare delivery ecosystem delivers less than stellar results for easily the highest costs globally. There is a wealth of potential innovations that could enable integration and coordination of health, education, and social services. Actual organizational integration would help, but is not necessary. What is needed is for people to perceive that they have easy, integrated access to best care practices and resources.

As the historical case studies illustrate, some elements of transformation are already in place. The case studies of potential innovations offer now proven approaches to further elements of transformation. Thus, the path forward includes many valuable policies, practices, and approaches. Nevertheless, the complexity of the healthcare delivery ecosystem will continue to impose substantial challenges. Transformation will likely always be a work in progress.

References

Asch, D.A., Muller R.W., and Volpp, K.G. (2012). Automated hovering in healthcare—watching over the 5,000 hours. *New England Journal of Medicine*, 367, (1), 1–3.

ATIA (2018). What is assistive technology? https://www.atia.org/at-resources/what-is-at/

Bailey, D.J. (2017). Value-based care alone won't reduce health spending and improve patient outcomes, *Harvard Business Review*, June 16

Bakker, D., Kazantzis, N., Rickwodd, D., & Rickard, N. (2016). Mental health smartphone apps. *JMIR Mental Health*, 3(1), e7, doi: 10.2196/mental.4984

Bartleby (2018). Better by design: Companies can make work easier for disabled employees, if they want to. *The Economist*, November 1.

Boer, F.P., (1999). *The Valuation of Technology: Business and Financial Issues in R&D*. New York: Wiley.

Boot, F.H., Dinsmore, J., Khasnabis, C., and MacLachlan, M. (2017). Intellectual disability and assistive technology. *Frontiers of Public Health*, 5 (10).

Boustany, K., Pennock, M.J., Bell, T., Boustani, M., and Rouse, W.B. (2016). *Leveraging Computer Simulation Models in Healthcare Delivery Redesign*. Indianapolis: Indiana University Health, Aging Brains Care Center.

Carroll, A.E. (2017). Don't nudge me: The limits of behavioral economics in medicine. *New York Times*, November 6.

Casey, C. (2012). Market for assistive technologies growing rapidly in US. http://www.ucdenver.edu/about/old_newsroom/newsreleases/Pages/Assistive-technologies-market-growing-at-rapid-rate.aspx

CMS (2020). *Trump Administration Drives Telehealth in Medicare and Medicaid*. Baltimore, MD: Centers for Medicare & Medicaid Services press release, October 14.

Deming, W.E. (2000). *Out of the Crisis*. Cambridge, MA: MIT Press.

Flexner, A. (1910), *Medical Education in the United States and Canada: A Report to the Carnegie Foundation for the Advancement of Teaching*. New York City: The Carnegie Foundation for the Advancement of Teaching, Bulletin No. 4.

Fowler, J.H. (2008). Dynamic spread of happiness in a large social network: Longitudinal analysis over 20 years in the Framingham Heart Study. *BMJ*, 337, a2338.

Goldsmith, J. and Bajner, R. (2017). 5 Ways U.S. Hospitals Can Handle Financial Losses from Medicare Patients, *Harvard Business Review*, November.

Haskins, R. and Margolis, G. (2014) *Show Me the Evidence: Obama's Fight for Rigor and Results in Social Policy*. Washington, DC: Brookings Institution.

Hoffman, N., Sterkenburg, P.S., and Van Rensburg, E. (2017). The effect of technology-assisted therapy for intellectually and visually impaired adults suffering from separation anxiety. *Assistive Technology*, in press.

Johns, M.M.E., Madhavan, G., Amankwah, F., and Nass, S. (eds) (2019). *Guiding Cancer Control: A Path to Transformation*. Washington, DC: National Academies Press.

Johnson, C.Y. (2018). The tech industry thinks it is about to disrupt health care. Don't count on it. *Washington Post*, February 9.

Jorge, J.A. (2001). Adaptive tools for the elderly: New devices to cope with age-induced cognitive disabilities. *NSF Workshop on Universal Accessibility of Ubiquitous Computing*, May 22-25, Alcacer do Sal, Portugal

Kahneman, D. (2011). *Thinking, Fast and Slow*. New York: Farrar, Straus and Giroux.

Keeney, R.L. and Raiffa, H. (1993). *Decisions with Multiple Objectives: Preferences and Value Tradeoffs*. Cambridge, UK: Cambridge University Press.

Kelleher, K., Reece, J. and Sandel, M. (2018). The Healthy Neighborhood, Healthy Families Initiative. *Pediatrics*, 135 (2), doi: 10.1542/peds.2018-0261.

LaMantia M.A., Alder C.A., Austrom M.G., Cottingham A.J., Litzelman D.K., Boustany K.C., and Boustani M.A. (2014). The Aging Brain Care Medical Home Program: Accomplishments and Lessons Learned at One Year. *Alzheimer's & Dementia: The Journal of the Alzheimer's Association*, 10(4), P209.

Licurse, A., Fanning, K., Laskowski, K., and Nadman, A. (2020). Balancing virtual and in-person health care. *Harvard Business Review*, November 17.

Mada (2018). Cognitive and learning disabilities. http://madaportal.org/e-accessibility/ux-design/cognitive-and-learning-disabilities

McAfee, A. and Brynjolfsson, E. (2017). *Machine, Platform, Crowd: Harnessing Our Digital Future*. New York: Norton.

McCue, T.J. (2017). Elderly and disabled assistive technology market to surpass $26 billion by 2024. *Forbes*, March 21, 2017.

NAP (2002). *Making the Nation Safer: The Role of Science and Technology in Countering Terrorism*. Washington, ED: National Academy Press.

NAP (2012). *Telehealth in an Evolving Healthcare Environment*. Washington, DC: National Academies Press.

NAP (2017). *The Promise of Assistive Technology*. Washington, DC: National Academies Press.

NAP (2018). *Aging and Disability: Beyond Stereotypes to Inclusion*. Washington, DC: National Academies Press.

Naylor, M.D. (2012). Advancing high value transitional care: The central role of nursing and its leadership. *Nursing Administration Quarterly*, 36, 115–126.

Naylor, M.D., Hirschman, K.B., Hanlon, A.L., et al. (2014). Comparison of evidence-based interventions on outcomes of hospitalized, cognitively impaired older adults. *Journal of Comparative Effectiveness Research*. 3 (3), 245–257.

NCHS (2019). *Long-Term Care Providers and Service Users in the United States, 2015-16*. Atlanta, GA: Centers for Disease Control and Prevention. Office of Vital and Health Statistics.

Nield, D. (2017). All the sensors in your smart phone, and how they work. *GIZMODO*, July 23, https://gizmodo.com/all-the-sensors-in-your-smartphone-and-how-they-work-1797121002

Nishman, P. (2018). *The Wearable Coach*. Vienna, VA: SourceAmerica.

Owuor, J., et al. (2018). Does assistive technology contribute to social inclusion for people with intellectual disability? A systematic review protocol. *BMJ Open*, 8 (2), e017533, DOI:10.1136/bmjopen-2017-017533

Park, H., Clear, T., Rouse, W.B., Basole, R.C., Braunstein, M.L., Brigham, K.L., and Cunningham, L. (2012). Multi-level simulations of health delivery systems. A prospective tool for policy, strategy, planning and management. *Journal of Service Science*, 4 (3), 253–268.

Patel, M.S., Volpp, K.G., and Asch, D.A. (2018). Nudge units to improve the delivery of health care. *New England Journal of Medicine*, 378 (3), 214–216.

Pennock, M.J., & Rouse, W.B. (2016). The epistemology of enterprises. *Systems Engineering*, 19(1), 24–43.

Pennock, M.J., Yu, Z., Hirschman, K.B., Pepe, K.P., Pauly, M.V., Naylor, M.D., and Rouse, W.B. (2018). Developing a policy flight simulator to facilitate the adoption of an evidence-based intervention, *IEEE Journal of Translational Engineering in Health and Medicine*, 6 (1), 1–12.

Pew Research Center (2017). 7 facts about Americans with disabilities. http://www.pewresearch.org/fact-tank/2017/07/27/7-facts-about-americans-with-disabilities/ft_17-07-27_disabledolderamericans/

PRB (2018). *Fact Sheet: Aging in the United States*. Washington, DC: Population Reference Bureau.

Rouse, W.B. (2007). *People and Organizations: Explorations of Human-Centered Design*. New York: Wiley.

Rouse, W.B. (2014). Human interaction with policy flight simulators. *Journal of Applied Ergonomics*, 45 (1), 72–77.

Rouse, W.B. (2015). *Modeling and Visualization of Complex Systems and Enterprises: Explorations of Physical, Human, Economic, and Social Phenomena*. Hoboken, NJ: John Wiley.

Rouse, W.B. and Cortese, D.A. (eds) (2010). *Engineering the System of Healthcare Delivery*. Amsterdam: IOS Press.

Rouse, W.B., Johns, M.E., and Cortese, D.A. (2010). Healthcare costs or investments? *Information • Knowledge • Systems Management*, 8 (1–4), 479–480.

Rouse, W.B., Johns, M.M.E., and Pepe, K. (2019). Service supply chains for population health: Overcoming fragmentation of service delivery ecosystems, *Journal of Learning Health Systems*, 3 (2), https://doi.org/10.1002/lrh2.10186.

Rouse, W.B., Johns, M.M.E., and Pepe, K. M. (2017). Learning In the healthcare enterprise. *Journal of Learning Health Systems*, 1 (4), https://doi.org/10.1002/lrh2.10024.

Rouse, W.B., and McBride, D.K. (2019). A systems approach to assistive technologies for disabled and older adults. *The Bridge*, 49 (1), 32–38.

Rouse, W.B., and McBride, D.K., (2021). Cost/Benefit Analysis for Human Systems Investments: Predicting and Trading Off Economic and Non-Economic Impacts of Human Factors & Ergonomics. In W. Karwowski and G. Salvendy, eds, *Handbook of Human Factors & Ergonomics* (5th Edition), New York: Wiley

Rouse, W.B., and McBride, D.K., (2022). Assistive Technologies for Disabled and Older Adults: Models of Use Cases, Market Economics, and Business Cases. In A. Madni and N. Augustine, eds, *Handbook of Model-Based Systems Engineering*. Berlin: Springer.

Rouse, W.B., Naylor, M.D., Yu, Zhongyuan, Pennock, M.P., Hirschman, K.B., Pauly, M.V., & Pepe, K.P. (2019). Policy flight simulators: Accelerating decisions to adopt evidence-based health interventions. *Journal of Healthcare Management*, 64 (4), 231-241.

Rouse, W.B., Pepe, K.M., and Johns, M.M.E. (2018). Population health as a network of services: Integration of health, education, and social services. In P. P. Maglio, et al., eds., *Handbook of Service Science* (2nd Edition). Berlin: Springer.

Rouse, W.B., and Serban, N. (2014). *Understanding and Managing the Complexity of Healthcare*. Cambridge, MA: MIT Press.

Rouse, W.B., and Spohrer, J.C. (2018). Automating versus augmenting intelligence. *Journal of Enterprise Transformation*, https://doi.org/10.1080/19488289.2018.1424059.

Sage, A.P. and Rouse, W.B. (eds) (2009). *Handbook of Systems Engineering and Management*. New York: Wiley.

Seervai, S. (2020). *A Monumental Effort: How Obamacare Was Passed—An Interview with Liz Fowler*. New York: The Commonwealth Fund, March 20.

Simon, H.A. (1956). Rational choice and the structure of the environment. *Psychological Review*. 63 (2), 129–138.

Simon, H.A. (1957). *Models of Man, Social and Rational: Mathematical Essays on Rational Human Behavior in a Social Setting*. New York: Wiley.

SourceAmerica (2018). *Commissary Helper: Installation and User Guide*. Vienna, VA: SourceAmerica.

Thaler, R.H. and Sunstein, C.R. (2008). *Nudge: Improving Decisions About Health, Wealth, and Happiness*. New Haven, CT: Yale University Press.

Tolk, A., Rouse, W.B., Pires, B.S., Cline, J.C., and Diallo, S.Y. (2021). *Using an Artificial Society to Evaluate Health Policies Addressing the Opioid Epidemic*. McLean, VA: The MITRE Corporation.

US DOL (2018). Employment Laws: Disability & Discrimination. https://www.dol.gov/odep/pubs/fact/laws.htm

VA (2018). *VA Expands Telehealth by Allowing Health Care Providers to Treat Patients Across State Lines*. https://www.va.gov/opa/pressrel/pressrelease.cfm?id=4054

Yu, Z., Rouse, W.B., Serban, N. and Veral, E. (2016). A data-rich agent-based decision support model for hospital consolidation. *Journal of Enterprise Transformation*, 6 (3/4), 136–161

5

Higher Education

This chapter addresses the following questions:

- What is the higher education ecosystem?
- What types of innovation are needed?
- Do potential innovations differ by institution?
- How might these innovations be enabled?
- How might enterprise transformation facilitate these innovations?
- How can such investments be economically justified?

The Ecosystem

Figure 5.1 provides a schematic view of the ecosystem of higher education. Schools are, of course, central, with primary and secondary schools feeding higher education. Students transition from schools to employers. Employers provide payrolls to employees and taxes to government. Government provides money as well as policies and regulations. Government money includes grants to schools, government-backed loans, and scholarships and grants. Family resources are also central.

Schools employ money to pay faculty members and staff, create and maintain infrastructure, acquire textbooks and other publications, and pay for various services. Schools are managed by Boards of Trustees for private institutions, or Boards of Regents or equivalent for public institutions. Faculty Senates, or equivalent, oversee curricula, faculty recruitment and promotions. Unions play central roles at some institutions.

Oversight is influenced by government policies and regulations. Licensing and accreditation organizations play central roles, often with regional or national organizations exercising oversight. Compliance functions have increasingly become central at most institutions. Faculty and staff members often spend significant time adhering to compliance policies and procedures.

The high-level view provided by Figure 5.1 is significantly elaborated in case studies later in this chapter. Figure 5.1 mainly serves to provide the broad context within which individual institutions have to operate. This context strongly influences the challenges and priorities institutional leaders have to address.

Figure 5.2 depicts a multi-level architecture of academic enterprises (Rouse, 2016). The practices of education, research, and service occur in the context of processes,

Transforming Public-Private Ecosystems. William B. Rouse, Oxford University Press.
© William B. Rouse (2022). DOI: 10.1093/oso/9780192866530.003.0005

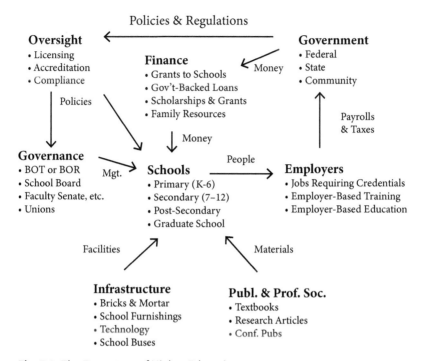

Fig. 5.1 The Ecosystem of Higher Education

structure, and ecosystem. Understanding the relationships among practices, processes, structure, and ecosystem provides the basis for transforming academia, leveraging its strengths, and overcoming its limitations. Later in this chapter, I address these relationships in terms of both conceptual and computational models of academic enterprises.

The architecture in Figure 5.2 helps us to understand how various elements of the enterprise system either enable or hinder other elements of the system, all of which are embedded in a complex behavioral and social ecosystem. Practices are much more efficient and effective when enabled by well-articulated and supported processes for delivering capabilities and associated information, as well as capturing and disseminating outcomes.

Processes exist to the extent that organizations (i.e., campuses, colleges, schools, and departments) invest in them. These investments are influenced by economic models and incentive structures, and are made in pursuit of competitive positions and economic returns. These forces hopefully coalesce to create an educated and productive population, at an acceptable cost.

When we employ Figure 5.2 to understand relationships among universities, the interesting phenomenon in Figure 5.3 emerges. The hierarchical structure of Figure 5.2 dovetails with the heterarchical nature of academic disciplines. The dotted

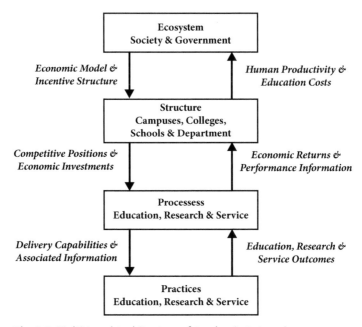

Fig. 5.2 Multi-Level Architecture of Academic Enterprises

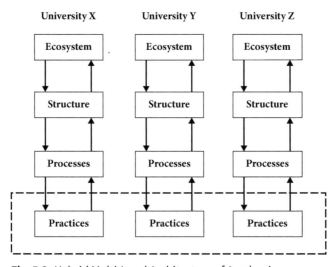

Fig. 5.3 Hybrid Multi-Level Architecture of Academia

rectangle in Figure 5.3 represents how faculty disciplines both compete and define standards across universities.

The disciplines define the agenda for "normal" science and technology, including valued sponsors of this agenda and valued outlets for research results. Members of faculty disciplines at other universities have an enormous impact on promotion and tenure processes at any particular university. Such professional affiliations also affect other types of enterprises, for example, healthcare. However, universities seem to be the only enterprise that allow external parties to largely determine who gets promoted and tenured internally. This has substantial impacts on understanding and modeling the performance of any particular university.

More specifically, the standards set at the discipline level determine:

- Agenda for "normal" science and technology
- Valued sponsors of this agenda
- Valued outlets for research results

Consequently, almost everyone chases the same sponsors and journals, leading to decreasing probabilities of success with either. In addition, each faculty member produces another faculty member every year or so, swelling the ranks of the competitors. Recently, retirements are being delayed to refill individuals' retirement coffers, which decrease numbers of open faculty slots.

As probabilities of success decrease, faculty members

- Write an increasing number of proposals
- Submit an increasing number of journal articles
- Resulting in constantly increasing costs of success
- Congested pipelines, which foster constantly increasing times until success
- Bottom line is less success, greater costs, and longer delays

The economic model of research universities discussed in one of the case studies later in this chapter enables exploration of these phenomena.

Universities can hold off these consequences by hiring fewer tenure-track faculty members, i.e., using teaching faculty and adjuncts. But this will retard their march up the rankings and hence slow the acquisition of talented students, who will succeed in life and later reward the institution with gifts and endowments. I later explore the tradeoff between controlling cost and enhancing brand value.

Alternatively, universities can pursue "niche dominance" and only hire tenure-track faculty in areas where they can leapfrog to excellence. This will, unfortunately, result in two classes of faculty—those on the fast track to excellence and those destined to heavy teaching loads. The first class will be paid a lot more because of the great risks of their being attracted away to enhance other universities' brands.

Stakeholders

Table 5.1 lists stakeholders and examples initially discussed in Chapter 2. Expanding a few of these categories of stakeholders, the number of stakeholders becomes substantially larger.

Table 5.1 Stakeholders in Higher Education.

Stakeholders	Examples
Constituencies	Congress, Students, Parents, Employers
Government Agencies	Federal, State & City Departments of Education
Agencies Workforce	Employees, Unions
Industry & Institutions	Institutions, Trustees, Regents, Publishers, Suppliers
Industry Workforce	Employees, Unions
Oversight Organizations	Accreditation & Licensing Organizations, AHEE
Advocacy Groups	Learning Disabilities, Education Trust, Stand for Children, etc.

AHEE = Association for Higher Education Effectiveness

Figures 5.2 and 5.3 suggest a broad range of stakeholders beyond those in Table 5.1. Figure 5.2 indicates a wide range of stakeholders beyond faculty members and students. In fact, increases in numbers of non-faculty staff members and administrators have been the primary drivers of increased costs of higher education (Rouse, 2016).

Figure 5.3 depicts central relationships among universities. Faculty members within each discipline at a particular university are evaluated for promotion and tenure by faculty members in each discipline at other universities. More specifically, universities effectively outsource the evaluation of their faculty members to other universities.

Faculty members know this and invest considerable time building relationships with faculty members at other institutions that will later be evaluating them. The very expensive process of preparing and submitting research articles is central to this distributed evaluation process. Consequently, one could argue that considerable resources only indirectly benefit students.

However, the reputation or brand value of a university is central to attracting the best students. Brand value is highly correlated with faculty members' publications and reputations. Consequently, as I later illustrate in detail, university leaders have to struggle with tradeoffs in investing in brand value and the implications of these investments in overall costs.

Past Innovations

Morrill Land-Grant Acts (1862)

The Morrill Land Grant Act of 1862 profoundly affected research universities in the United States, leading to transformation, or Americanization, of the Humboldt model for research universities. The American version of this German model was organized more democratically, had participatory governance, and was managed by deans and presidents appointed by trustees. In contrast, the German model invested ultimate power in the senior faculty members who elected the chancellor or rector from among their peers.

The Morrill Land-Grant Acts, named for Representative Justin Smith Morrill of Vermont, are United States statutes that enabled the creation of land-grant colleges that would teach agriculture and engineering. The purpose of the land-grant colleges was, "Without excluding other scientific and classical studies and including military tactics, to teach such branches of learning as are related to agriculture and the mechanic arts, in such manner as the legislatures of the States may respectively prescribe, in order to promote the liberal and practical education of the industrial classes in the several pursuits and professions in life." These acts include the Morrill Act of 1862 and the Morrill Act of 1890.

The Morrill Act of 1862 allocated 30,000 acres of federal land per state based on the number of senators and representatives each state had in Congress. This land, or the proceeds from its sale, was to be used toward establishing and funding the requisite educational institutions. If the federal land within a state was insufficient to meet that state's land grant, the state was issued "scrip" which authorized the state to select federal lands in other states. For example, New York selected valuable timberland in Wisconsin to fund Cornell University. The resulting management of this scrip by Cornell yielded one third of the total grant revenues generated by all the states, even though New York received only one-tenth of the 1862 land grant. Overall, the 1862 Morrill Act allocated 17,400,000 acres of land.

The Act was first proposed in 1857, and was passed by Congress in 1859, but President James Buchanan vetoed it. Morrill resubmitted the act in 1861 with the amendment that the proposed institutions would teach military tactics as well as agriculture and engineering. Aided by the secession of many states that did not support the Act, this reconfigured Morrill Act was signed into law by President Abraham Lincoln on July 2, 1862.

A second Morrill Act in 1890 was aimed at the former Confederate states. This Act required each state to show that race was not an admissions criterion, or otherwise to designate a separate land-grant institution for persons of color. Among the seventy colleges and universities that benefitted from the Morrill Acts are several HBCUs—Historically Black Colleges and Universities. Though the 1890 Act granted cash instead of land, it established that colleges under the 1890 Act had the same legal standing as the 1862 Act colleges. Hence, the phrase land-grant college properly applies to both groups.

The land grants, especially the proceeds from the land, enabled enormous investments in what became flagship state universities. The University of Arizona, University of Florida, University of Illinois, University of Maryland, Ohio State University, Pennsylvania State University, University of Wisconsin and, all told, more than 70 institutions became land-grant colleges—most of them are now universities. This, of course, provided a huge boost to education in agriculture and engineering.

Agricultural Extension Service (1914)

Rep. Asbury F. Lever of South Carolina introduced this bill in the U.S. House of Representatives, while Sen. Hoke Smith of Georgia introduced a similar bill in the Senate. The result was the Smith Lever Act of 1914. The Act formalized the U.S. Department of Agriculture's partnership with land-grant universities to conduct research and provide education in agriculture. Congress created the extension system to support rural agriculture, where half the U.S. population lived and a third of the population was engaged in farming.

This helped enable the American agricultural revolution, which dramatically increased farm productivity, allowing fewer farmers to produce more food. The extension service's first big challenge came during World War I, when it helped the nation meet its wartime needs by increasing wheat acreage significantly. The extension service encouraged farm production, marketing, and conserving of perishable products by canning, drying, and preserving.

Throughout the Great Depression, universities and extension services focused on farm management for individual farmers. Extension agents taught farmers about marketing and helped farm groups organize both buying and selling cooperatives. At the same time, extension home economists taught farm women skills that helped many farm families survive the economic depression.

During World War II, the extension service worked with farmers to secure the production increases essential to the war effort. During the post war, the number of farms decreased by 60 percent but production dramatically increased. Over the next 50 years, productivity went from one farmer supporting 15 people to one supporting 140 people. The extension service still plays an important role in American life.

I encountered the extension service as I grew up in Rhode Island and became involved in 4-H. Aquidneck Island, where I lived, had many farms growing potatoes, sweet corn, tomatoes, and other vegetables. When I went to the University of Rhode Island, I experienced how this land-grant university supported the state's agricultural sector using extensive farmland and conducting a range of experiments.

When I joined the faculty of the University of Illinois at Urbana-Champaign, I encountered agriculture at a completely different scale. This land-grant university focused on corn and soybean production, also employing extensive farmland and experimental practices. The university was immersed in a vast green carpet of corn and soybeans stretching for many miles beyond this small city. Both universities were earnestly and totally committed to research and education that supported the agricultural sectors of their states.

GI Bill (1944)

President Franklin Roosevelt sponsored the Servicemen's Readjustment Act of 1944, known as the GI Bill. It was motivated in part by the plight of service men returning from World War I, receiving $60 and a train ticket home. Bonuses were declared, based on number of days served, but payments were often delayed for decades. World War I veterans were quite unhappy with this treatment.

Millions of World War II veterans would have flooded the job market. Instead, the GI Bill enabled them to opt for education. Veterans accounted for 49 percent of college admissions in 1947, the peak year. By the time the original GI Bill ended in 1956, nearly 50 perent of World War II veterans had enrolled in an education or training program.

At the University of Illinois in 1946, more than 23,000 students hoped to register. This represented an 80 percent increase in enrollment from the previous year and 8,000 more than the Urbana campus could accommodate. Accommodating this surge in demand required hiring substantial numbers of faculty members and, of course, greatly expanding facilities.

When I joined the Illinois faculty in 1974, many of the senior faculty members were those who had been hired during this surge. These were predominantly teaching faculty, although they had tenure—one of the ways they were lured into faculty positions. However, by the late 1960s and 1970s, the emphasis had shifted to science and engineering research. I was part of the new wave of research-oriented faculty members.

The GI Bill greatly expanded the footprint of U.S. universities. As those hired in the 1940s and 1950s retired, they were replaced with research-oriented faculty members and the academic research enterprise steadily grew. It helped that institutions such as the National Science Foundation and National Institutes of Health were emerging to support this growth.

National Science Foundation (1950)

The pre-World War II 20th century provided a hotbed of research in physical sciences and mathematics. Physics and computing are of particular note. However, the modern research university, particularly in the U.S., emerged following World War II. Vannevar Bush, a 20th century leader in engineering and science, was instrumental in defining the vision.

Bush articulated the central principles in *Science: The Endless Frontier* (Bush, 1945):

- The federal government shoulders the principal responsibility for the financial support of basic scientific research
- Universities—rather than government laboratories, non-teaching research institutes, or private industry—are the primary institutions in which this government-funded research is undertaken
- Although the federal budgetary process determines the total amount available to support research in various fields of science, most funds are allocated not

according to commercial or political considerations but through an intensely competitive process of review conducted by independent scientific experts who judge the quality of proposals according to their scientific merits alone.

Bush's leadership led to President Truman's establishment of the National Science Foundation (NSF) via the National Science Foundation Act of 1950. NSF's stated mission is "To promote the progress of science; to advance the national health, prosperity, and welfare; and to secure the national defense." The NSF is certainly not the primary government agency for the funding of basic science and engineering, as many envisioned in the aftermath of World War II. Specialized agencies such as the National Institutes of Health (medical research), U.S. Atomic Energy Commission (nuclear and particle physics), National Aeronautics and Space Administration (space science), and the Defense Advanced Research Projects Agency (defense-related research) dominate support for these major research areas. Nevertheless, the NSF funds approximately 20 percent of all federally supported basic research conducted by the United States' colleges and universities. Thus, Bush's vision has, at least in part, long been realized.

Perhaps not surprisingly, Bush's home university, the Massachusetts Institute of Technology (MIT), was very successful in adopting his principles. James Killian, MIT president from 1949 to 1959, notes that "From MIT's founding, the central mission had been to work with things and ideas that were immediately useful and in the public interest. This commitment was reinforced by the fact that many faculty members had had during the war direct and personal experience in public services." (Killian, 1985)

He reports that MIT's relationship with the federal government reached new heights with World War II:

- MIT took on critical challenges, e.g., the Sage missile defense system and the Whirlwind computing project
- Faculty and alumni served in important advisory roles in the federal government
- Faculty, including two MIT presidents, served in senior executive positions, on leave from MIT

As a consequence, MIT became and remains a national resource, perhaps the key player in "big science." In the process, MIT was transformed into a university.

A handful of other leading institutions such as The University of California at Berkeley, California Institute of Technology, University of Illinois, and Stanford University, joined MIT in leading the way to define the nature and "rules of the games" for research universities.

Total federal research funding now exceeds $40 billion annually, with roughly $20 billion from NIH, $5 billion from NSF, and $5 billion from the DoD. This accounts for roughly 60 percent of all university research expenditures. Clearly, Bush's legacy is immense.

Bayh-Dole Act (1980)

Sen. Birch Bayh of Indiana and Sen. Robert Dole of Kansas sponsored the Bayh–Dole Act, or Patent and Trademark Law Amendments Act, of 1980. This legislation changed the procedures by which federal contractors could retain ownership of inventions produced with federal funding. Before this Act, federal contractors were required to assign inventions to the federal government unless the funding agency determined that the public interest was better served by allowing the contractor or inventor to retain rights. Bayh–Dole uniformly permits non-profit organizations and small businesses to retain ownership of inventions made under contract. Another change was authorization of federal agencies to grant exclusive licenses to inventions owned by the federal government.

This legislation soon led to formation of Intellectual Property and Technology Transfer Offices, or equivalent, by many universities to commercially exploit the results of federally funded research. In addition, corporately funded research often results in jointly owned intellectual property (IP). Universities have come to increasingly control IP, although they have a poor track record of exploiting it.

Gatorade has provided enormous income to the University of Florida and Genentech has been a windfall for the University of California at San Francisco. However, the number of major successes like these are dwarfed by the vast numbers of ideas that never lead to any revenues and profits for the licensee or royalties for the university. Perez-Pena (2013) reports that patenting and licensing are seldom profitable. Revenues generated are seldom greater than the costs of running the IP patenting and licensing function. Further, rigid IP policies tend to alienate sponsors.

In some cases, IP takes the form of patents, but more often it is embodied in the know-how of the researchers. Either form of intellectual property may result in spin-off businesses that create jobs, revenue, profit, and perhaps public stock offerings. Spin-offs enabled MIT research, by 1997, to foster the formation of 4,000 companies employing 1.1 million employees with sales of $232 billion (BankBoston, 1997).

Many universities require faculty members, and sometimes students, to sign agreements that indicate the university owns any IP created. One university forces faculty to agree to the university owning any know-how gained while in the university's employ. One IP lawyer told me that owning the know-how of others is completely unenforceable.

Faculty members are usually allowed to consult one day per week and any IP created for consulting clients is not subject to such university agreements. Faculty who spin off technologies to launch new business ventures are usually encouraged, but the "rules of this game" vary greatly, with differing levels of incentives and impediments.

My experiences in forming several university spin-offs are quite varied. When I cofounded Search Technology, while a professor at the University of Illinois, my department chair told me that he was OK with it, but not to let the dean find out as he would consider it to be a major distraction. In contrast, when I became chair of the School of Industrial and Systems Engineering at Georgia Tech, the provost told me that he hoped I would continue to be involved in my company, Enterprise Support Systems.

University revenues from patents and licensing now exceed $2 billion annually, which is only a few percent of their annual research expenditures. Just two companies—IBM and Qualcomm together—significantly exceed $2 billion annually. Nevertheless, occasional homeruns benefit a handful of otherwise well-resourced universities.

Potential Innovations

I have spent 50 years involved with universities except for a 13-year period founding and growing two high technology companies, both spin-offs from academic research. I have held faculty positions at six universities, usually in leadership roles heading research centers. I have held a couple of administrative positions as division head and school chair. I have served as advisory board member, consultant, and invited speaker at over 50 universities.

The case studies of potential innovations discussed in this chapter were seeded by my Advisory Board when I was Executive Director of the Tennenbaum Institute at Georgia Tech. We were researching best practices for enterprise transformation in aerospace, automotive, computer and healthcare industries. The Board was populated with senior industry executives from these industries.

Several Board members repeatedly asked, "Why don't you apply your enterprise transformation methods and tools to yourself? When are you going to focus on transforming academia?" These questions stuck with me and, a few years later, I picked up the gauntlet. The result was *Universities as Complex Enterprises: How Academia Works, Why It Works These Ways, and Where the University Enterprise Is Headed* (Rouse, 2016).

Case Studies

In the last chapter of the 2016 book, I outlined and illustrated an economic model of research universities that provided the first case study in this chapter. This led to rich interactions with John Lombardi, who has held senior leadership positions at five major universities. He provided data sets that enabled assessing the extent to which university strategy depends on the resources available. That is the second case study.

We next then joined forces with Mike Johns, who has also held senior leadership positions at several major universities. We now had a rich experience base in humanities, medicine, and engineering. The third case study considers opportunities for transformational investments in these three academic areas, particularly in the challenging times associated with the pandemic.

The fourth cases study moves from strategic decisions by university leaders to student decision making with regard to choosing academic majors. How might policies and resources affect students' choices for STEM (science, technology, engineering, and mathematics) majors? What roles should government play and what should be the roles of educational institutions?

Thus, the four case studies of potential innovations include:

- The Future of Research Universities
- Impacts of Resource Demographics
- Opportunities for Transformational Investments
- Enhancing the STEM Talent Pipeline

Each of these case studies of potential innovations is rather substantial. Consequently, a full section of this chapter is devoted to each case.

The Future of Research Universities

Research universities face enormous strategic challenges as the costs of education steadily increase far beyond increases in the cost of living. They also face increasing global competition. This section elaborates the four scenarios in Table 5.2 for the future of research universities:.1

Scenario development should be based on best practices on this topic (Fahey & Randall, 1998; Schoemaker, 1995; Schwartz, 1991). All of the pundits begin by defining the forces that drive the future. There are—at least—four strong driving forces that will affect academia's future:

- Competition among top universities will become increasingly intense, both for talent and resources—there will be a clash of the titans
- Globalization will result in many academic institutions, particularly in Asia, achieving parity in the competition—it will become hot, flat, and crowded
- Demographic trends foretell an aging, but active populace leading to an older student population—higher education will need to become a lifespan mecca
- The generation of digital natives will come of age, go to college and enter the workforce—there will be no choice but become a networked university

We cannot escape these forces; nor can we fully predict the ways in which they will interact to shape the world over the next couple of decades. We can be sure, however, that for academic institutions to compete in this future, their strategies must be sufficiently robust to accommodate these forces. If, instead, they focus on just one scenario—for example the clash of titans that most closely resembles business as usual, perhaps on steroids—they will almost certainly be at a competitive disadvantage in the future.

Table 5.2 Four Scenarios for Future Research Universities.

	Clash of Titans	Hot, Flat & Crowded	Lifespan Mecca	Network U.
General Description	Academic institutions continue to battle with leaders for dominance, as well as competing with premier international universities for global rankings	Global parity emerges in graduate education in science and technology, particularly for traditional disciplines and sub-disciplines; greater collaboration among institutions emerges; demand for higher education in the U.S. will nevertheless increase substantially	Demand for postgraduate and executive education surges as career changes become quite common; demand steadily grows for education and arts by an increasingly urban older population	Social technology prevails; access to the best content and faculty is universal; nevertheless, students go to college to learn and mature; however, the classroom experience is now highly interactive, both remotely and face-to-face
Dominant Issue	The competition for talent becomes fierce, with well-endowed chairs becoming the minimum for attracting talent; top students at all levels expect and get near-free education	Many of the best jobs are in Asia; scarcity and constraints dominate sustainability debates; clashes of belief systems create political turmoil and security concerns; meeting demands presents strong challenges	Two or three MS or MA degrees become common across careers, as do often required certificate programs; multiple artistic performance and sporting events per day become common	Students and faculty have broad and easy access to knowledge, often via other people; with the "best in class" universally available, local faculty play more facilitative roles in small (10-20) "high touch" discussion groups

Continued

Table 5.2 *Continued*

	Clash of Titans	Hot, Flat & Crowded	Lifespan Mecca	Network U.
Economic Implications	The top players continue to dominate receipt of Federal funds, with considerable pushback from other players; costs of facilities and labs soar, much of which must be raised from philanthropic sources	Federal and state support diminish as portions of budget; industrial and philanthropic support are increasingly competitive; sponsors become sensitive to where resources are deployed; undergraduate tuition stabilizes and increases are less and less acceptable	Tuition revenues soar for executive programs and graduate education programs popular with elders; revenues from artistic performance and sports venues become significant portions of university budgets	More teaching professionals are needed for recitation-sized classes; teaching skills are at a premium; increasing numbers of high-quality programs result in strong downward pressure on tuition and fees; faculty research becomes near totally externally funded
Social Implications	University cultures are sustained, with adaptations for a decreasingly Caucasian male population—for both students and faculty—but one that is committed to the values and sense of purpose that has been central for recent decades; changing demographics impacts how alumni best relate to their alma maters	Global footprints of top universities increase by necessity; social, cultural, and ethnic diversity of faculty and students increases in turn; traditional business practices, e.g., promotion and tenure, must change to accommodate diversity	Median age of students increases substantially, changing the campus culture substantially; older students in particular expect and get high quality, user-friendly services; diversity of faculty increases substantially to satisfy diversity of demands	Students and faculty are networkers *par excellence*; both within and across institutions; students' evaluations of teaching effectiveness play an increasing role; students seamlessly transition from K-12 to university to lifespan education

Clash of Titans

I have worked at, consulted with, or served on advisory boards of quite a few top universities. Every one of them pays attention to their *US News & World Report* ranking. They aspire to battle with the titans of higher education, and hold their own. This scenario has universities continuing that clash, perhaps clawing their way to higher rankings, albeit in an increasingly competitive environment.

Hot, Flat and Crowded

Tom Friedman (2005) has argued that the world is flat and we should no longer assume business as usual—his revision of this best seller included a chapter on Georgia Tech and how they transformed education in computing. More recently, Friedman (2008) has argued that the world will be hot, flat, and crowded. In this scenario, academic institutions have to compete with a much wider range of players in a global arena.

Lifespan Mecca

It is easy—and convenient—to assume that the students of the future will be much like the students of today. However, CSGNET (2007) reports that over the past decade the number of graduate students 40 years old and older has reached record numbers. From 1995 to 2005, the number of post-baccalaureate students age 40 and older at U.S. colleges and universities jumped 27 percent. And during the next two decades, the number of older citizens will rise at even faster rates than the number of those 24 and younger, which suggests that the number of post-baccalaureate students age 40 and over very likely will continue to grow. In this scenario, universities have to address a "student" population with more diverse interests and expectations rather different from students of the past and current eras.

Network U.

Technology is increasingly enabling access to world-class content in terms of publications, lectures, and performances. Higher education can leverage this content to both increase quality and lower costs (Kamenetz, 2009; North, 2009). This technology has also spawned the generation of "digital natives" that is always connected, weaned on collaboration, and adept at multi-tasking. In this scenario, academia has to address different types of student using very different approaches to delivering education and conducting research.

Framing the future 20 years from now is quite difficult. Yet, this is essential if academic institutions are to focus their competencies and resources on the possible futures in which our students—and all of us—will have to compete. Our abilities to understand and manage the inherent uncertainties associated with these futures can be an enormous competitive advantage. We need to enhance these abilities to maintain our competitive position in global education.

Economic Model

This section summarizes a computational model for predicting how various strategic decisions will affect research universities as they address the four scenarios. The goal was to enable university leaders to explore alternatives and tradeoffs in their strategies for the future (Rouse, 2016).

The conceptual organization of the overall model follows the multi-level architecture in Figure 5.2. This architecture was used to identify the phenomena to be represented in this model. It is important to note however that the computational framework—a set of linked spreadsheets—does not explicitly employ the structure in Figure 5.2.

The hybrid architecture shown in Figure 5.3 portrays the conceptual impact that universities have on each other. This might suggest that an integrated model would require representation of multiple universities. To avoid such complications, other universities are represented in terms of their aggregate demands for sponsored research and journal publications. These aggregate demands were projected based on data provided by government agencies and journal publishers.

Figure 5.4 portrays the overall flow of variables within the economic model. Not every connection is portrayed, as the figure would become hopelessly messy. Of particular note, students' applications and enrollments are driven by a tradeoff between net tuition and brand value. Somewhat simplistically, students seek to matriculate at the highest brand value university that they can afford.

Figure 5.5 shows how all the models come together, with the variables within each model listed. The financial model that follows Figure 5.4 is not shown in Figure 5.5 as it draws revenue and cost data from all the other models. Showing all these linkages would also make this figure quite messy.

Scenario Projections

Table 5.3 shows a subset of the variables that are affected by the four scenarios summarized earlier. To project the outcomes for each scenario, I used initial conditions for each scenario that achieved NPV = 0. Rather than fixing initial tuition and its rate of growth, I could have adjusted tuition each year to create zero deficits. However, this would make it difficult to compare scenarios.

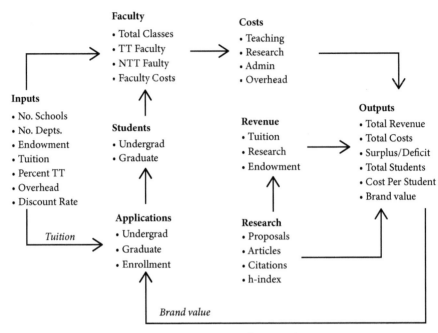

Fig. 5.4 Overall Structure of Economic Model of Research Universities

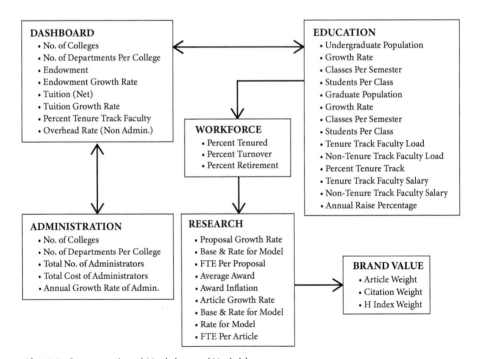

Fig. 5.5 Computational Modules and Variables

Table 5.3 Selected Variables Versus Scenarios.

	Baseline	Clash of Titans	Hot, Flat & Crowded	Lifespan Mecca	Network U.
Overall					
Endowment	$150M	$150M	$150M	$150M	$150M
Endowment Growth Rate	5%	8%	4%	4%	2%
Tuition (Net)	?	?	?	?	?
Tuition Growth Rate	3%	5%	2%	2%	1%
Percent Tenure Track Faculty	50%	80%	30%	30%	20%
Overhead Rate (Non Admin)	50%	50%	50%	50%	50%
Admin					
Annual Growth Rate of Admin	5%	6%	3%	3%	−5%
Proposals					
Average Award	$100K	$100K	$100K	$100K	$100K
Award Inflation	3%	3%	3%	3%	3%
Teaching					
Undergraduate Population	4,000	4,000	4,000	4,000	4,000
Growth Rate	2%	2%	2%	2%	2%
Graduate Population	4,000	4,000	4,000	4,000	4,000
Growth Rate	4%	6%	−4%	6%	10%
Faculty					
Tenure Track Faculty Load	2	2	2	2	2
Non-Tenure Track Load	4	4	4	4	4
Workforce					
Percent Tenured	70%	50%	30%	30%	10%
Percent Turnover	5%	5%	10%	10%	10%
Percent Retired	10%	10%	10%	10%	10%

Clash of Titans. In this scenario of business as usual on steroids, tuition grows steadily by 5 percent annually. Endowment grows steadily by an aggressive 8 percent. Percent tenure track is 80 percent to increase brand value. Percent tenured after the 6th year is 50 percent. The goal is to retain only the most productive faculty members. The undergraduate population grows slowly at 2 percent while the graduate population grows steadily at 6 percent. Administrative costs grow steadily at 6 percent as they have in recent years.

Hot, Flat and Crowded. With competition among global universities intensifying, graduate enrollment decreases by 4 percent annually reflecting foreign students making different enrollment choices than in the past. Fewer graduate students result in a reduction of tenure track faculty to 30 percent. Tuition growth is limited to 2 percent and endowment growth slows to 4 percent. Growth of administrative costs is reduced to 3 percent.

Lifespan Mecca. Enrollment of older students seeking career changes or pursuing retirement interests results in the graduate population growing at 6 percent per year. The undergraduate population grows more slowly at 2 percent. Tuition increases are limited to 2 percent as much of this growth comes from people who are unwilling to pay constantly escalating tuitions. The percent tenure track faculty decreases to 30 percent because the MS and perhaps MA degrees being sought require more teaching faculty. Endowment grows slowly at 4 percent. Growth of administrative costs is limited to 3 percent.

Network U. Increased online offerings results in the graduate population growing quickly at 10 percent annually, while undergraduate population grows more slowly at 2 percent. Classes become small discussion groups; class sizes vary from traditional numbers to much larger. The percent tenure track faculty decreases to 20 percent as the research enterprise becomes more focused on niches of excellence rather than trying to compete across the board. Tuition growth is necessarily limited to 1 percent in this highly competitive environment. Endowment grows very slowly at 2 percent, as most alumni have never set foot on campus. Administrative costs necessarily must decline by 5 percent annually.

Comparison of Projections

Figures 5.6–5.8 show the results of using the variable choices in Table 5.3 as inputs to the overall economic model of the university enterprise. Figure 5.6 portrays student population at year 20 and tuition for NPV equals zero. Note that the tuition does not differ greatly for each scenario. This is due to the model automatically adjusting the number of faculty members to meet demands. This is, of course, easier for non-tenure track faculty members than for those who are tenured.

The student population is depressed for Hot, Flat and Crowded as graduates students choose to enroll at globally equivalent but less expensive universities. Lifespan Mecca attracts older American students that swell the graduate ranks. Not surprisingly, Network U leads to dramatic growth of online graduate students.

Figure 5.7 portrays the brand value for each scenario. Brand value for Clash of Titans dwarfs the other scenarios, the closet being the Baseline. The other three scenarios drive needs to move away from emphases on graduate research conducted on campus. I have found that faculty members often have great difficulty thinking about such alternatives.

We would expect the technology-enabled Network U. to have large classes of remotely connected students, probably very large for lectures and smaller for discussion sections. However, even the discussion classes are likely to be much larger

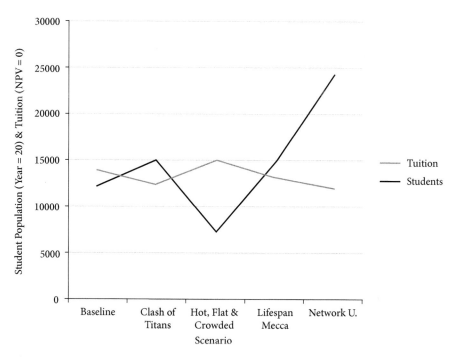

Fig. 5.6 Student Population (Year = 20) and Tuition (NPV = 0)

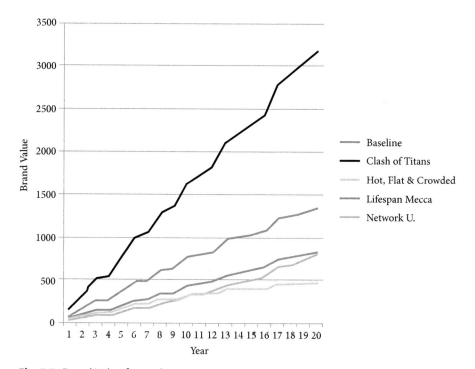

Fig. 5.7 Brand Value for Each Scenario

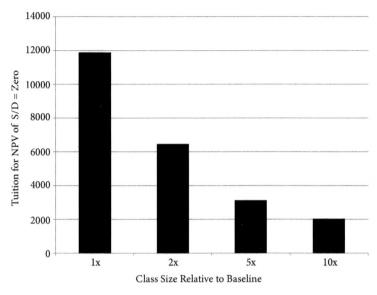

Fig. 5.8 Tuition (NPV = 0) for Class Sizes Relative to Baseline

than traditional campus classes. Figure 5.8 shows tuition versus class size in terms of numbers of times larger than the Baseline.

The impact is fairly dramatic. As class sizes increase, the overall model automatically reduces numbers of faculty members, which consequently substantially reduces costs. A rapidly growing student body (see Figure 5.6) while costs of delivery are plummeting enables cutting tuition from $12,000 per semester to $2,000.

Thus, an undergraduate degree would cost $16,000 in total, assuming it requires eight semesters to earn enough credits to graduate. Of course, by this point the notion of semesters may be completely obsolete. Pricing will probably be by the course. How courses are bundled will be up to each student. Alternatively, pricing might be by the module, with students mixing and matching the modules to gain the knowledge and skills they seek.

These tuition numbers may seem ridiculously low. However, Georgia Tech's online MS degrees in computer science and data analytics have tuitions of $10,000 for the whole degree. They have 10,000 students enrolled and generate a tidy surplus. It helped greatly that AT&T and Accenture invested several million dollars to create these offerings.

This scenario easily causes one to consider what the university should do with its sizable investment in bricks and mortar. One possibility is that this infrastructure mainly serves the resident undergraduate student population, while the graduate population needs limited numbers of traditional classrooms and, of course, no dormitories and dining halls.

An overall comparison of these scenarios is as follows:

- Baseline: Keeps revenues and costs balanced across years with modest brand value; lower than Clash of Titans but higher than the other three scenarios
- Clash of Titans: Begins with slight deficit and then generates growing surplus as student population grows; brand value is strong due to high percent of tenure track faculty
- Hot, Flat & Crowded: Leads to declining graduate enrollments and, in later years, steadily increasing deficits; brand value plummets
- Lifespan Mecca: Leads to strong growth of graduate enrollments and essentially zero deficits; brand value increases, relative to Hot, Flat and Crowded, because of more faculty members being needed to serve increased enrollments
- Network U: Leads to exploding graduate enrollments; increasing class sizes, enabled by technology, dramatically lowers costs; brand value steadily decreases as larger class sizes lead to reduction of faculty size; initial deficits are replaced in later years by huge surpluses

Policy Implications

What are the strategic and tactical policy implications of the results found for this set of scenarios? These implications can be considered at two levels—across scenarios and within scenarios. The within-scenario challenges and opportunities are likely to influence how across-scenario issues are best addressed.

Across Scenarios. My experience has been that research universities most readily relate to Clash of Titans. If strong growth of the graduate student population is accompanied with large, yet acceptable, tuition growth as well as endowment growth, the above results show that pursuit of this scenario is fully viable. Problems will arise, however, if the other scenarios become salient.

The loss of graduate revenues portended by Hot, Flat and Crowded could be quite difficult to sustain. I recently asked a Provost, "What would be the consequences if, for some political or economic reasons, all the Chinese graduate students disappeared?" He responded that, "We would lose $35 million in annual tuition revenues."

I asked, "What is Plan B?" He said, "Well, all research universities would be in this situation." I replied, "That does not sound like a Plan B." To be fair, the university in question is working to diversify its foreign graduate student population, which would decrease the chances of a single point of failure. Better yet would be approaches to encouraging more American graduate students, but this would require investing scarce resources in much larger stipends.

Lifespan Mecca could help this situation substantially, as the results shown above indicate. Professional educational offerings, supported by students' employers, plus affordable lifelong learning offerings could replace the graduate students lost to Hot, Flat and Crowded. However, they would not be research students. Nevertheless, developing these offerings would be good hedges against the downside of Hot, Flat and Crowded.

Network U could change the whole fabric of the university. "Guides on the side" would replace many or most the "sages on the stage." Flipped class would become a norm. Online enrollment would soar. Faculty members' interpersonal skills would become core competencies. Students' sense of affiliation would mainly relate to the value being provided by the education. The value of campus amenities and athletics would diminish.

One might embrace this scenario or simply choose to hedge against it. This would, at least, involve investing in capabilities to provide high value online offerings. One hybrid possibility would be investing in these capabilities to provide the Lifespan Mecca offerings noted above. This would provide the competencies, as well as some infrastructure, to enable scaling up when Network U becomes increasingly prevalent.

The bottom line is that one cannot just choose one of the scenarios. All of them must be addressed if only to define early warning signals of their emergence. More strategically, investments in Lifespan Mecca and Network U constitute hedges against Hot, Flat and Crowded. A balanced investment portfolio across all scenarios is likely to be the best approach. It will mean that one cannot put all the eggs in the Clash of Titans basket, as that could be quite risky.

Within Scenarios. Clash of Titans presents a particularly difficult challenge. The current success model at most research universities requires faculty members to work harder and harder to achieve less and less success. Universities need to broaden their views of "gold standard" sponsors beyond NIH and NSF to include other first-rate sponsors such as the National Aeronautics and Space Administration and the Office of Naval Research. Private foundations and industry sponsorship should be increased.

Universities also need to broaden their views of "gold standard" journals beyond current "A" journals. They should emphasize citations rather than impact factors, which have been shown to be irrelevant. A paper that earns 100+ citations in a low impact factor journal should be seen as a home run, not something to be dismissed.

University Presidents, Provosts, Deans, and Promotion and Tenure Committees need to communicate these changes to their faculties, particular junior faculty members. If everyone continues to pursue the old success model, there will be a lot less success, leading to pervasive frustration of junior faculty and much waste of human and financial resources. The outsourcing of evaluations of junior faculty needs to be tempered by more internal assessments.

Many universities have envisaged keeping Hot, Flat and Crowded at bay by creating global campuses, the idea being that those who eschew matriculating in America can earn the same credential in Dubai or Singapore. There are merits to this idea, but also limits. I have experienced many faculty members of foreign extraction advocating the launch of a new campus in their native country. Campus leadership has encouraged this to the extent that the talent on the home campus was often diluted. Having a branch of CMU or MIT in every country is inevitably unsustainable, particularly in terms of brand value and quality of education.

On the other hand, making a Network U version of CMU and MIT globally accessible makes much more sense. An interesting hybrid involves pursing a year or two online and the rest of the degree on campus. The key is for the university to make the investment to assure high quality online offerings that lead to the advertised knowledge and skills. This is not simply a matter of putting one's PowerPoint slides on the web. Proactive engagement of students in the learning experience requires that educators design this experience, monitor its evolutions and constantly improve it.

Lifespan Mecca requires careful attention to what students, ranging from mid-career professionals to eager-to-learn retirees, want and need to gain to achieve their educational aspirations, for example, promotions, new jobs, or simple mastery of history, music, or political science. Many traditional faculty members do not like to teach professionals and see history, music, and political science as "service courses." Success in this arena, therefore, may mean many fewer traditional faculty members.

Summary. Developing a strategy for addressing each scenario is necessary before one ponders how investments in these strategies might be leveraged across scenarios. The key point is that one does not know what mixture of these scenarios will emerge over the next 10-20 years. One's strategy across these scenarios needs to leverage opportunities while also hedging the downsides associated with these futures.

Impacts of Resource Demographics

To what extent do the projections of the last case study depend on the resources an institution has to respond to the forces of change? The economic model of research universities was extended to address this question (Rouse, Lombardi & Craig, 2018). There are three forces of particular interest. They may work independently, but also may have combined effects on projected results:

- S1: Competition for federal dollars and publication in top journals is steadily increasing. The current success model at most research universities requires faculty members to work harder and harder to achieve less and less success, proposal writing consuming increasing time and publication preparation receiving decreasing attention.
- S2: Foreign student applications to graduate programs have decreased in recent years due to competition from other countries and, more recently, concerns about U.S. immigration policies. These professional master's degrees are typically "cash cows" for research universities, subsidizing many other aspects of the enterprise.
- S3: Highly polished, well-done MOOCs (Massive Open Online Courses) will increasingly succeed. Once the credentials associated with success in these online courses are acceptable to employers, it is easy to imagine a massive

shift away from traditional classrooms for some categories of students, especially those seeking professional credentials and master's degrees where distance learning is already recognized and increasing common.

We have extended and used the computational model to explore the implications of these forces for four specific research universities, two public and two private institutions. Well-resourced universities, such as the most successful among the top 100–200, will likely cope in different ways. Institutions that almost totally depend on tuition dollars, which typically fall outside the top group, will struggle to keep tuition competitive while avoiding large deficits.

Using 2016 data from the Center for Measuring University Performance (MUP) (Lombardi, et al., 2000–2016), Table 5.4 was populated. The data in the first three columns were provided by the MUP project. The data in the remaining columns were gleaned from each university's website. We do not show the identity of each institution, but the model was explicitly fit to particular universities. Fitting the model to specific institutions has not been attempted before this study, in part due to not having the MUP data.

Fitting the model to a particular university involved the following steps:

1. Input parameters from Table 5.4
2. Apply 50 percent discount to advertised undergraduate tuition at private institutions or 20 ercent for public institutions.
3. Adjust average award to match overall federal research $
4. Adjust class sizes to achieve near zero NPV of surplus/deficit; this is the break-even assumption—thus, NPV = 0 at Year 0 for all scenarios
5. Revisit steps 3 and 4 as needed

The iterative nature of steps 3 and 4 is due to the faculty being automatically sized by the model to meet educational demands. When class sizes increase, faculty numbers

Table 5.4 High Level Characteristics of Four Research Universities.

	Federal $ M	Endow-ment $ M	State $ M	UG Students	UG Tuition	Grad Students	Grad Tuition	No. Col-leges	Departments Per College
Large Public	800	10,000	300	29,000	15,000	15,000	24,000	19	18
Large Private	700	20,000	0	7,000	50,000	9.000	50,000	7	16
Small Public	60	600	100	16,000	15,000	5000	24,000	8	6
Small Private	50	900	0	000	50,000	2000	50,000	4	6

Note: Large and small denote resources rather than numbers of students

Table 5.5 Model Parameters Fit to Four Institutions.

	State Funding Growth %	% Tenure Track Faculty	Overhead Rate on Funded Research	Average Undergrad Class Size	Average Graduate Class Size	Average Award Size
Large Public	2%	70%	60%	80	28	$330K
Large Private	NA	80%	60%	16	8	$260K
Small Public	2%	30%	50%	65	45	$210K
Small Private	NA	70%	50%	40	29	$150K

decrease, fewer proposals are submitted, and fewer awards received. This requires increasing the average award size for the university to match the overall numbers in the first column of Table 5.4. Note that because graduate tuition is much higher, projections are more sensitive to sizes of graduate classes.

Table 5.5 shows the best-fit parameters that resulted from the fitting process. Common assumptions across all institutions included undergraduate population growth rate of 3 percent, undergraduate tuition growth rate of 3 percent, graduate population growth rate of 4 percent, graduate tuition growth rate of 5 percent, endowment growth rate of 6.5 percent, endowment earnings of 5 percent, and discount rate of 4 percent. Sensitivity analyses showed that overall results are not very sensitive to these assumptions in terms of plus or minus 1 percent. Negative values, in contrast, have a much larger impact.

Model Projections

The three scenarios are succinctly defined as follows: 1) S1: Status Quo, 2) S2: Graduate Student Population Declines by 5 percent annually, and 3) S3: Graduate Tuition Declines to $10,000 Due to Online Offerings. The results for these three scenarios are summarized in Figures 5.9 and 5.10. Note that class size is varied—to 10X or 1,000—for the three instances of S3 rather than adding a fourth and fifth scenario. This reflects that fact that the external competitive driver is the same in all three cases. What differs is the institution's response to the scenario.

S3:$10K is the worst scenario, resulting in negative NPV (S/D) for everyone, because the number of students does not decrease while revenue decreases substantially. Three of the cases—S2, S3:10x, and S3:1K—lead to substantially reduced numbers of faculty, which undermines institutional publishing productivity and, hence, brand value. S3:1K is the most profitable because the number of students does not decrease but faculty numbers are cut by over 90 percent. Brand value, of course, plummets but only in a relative manner.

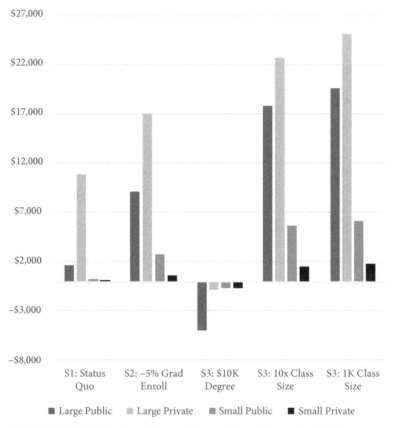

Fig. 5.9 NPV (S/D) for Four Universities and Three Scenarios ($ Million)

Institutions with significant resources are simply not going to let these futures happen to them. As discussed below, high-resource institutions have been the "first movers" in enabling S3: $10K. Thus, they are cannibalizing their professional masters "cash cows" before others do. They are likely to become the infrastructure platforms for others' educational content. They may also be content providers to resource poor institutions. This raises the possibility that these resource poor institutions will disappear or be absorbed by others (Azziz, et al., 2017).

Scenario 1: Status Quo. In this scenario, the number of proposals submitted grows exponentially to compensate for declining success rate, which leads to the number of articles submitted declining exponentially, due to lack of faculty time, which leads to a plateauing of brand value. More specifically, assuming a faculty member needs to secure an NSF award every other year, they need to submit 2 proposals in year 1 and 7 proposals in year 20. As proposals take precedence over publications, this faculty

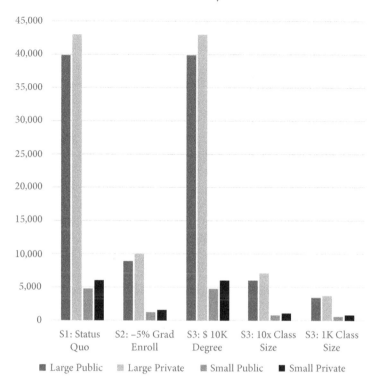

Brand Value:
20 Year Outlook by Scenario

Fig. 5.10 Brand Value at Year 20 for Four Universities and Three Scenarios

member will submit 4 articles in year 1, with 1 being accepted, and 0 in year 20, with of course none being accepted.

One might argue that just writing proposals rather than papers would hurt a faculty member's career. However, once tenured, this risk is less. Further, funds from contracts and grants are needed to support graduate students and avoid large teaching loads. The intellectual work associated with proposal writing is likely to be more attractive than teaching, for example, 2–3 courses per semester, which can be the fate for faculty members who are judged to not be "research active."

The consequence of these dynamics is increasing subsidization of the research enterprise, which has to come from other revenues. For private institutions with small endowments, this subsidy must come from tuition revenue. This may translate into student debt, due to increasing tuitions being used to partially fund the research enterprise. These phenomena are illustrated in detail in (Rouse, 2016).

This scenario is, of course, not sustainable. Institutions may decide to redistribute the tasks of proposal preparation and article submission to different personnel, although this may to be difficult for institutions with fewer resources. Beyond that, Promotion and Tenure Committees might not credit the faculty with success in securing funding and publishing articles.

As noted earlier, universities could also help themselves by broadening their success models beyond NIH and NSF. The belief that a junior faculty member has to secure a grant from one of these agencies to gain tenure leads to their submitting large numbers of unsuccessful proposals. Intellectual outcomes are what really matter, not the source of the funds. The model for brand value considers publications, citations, and *h-index*, not sources of funding. Funding enables research, which enables publications, that lead to citations and hence *h-indices*. Universities are paying dearly, in terms of increasing subsidies, by clinging to NIH and NSF.

Shneiderman (2018) discusses an approach to creatively rethinking universities' research success models. His focus on combining basic and applied research would likely enable significantly decreased costs of securing research funding. There is a risk, however, that applied research might lead to fewer articles contributing to brand value. Technical reports, for instance, are usually not well cited.

Beyond such changes within universities, research-sponsoring agencies could lower costs of research by changing procurement processes. For example, they could, and several do, require brief white papers with an initial articulation of an idea. For ideas that have a high probability of being funded, investigators are encouraged to submit proposals. Current peer review processes at agencies such as NIH and NSF tend to reinforce reigning academic paradigms and discourage proposals outside the norm, e.g., (Carroll, 2017). These processes need to be rethought.

Scenario 2: Declining Graduate Enrollments. In this scenario, we see that declining enrollment results in declining size of faculties, which leads to fewer faculty members' research having to be subsidized, which leads to fewer publications and significantly decreased brand value. However, the key element for institutions of any size is not necessarily the total number of faculty but the number of research effective faculty. An institution with 200 TT faculty and 50 teaching faculty can achieve the same brand value as an institution with 200 TT faculty and 200 teaching faculty.

This scenario involved 5 percent annual decreases of graduate enrollments, reflecting an observed trend over the past few years, as well as recent turmoil over immigration. Realistically, top players will not experience such decline, while lower players will see greater declines. The top institutions will retain their ability to pick the best foreign applicants. Fewer applicants overall will mean that the top institutions will consume a greater portion of the pool.

Scenario 3: Declining Graduate Tuitions. In this scenario, decreased graduate tuition, due to high-quality online offerings, results in substantial deficits, but brand value is sustained if class sizes are maintained at S1 levels. Deficits are highly affected by attempts to maintain the research enterprise. The magnitude of graduate and post-baccalaureate certificate tuitions as a key support to tuition-driven institutions and a profit center for all institutions will surely decline with the continued improvement in technology-enabled instruction, although the enhanced quality of technology can be expensive. Several contemporary initiatives have involved substantial up-front corporate investments, and subsequent enrollment of large numbers of their employees (Goodman, et al., 2016).

Scale here will be critical as institutions increasingly outsource the infrastructure for distance education offerings to organizations that can provide cost-effective operations. A key element in this and the other S3 alternatives will be the ability to link distance programs to high value brands. This is an increasingly evident trend in the field as commercial providers offer institutionally branded programs on a common technology platform.

A modification of scenario 3 that captures the effects of increasing graduate class sizes by 10X yields very positive results that differ across institutions due to baseline S1 class sizes. The declining size of faculty, due to larger classes, increases surplus but erodes brand value. How much brand value will suffer as a result of changes in the scale of graduate education will depend on the mix of programs. Some fields have key quality metrics linked to small class size. Others fields may not have such issues with class size.

An additional modification to scenario 3, which projects the impact of increasing graduate class sizes to 1,000 per class yields increasingly positive results, although the further decline of the size of faculty, due to yet larger classes, substantially erodes brand value. A hybrid model would have such large classes for introductory courses but shrink class size to more traditional levels for advanced courses.

It is of particular note that the top institutions are driving all variations of scenario 3, with Coursera, edX and Udacity being prime examples. These institutions have the resources to enable large experiments. In addition, they can attract major commitments from industry to underwrite these experiments and seed enrollments. AT&T and Accenture's large commitments to Georgia Tech for high quality MS degrees in computer science and data analytics, mentioned earlier, illustrate how $10,000 MS degrees can be possible. Lower-level players, where tuitions from professional graduate degrees are their only "cash cow," are at substantial risk.

Assuming class sizes of 1,000 raises the prospect of there not being enough students to fill these classes. However, $10,000 professional MS degrees are likely to spur dramatic increases in demand, in part because this price point will easily fit within many large corporations' education budgets (Goodman, et al., 2016). Nevertheless, the higher brand value institutions may dominate this market, to the significant detriment of the lower brand value institutions.

Overall, all these scenarios result in decreased research productivity due to diminishing returns for S1, as well as dramatically declining faculty sizes for S2 and S3. All four institutions that illustrate these scenarios benefit financially by decreasing subsidies of research, but the dramatic decrease of research output should certainly be a national concern. Using student debt, at least in part, to subsidize the re-search enterprise is not in the national interest. Some rethinking seems definitely warranted.

Comparing Institutions. How do the different scenarios affect the four institutions studied? Brand value decreases due to diminishing returns from research sponsors affects all institutions similarly. The ratios of the brand value of large institutions to small institutions range from 4.7 to 7.7 across the scenarios. Thus, the top-ranked institutions will likely remain on top. The substantially declining research productivity of all four institutions should be a major concern in terms of economic development, national security, etc.

The change of NPV differs significantly across large and small institutions, particularly for S3. The two large institutions average NPV = -$2.8 billion, while the two small institutions average NPV = -$2.3 billion. The year 20 revenues for the large institutions average $6.8 billion, while the two small institutions average $1.0 billion. Clearly the small institutions are not in a position to weather such losses due to technology transforming their graduation education business.

Summary

It is unknown what mix of these scenarios will actually emerge. Universities need strategies and investments that enable robust responses to whatever mix emerges. Models such as the one extended and exemplified here, and more fully explored in (Rouse, 2016), provide institutional leaders with a method of exploring the impacts of various policy decisions within their institutions, as well as assessing the impact of changes in the external environment on their institution.

Predictions for the three scenarios serve as warnings about what might happen if universities persist with their current strategies. Meyer and Zucker (1989) discuss the notion of "permanently failing organizations," where persistence compensates for lack of performance. Muddling through will not work when faced with the scenarios outlined here as losing billions of dollars is not a realistic option for many institutions.

Fundamental change is in the offing. Higher education cannot sustain its current cost structures. The limits of tuition increases will inevitably be reached, significantly facilitated by increasingly powerful and sophisticated technology platforms, likely offered by institutions with high brand values. Many educational institutions will need to reconfigure their operations, restructure their financial models, or disappear amidst "creative destruction" (Schumpeter, 1942).

Opportunities for Transformational Investments

There are always challenges, particularly in organizations with many perceptive and creative people who can always think of new offerings, often with little revenue to support them. There are, in addition, several other concerns that consume the attention and time of academic institutions. This case study considered these concerns and possible investments to address them (Lombardi, Johns, Rouse &. Craig, 2020; Lombardi, Craig, Johns & Rouse, 2020).

Challenges

K-12 Deficiencies. Evidence of poor preparation is pervasive but especially in terms of completion rates. However, the demand that everyone who enters should graduate and get a degree disguises some of this. Institutions spend very large amounts on support services to compensate for the poor preparation of many of their students.

Increasing Demands for Services. Beyond the normal educational services, there are health services, including mental health, career counseling, placement services, dispute resolution services, managing intramurals and clubs, etc. These services require staffing, facilities, and budgets. This obviously increases costs, but seldom revenue. Consequently, tuitions and fees have to cover these costs.

Increasing Oversight & Compliance. Activities associated with university accreditation, discipline-specific accreditation, certifications of workload distributions, auditing of travel expense reports, compliance with policies and procedures, e.g., format requirements for promotion and tenure cases, and sundry other forms, signatures, etc. consume significant faculty and staff time. The worst situation is a culture of compliance laced with administrative incompetence.

Increasing Contingent Faculty. Universities' budgetary challenges have resulted in increased reliance on adjuncts and part-time faculty whose salaries are contingent on adequate enrollments in the courses they are slated to teach. Further, their salaries are substantially lower than tenure track faculty. Consequently, 25 percent of adjuncts across the US are receiving some form of public assistance, typically food stamps and Medicaid. This situation has prompted unionization efforts for faculty, staff, and graduate students, which tends to undermine the collegial climate that was highly valued.

Costs-Benefits Questioned. The costs of higher education have risen much faster than incomes and the other costs of living. As a result, student loan debts now exceed U.S. credit card debts. This has caused students and parents to question the benefits of higher education. The return on investment (ROI) on an earned degree is still quite positive. However, seeing this return depends on completing the degree. It does seem that the "tuition bubble" will burst at some point (Rouse, Lombardi & Craig, 2018)

Improving Educational Technology. The pandemic has caused many to recognize that online learning is better than expected. With adequate investments, online programs can provide functions and features that are seldom available in traditional classrooms. These programs can often be hosted on platforms developed by major institutions, e.g., Coursera, edX, and Udacity. The technology enables much larger classes, e.g., 10,000 in Georgia Tech's online MS in computer science. This enables much lower tuition, e.g., $10,000 for the whole MS degree at GT.

Table 5.6 Strategies Versus Cohorts.

Strategies	Cohorts		
	Strong	Decent	Marginal
Sustain Current Business Model	Recognizes Needs to Evolve	Priority But Will Entertain Changes	Highest Priority If Possible
Experiment, Learn Quickly & Adapt	Leads Delivery Innovations	Fast Follower of Successes	Slow Follower of Successes
Disrupt Current Business Model	Resources Available	Resources Unavailable	Resources Unavailable
Move Online With Contingent Faculty	Selectively Attractive	Increasingly Attractive	Increasingly Necessary

Decreasing Foreign Students. Increasing equity of foreign institutions, immigration headaches in the U.S., and now pandemic worries will steadily decrease enrollments of full tuition paying foreign students, threatening almost $50 billion of revenue to U,S, universities. Educational technology can enable recruiting students without their being in the U.S., but the acceptable tuitions for such offerings will likely challenge many institutions.

Possible Futures

The last case study illustrated the impacts of resource availability on institutions' strategic options. We used similar metrics to sort all universities into strong, decent, and marginal university cohorts—in terms of resources available to adapt to change (Lombardi, Craig, Johns & Rouse, 2020).

As shown in Table 5.6, institutions in the strong cohort have the resources—and confidence—needed to lead experimentation and evolution of innovative new business models. Institutions in the decent cohort understand change is in the offing and will be a faster follower of successes to the extent that resources allow. Institutions in the marginal cohort will struggle to sustain their current business model, which is seriously threatened.

Disciplinary Differences

Different disciplines will address change in different ways, in part greatly dependent on the university cohort in which they are located. As indicated earlier, we have explored the impacts of change on humanities, medicine, and engineering. We expect that schools of business and law will also face similar challenges. Nevertheless, the investments by discipline may differ significantly as shown in Table 5.7.

Table 5.7 Example Investments in Innovations Versus Disciplines.

Potential Investments	Discipline		
	Humanities	Medicine	Engineering
High-quality online offerings to support both virtual and in-person education, including support for group work	High quality virtual materials from selected pre-industrial civilizations representing Asia, Africa, North and South America, Europe, and Middle East,	Virtual classrooms for both lecture and small group discussion, including the "art of clinical reasoning" and actual "rounds" on patients virtually with focus on developing tacit knowledge	High-quality online offerings, with seasoned, talented instructors interspersed with demonstrations, experiments, and group discussions and work
Advanced interactive technology to support experiences, demonstrations, experiments. etc.	Augmented reality-based interactions with art, history, geography, culture, language to enable students to experience other times, places and cultures	AI-based patient simulators so students can experience any disease and morbidity despite no current patient having it, including all types of personalities and even disabilities not associated with the disease or morbidity	Computational laboratories for every engineering discipline that provide access to hardware such as robots, powertrains, electronics, integrated circuits, and manufacturing processes
Advanced technology for accessing data, information, and knowledge	Easily accessible databases of texts, material culture, artifacts. Virtual reproductions of art, music, theater, popular culture with capability for individual interaction to create virtual experiences within the cultural context of the objects to engage particular themes, values, and behaviors	Content aggregation, text analytics, and machine learning for access and interpretation of millions of published articles across the breadth of medicine and related sciences	Content aggregation, text analytics, and machine learning for access and interpretation of millions of published articles across the breadth of engineering and science
Process modeling and reengineering across every process in the institution to streamline services and decrease costs	Evaluate tradeoff between student-mentor engagement with humanistic subjects and large-scale technology enabled humanistic activity	Reduce redundancy and non-relevant clinical experiences in medical school and residency training to reduce student costs and years needed to enter clinical practice	Represent student flows through each curriculum in terms of knowledge, skills and experiences gained and the costs of delivering these outcomes; focus on increasing efficiencies without losing quality

Online Education. All disciplines will necessarily have to entertain greater use of online teaching as the response to the pandemic has prompted. However, disciplines may differ in emphases. Some of these differences will be driven by the differing content employed in the curricular of these differences. Also of great importance, will be the extent that face-to-face interactions are central to each discipline and the extent to which these interactions can be technologically mediated.

Interactive Technologies. Advanced technology can enable compelling interactive portrayals of phenomena ranging from chemistry and physics, to human physiology and behaviors, to social and cultural interactions. These interactive technologies can augment reality and provide profound educational experiences. The quality of these immersive portrayals has steadily improved and the costs, at least on widely available platforms, have progressively decreased. The economics of such technologies depend, however, on the number of students across which costs can be amortized.

Knowledge Management. Information access and knowledge management are challenges across disciplines, although the nature of data and knowledge artifacts differ substantially across disciplines. In particular, the technological infrastructure associated with science and technology has benefitted from enormous investments. Humanities have seen important investments and innovations but not at all on the same scale. Of particular note, the data and knowledge artifacts of the humanities were seldom originally created digitally.

Process Improvement. Process modeling and improvement initiatives are significantly affected by two factors. One is the extent to which educational processes are interwoven with operational processes. This is greatest for medicine where much of education happens during delivery of clinical services. In engineering, considerable research happens with industry and undergraduate cooperative education programs are pervasive. Humanities have few similar processes and thus can be approached in a more straightforward manner.

The second factor is scale. When an undergraduate major, e.g., in electrical, industrial, or mechanical engineering, has well over 1,000 students in one department, technology investments can be amortized across many students and, thereby, justify much greater investments. If such institutions are also well resourced, i.e., the strong cohort, the human and financial resources can be marshaled to undertake these investments.

Impacts on Ecosystem of Higher Education

Increased enrollments can be expected due to technology-enabled easier access and potentially lower priced tuitions—see Georgia Tech example. With continuing pressures to control costs, there will be a steadily decreasing tenure track faculty workforce, with the possible exception in institutions in the strong cohort.

Technology and outsourcing will result in steadily decreasing staff positions. Decreased investments in bricks and mortar will inevitably lead to fewer support staff.

Overall university employment will decline, with possible exceptions in medicine where clinician deficits are projected, and possibly engineering with steadily increasing demands for STEM education.

Impacts on U.S. Global Competitiveness

The overall result will be a better-educated workforce due to increased enrollments. There will be increased workforce diversity due to easier access and lower prices. This will lead to an increasingly healthy, educated, and productive workforce that is competitive in the global marketplace.

With faculty positions becoming scarcer, there will be increased placement of PhD graduates in industry and government. This will lead to enhanced technology transfer and innovation due to broadened placement of research talent. Industry and government demand for professional graduate degrees will increase with easier access and lower prices.

Enhancing the STEM Talent Pipeline

The three case studies thus far discussed in this chapter have focused on strategic options available to institutional leaders. This case study shifts gear to consider choices available to students and the factors that influence these choices. The future of academia depends on the confluence of these two sets of choices.

The topic of how students choose college majors has received extensive study. It is much more complicated than might appear on the surface, involving interactions of the aspirations, aptitudes, and attitudes of students in middle school, high school, and early years of college. Relative to pursuing STEM (science, technology, engineering, and mathematics) majors, it is not a simple question of whether they liked and were proficient in high school mathematics.

There is an extensive literature on this topic. Table 5.8 provides a sampling. The issues range from the institutions where students seek admission, to what academic majors they choose to pursue, to what motivates STEM majors, to what behavioral and social phenomena encourages particular choices. This case study addresses this range of perspectives.

Factors Affecting Choice of Institution

A university's brand value plays an important role in several phenomena. It affects students' choices of where to apply and, if accepted, enroll. Many factors

Table 5.8 Factors Associated with Students Choices.

Topic Addressed	Source
Factors affecting choice of institution	Hoyt & Brown (2003)
Factors affecting choice of institution	Stark & Scholder (2011)
Factors affecting choice of institution	Noel-Levitz (2012)
Factors affecting choice of majors	Malgwi, Hover, & Burnaby (2005)
Factors affecting choice of majors	Williams (2007)
Factors affecting choice of majors	Fizer (2013)
Factors affecting choice of majors	SalahJaradat (2015)
Factors affecting choice of majors	Haggag, Patterson, Pope, & Feudo (2019)
Factors affecting choice of STEM majors	Wang (2013)
Factors affecting choice of STEM majors	Phelps, Camburn & Min (2018)
Factors affecting choice of Engr. majors	Zahorian, Elmore, & Temkin, (2013)
How soft skills affect choices	Koch, Nofziger, & Nielson (2015)
Behavioral barriers & interventions	Lavecchia, Liu, & Oreopoulos (2015)

affect students' choices, but brand value and costs dominate (Hoyt & Brown, 2003; Noel-Levitz, 2012).

Stark and Scholder (2011) present a methodological approach comparing "stated" versus "derived" importance—what students said versus what they actually did. They find that derived performance better predicts choices, often including factors that students indicated did not greatly matter.

These three reports are from consultants engaged with supporting university enrollment management functions, which have become increasingly sophisticated, although a bit derailed by the pandemic. Their statistical models are useful for predicting how many students will enroll; less so for which students will enroll.

Factors Affecting Choice of Majors

Several articles report findings on factors that affect college majors chosen, across all majors, not just STEM.

Malgwi, Hover, and Burnaby (2005) report on 3,800 students in a northeast business school. Factors affecting choice of major include interest in the subject, aptitude for the subject (women), and potential for career advancement and compensation (men). Changes of major were due to positive factors associated with the new major, rather than negative factors associated with the old major.

Williams (2007) reports on students' characteristics and external influences affecting choices of majors. Student characteristics include personal associations with major, level of professional aspirations, aptitude, and high school experiences. External influences include significant persons (family and friends, high school personnel, and professionals in the field), exposure to the major (publications, family associations, and personal experiences) and college factors (recruitment, personal contact, and reputation).

SalahJaradat (2015) performed a multi-dimensional analysis of undergraduate choices of major in a private university. Correlations with college reputation, teachers, school advisor, job opportunities, interest in the subject, and aptitude were all in the 0.1-0.2 range. This suggests that, at least for this population, no one or two factors dominated.

Fizer (2013) reported on factors affecting choice of academic majors in agriculture. The most frequently reported factors were family (22%), a career that is personally rewarding (21%), experience with Future Farmers of America and 4-H (20%). Of course, these students had already chosen to pursue careers in agriculture, just not their majors.

Haggag, Patterson, Pope, and Feudo (2019) found that student choices of majors at West Point were affected by rather subtle factors. Assignments to early morning sections of general education subjects resulted in 10% decreases in the likelihood of choosing to major in that subject. Fatigue from back-to-back courses prior to a general education subject resulted in decreases in the likelihood of choosing to major in that subject.

These findings are all relatively consistent, although at differing levels of resolution. Clearly more factors are involved than interest in the subject and aptitude for the subject. There are significant social factors that influence students' choices.

Factors Affecting Choice of STEM Majors

Wang (2013) reports on factors affecting choices of STEM majors. Not surprisingly, intentions to major in STEM play a significant role. Exposure to math and science courses, as well as high school math achievement play roles. Math self-efficacy beliefs are also important. Initial post-secondary experiences can reinforce STEM choices. Finally, receipt of financial aid plays an obvious role.

Phelps, Camburn and Min (2018) report that academic preparation and orientation is a strong predictor of choosing STEM majors. Students who take pre-college engineering courses have a 60 percent increase in likelihood of STEM enrollment. Early relevant post-secondary experiences also increase this likelihood.

Zahorian, Elmore and Temkin (2013) discuss the choices of majors by 300 engineering freshmen. Three factors were rated by students as most important in their major selection process: personal academic interests, potential for societal contributions, and job prospects. Of course, these students had already chosen to pursue careers in engineering, just not their majors.

Clearly, the likelihood of pursuing STEM in general, or engineering in particular, is greatly enhanced by high school experiences such as pre-college engineering courses. Early relevant post-secondary experiences also have an impact. I remember my experiences working in my uncle's plumbing company and how installing and maintaining various plumbing and heating systems greatly increased my interest in mechanical engineering. I wanted to really understand how and why these systems functioned.

Behavioral Factors Affecting Choices

Koch, Nofziger and Nielson (2015) argue for looking beyond cognitive skills as measured by achievement tests. They report that soft skills are also important to academic success. These soft skills include self-control, willingness to compete, intrinsic motivation, and self-confidence. They suggest that educational investments should consider how both cognitive and soft skills will be engendered.

Lavecchia, Liu and Oreopoulos (2015) provide a very impressive and comprehensive review of literature on behavioral barriers to academic success and interventions to overcome these barriers. Behavioral barriers include students focusing too much on the present and relying too much on the routines of education. These barriers impede students' inclinations to consider their futures. Some students focus too much on avoiding negative identities rather than deeper aspects of alternative futures. Overall, students are more likely to make poor choices with many options or little information.

The authors provide a very useful compilation of interventions proven to help overcome behavioral barriers, with research literature cited for each suggestion. Five in-depth tables include:

- Interventions that aim to offset immediate costs with immediate benefits
- Interventions to help reduce inertia and change routine for students
- Interventions to help reduce inertia and change routine for parents
- Interventions to help reduce inertia and change routine by changing defaults and adding structure
- Interventions that strengthen positive identities

Clearly, these findings from behavioral economics argue for addressing the whole student, both to enable success in general as well as to support STEM aspirations where warranted. Interestingly, this finding is very similar to the need to address the whole patient discussed in Chapter 4.

Overall Findings

Table 5.9 provides an overall, qualitative summary of the findings of this case study. The primary considerations change as students proceed on their educational and

Table 5.9 Students' Decisions, Considerations and Skills.

Decision	Primary Considerations	Soft Skills & Behavioral Barriers
Going to College	Other options, e.g., work, military, gap year or equivalent	Imagine futures, career aspirations
Where to Apply	Reputation, selectivity, financial aid, location	Imagine futures, social features
Where to Enroll	Majors available, financial aid	Imagine futures, social features
General Major	Role models, interests, aptitude, motivation	Imagine futures, assess skills
Specific Major	Knowledge, role models, interests, aptitude, motivation	Imagine futures, assess skills
Career Path	36% in jobs with title engineer; 90% in jobs using engineering skills (NAP, 2018)	Imagine futures, assess skills

career paths. Soft skills and overcoming behavioral barriers become increasingly important. Note the final row of Table 5.9—a student's degree does not dictate his or her future jobs

As indicated earlier, this case study was motivated by a desire to understand how government policies could enhance the STEM talent pipeline. The policy implications include the following:

- STEM preparation needs to start before college; middle school is ideal
- STEM motivation needs to start before college; middle school is ideal
- STEM investments in high school and middle schools increase talent pool
- STEM investments need to take into account both cognitive and soft skills
- Programmatic investments need to be balanced with financial aid

Approach to Transformation

Responsibilities for education in the U.S. are highly distributed among federal, state, and city governments, as well as public and private institutions. The federal government led the desegregation of schools in the 1950s. It is also a source of funds via grants and other mechanisms.

However, the federal government cannot dictate whether math and science are taught at various grade levels and how this content is presented. States have some control over content, e.g., via approved course textbooks, but local school districts have final say.

Federal monies provide a small percentage of school budgets. Of the remaining lion's share of budgets, roughly half comes from state resources, including income taxes, sales tax, and fees, and half comes from local resources, primarily through the property taxes of homeowners in the area. Local control of schools predominates.

For the above reasons, it does not make sense to aspire to transform the overall U.S. education system. There are far too many stakeholders and a far-ranging set of perspectives. Yet, the ecosystem of higher education, the focus in this chapter, is almost totally dependent on the outcomes of the K-12 system. As indicated in the third case study, an increasing percentage portion of higher education resources have to be devoted to remediating unprepared K-12 graduates.

One approach to this is for institutions of higher education to found and operate their own high schools. This is not a new idea. The University of Illinois at Urbana-Champaign founded University Laboratory High School in 1921. Much more recently, Purdue University and the City of Indianapolis founded Purdue Polytechnic High School in 2017. South of the border, the Monterrey Institute of Technology sponsors several high schools that share one or more national curricula: bicultural, multicultural and/or International Baccalaureate. I have lectured at their Tolucca campus several times and found the students most impressive.

This cannot be the primary approach to transformation, but it serves to illustrate an important point. Given the very distributed nature of governance and funding of education in the U.S., a portfolio of bottom-up innovations will likely be the best, albeit slow, path to transformation. The federal government can motivate and invest in these innovations but not control them.

It would be very helpful if higher education would team with K-12 to foster and mature this portfolio of innovations. Once innovations are proven at initial K-12 schools, grants and assistance could be provided to other schools to promote their adoption. Communities of interest formed around particular innovations could capture lessons learned and enable continual improvement.

Economic Valuation

The economics of higher education was one of the motivations for my interest in the case studies reported here. The leading indicators of how the tuition bubble might burst led to my book **Universities as Complex Enterprises** (Rouse, 2016). Subsequent studies, reported earlier, led me to realize several key differences among institutions and disciplines.

Yet, the fact remains that higher education is far too expensive. Subsidizing uncontrolled university budgets with student debt is a terrible strategy. Students struggling with debt delay getting married, buying homes, and having children. These unfortunate consequences undermine economic growth and, of course, undermine people's confidence in their futures.

The pandemic has clearly demonstrated that technologically-enabled education is feasible, although far from comprehensively acceptable. Once the pandemic is tamed,

I expect that the "new normal" will be some hybrid of face to face and online. This will enable the types of economic efficiencies discussed earlier in this chapter. Competition will force universities to lower prices. Lower prices will result in more students seeking education.

The value of bricks and mortar will be diminished. The number of classes where a faculty member lectures to 10-20 students will steadily decrease. I expect, as noted earlier, the "sage on the stage" will increasingly be replaced by the "guide on the side." The number of graduate programs producing would-be sages will decrease, while those yielding capable guides will hold their own.

For other than the best resourced institutions, the coming years will be economically disruptive. Those who embrace the maxim "never waste a crisis" will embrace the opportunity to innovate and transform. There will be winners, with hopefully students at the head of the line.

Conclusions

This chapter has explored the ecosystem of higher education in considerable detail. Historical innovations were reviewed and potential future innovations were outlined. It is essential to realize that this ecosystem is not composed of 5,000 cookie cutter institutions and 30,000 cookie cutter high schools—24,000 public and 6,000 private schools. There is enormous variety, particularly in terms of the availability of resources.

Yet, there is an agreed-upon overarching goal. We want to foster a healthy, educated, and productive population that is competitive in the global marketplace. Chapter 4 addressed health and this chapter has addressed education. Next, we need an environment conducive to these ends while also providing the energy needed to enable it.

References

Azziz, R., et al. (2017). *Mergers in Higher Education: A Proactive Strategy to a Better Future?* New York: TIAA Institute

BankBoston (1997). *MIT: The Impact of Innovation.* Boston, MA: BankBoston

Bush, V. (1945). *Science—The Endless Frontier: A Report to the President on Program for Postwar Scientific Research.* Washington, D.C. National Science Foundation

Carroll, A.E. (2017). Why the medical research grant system could be costing us great ideas. *New York Times,* June 18

CSGNET (2007). *Data Sources: The Rise of "Older" Graduate Students.* http://www.cgsnet.org/portals/0/pdf/DataSources_2007_12.pdf

Fahey, L. and Randall, R.M. (eds) (1998). *Learning from the Future: Competitive Foresight Scenarios*. New York: Wiley

Fizer, D. (2013). *Factors Affecting Career Choice of College Students Enrolled in Agriculture*. Martin, TN: University of Tennessee, MS Thesis

Friedman, T.L. (2005). *The World Is Flat*. New York: Farrar, Straus and Giroux

Friedman, T.L. (2008). *Hot, Flat, and Crowded*. New York: Farrar, Straus and Giroux

Goodman, J., Melkers, J., and Pallais, A. (2016). *Can Online Delivery Increase Access to Education?* Working Paper No. W22754. Cambridge, MA: National Bureau of Economic Research

Haggag, K., Patterson, R.W., Pope, N.G., and Feudo, A. (2019). *Attribution Bias in Major Decisions: Evidence for the United States Military Academy*. West Point, NY: United states Military Academy

Hoyt, J.E. and Brown, A.B. (2003). Identifying college choice factors to successfully market your institution. *C&U Journal*, Spring, 3–10

Kamenetz, A. (2009). *Who Needs Harvard*? Fast Company, September

Killian, J.R., Jr. (1985). *The Education of a College President: A Memoir*. Cambridge, MA: MIT Press

Koch, A., Nofziger, J., and Nielson, H.S. (2015). Behavioral economics of education. *Journal of Economic Behavior & Organization*, 115, 3–17

Lavecchia, A.M., Liu, H., and Oreopoulos, P. (2015). *Behavioral Economics of Education: Progress and Possibilities*. Bonn: Institute of Labor, Discussion Paper No. 8853

Lombardi, J., et al., (2000–2016). *The Top American Research Universities: Annual Report, 2000–2016*. Arizona State University and University of Massachusetts Amherst (http://mup.asu.edu)

Lombardi, J.V., Craig, D.D., Johns, M.M.E., and Rouse, W.B. (2020). The unrecognized complexity of higher education. *Annual Report of the Center for Measuring University Performance*. Amherst, MA: University of Massachusetts

Lombardi, J.V., Johns, M.M.E., Rouse, W.B., and Craig, D.D. (2020). The complexity of higher education, *The Bridge*, in press

Malgwi, C.A., Hover, M.A., and Burnaby, P.A. (2005). Influences on student's choices of college major. *Journal of Education for Business*, 80 (5), 275–282

Meyer, M.W. and Zucker, L.G. (1989). *Permanently Failing Organizations*. Washington, DC: Sage Publications

NAP (2018). *Educational and Career Pathways of Engineers*. Washington, DC: National Academy Press

Noel-Levitz (2012). *Why Did They Enroll? The Factors Influencing College Choice*. Iowa City, IA: Ruffalo Noel Levitz

North, G. (2009). *MIT Calls Academia's Bluff*. www.LewRockwell.com

Perez-Pena, R. (2013). Patenting their discoveries does not payoff for most universities. *New York Times*, November 20

Phelps, L.A., Camburn, A.M., and Min, S. (2018). Choosing STEM college majors: Exploring the role of pre-college engineering courses. *Journal of Pre-College Engineering Education Research*, 8 (1). 1–24

Rouse, W.B. (2016). *Universities as Complex Enterprises: How Academia Works, Why It Works These Ways, and Where The University Enterprise Is Headed*. New York: Wiley.

Rouse, W.B., Lombardi, J.V, and Craig, D.D. (2018). Modeling research universities: Predicting probable futures of public vs. private and large vs. small research universities. *Proceedings of the National Academy of Sciences*, 115 (50), 12582–12589

SalahJaradat, M. (2015). What really matters in choosing a college major. *International Journal of Arts and Commerce*, 4 (2)

Schoemaker, P.J.H. (1995). Scenario planning: A tool for strategic thinking. *Sloan Management Review*, Winter, 25–40

Schumpeter, J. (1942). *Capitalism, Socialism and Democracy*. New York: Harper & Brothers

Schwartz, P. (1991). *The Art of the Long View: Planning for the Future in an Uncertain World*. New York: Currency Doubleday

Shneiderman, B. (2018), The twin-win model: A human-centered approach to research success. *Proceedings National Academies of Science*, 115 (50), 12590–12594

Stark, R. and Scholder, T. (2011). *What Drives Student Choices? Applying Behavioral Economics to Higher Education*. Concord, MA: Maguire Associates, Inc.

Wang, X. (2013). Why students choose STEM majors: Motivation, high school learning, and postsecondary context of support. *American Educational Research Journal*, 50 (5). 1081–1121

Williams, K.B. (2007). *Factors Influencing Choice of Academic Major: A Comparison of Agricultural and Non-agricultural Degree Programs*. Lubbock, TX: Texas Tech University, PhD Dissertation

Zahorian, S., Elmore, M., and Temkin, K.J. (2013). Factors that influence engineering freshmen to choose their engineering major. *Proceedings of the 120th ASEE Annual Conference & Exposition*, Atlanta, Georgia, June 23–26

6
Energy and Climate

This chapter addresses the following questions:

- What is the energy and climate ecosystem?
- What types of innovation are needed?
- How might these innovations be enabled?
- How might enterprise transformation facilitate these innovations?
- How can such investments be economically justified?

The Ecosystem

The energy and climate ecosystem is clearly the most extensive addressed thus far in this book. I begin by looking at the overall system that needs to be influenced. This broad perspective can facilitate addressing the challenges of climate change and likely consequences.

As shown in Figure 6.1, the Earth can be considered as a collection of different phenomena operating on different time scales (Rouse, 2014a). Loosely speaking, there are four interconnected systems: environment; population; industry; and government. In this notional model, the population consumes resources from the environment and creates by-products. Industry also consumes resources and creates by-products, but it also produces employment. The government collects taxes and produces rules. The use of the environment is influenced by those rules.

Each system component has a different associated time constant. In the case of the environment, the time constant is decades to centuries. The population's time constant can be as short as weeks to months, as the pandemic has illustrated. Government's time constant is longer, thinking in terms of years. Industry is longer still, in the order of decades. These systems can be represented at different levels of abstraction and/or aggregation as shown in Figure 6.2

The levels of this ecosystem have fairly well-entrenched perceptions and priorities:

- *Society*: Elected officials have great difficulty trading off short-term versus long-term costs and benefits, due to a large extent to the concerns, values and perceptions of their constituents—citizens and companies.

Transforming Public-Private Ecosystems. William B. Rouse, Oxford University Press.
© William B. Rouse (2022). DOI: 10.1093/oso/9780192866530.003.0006

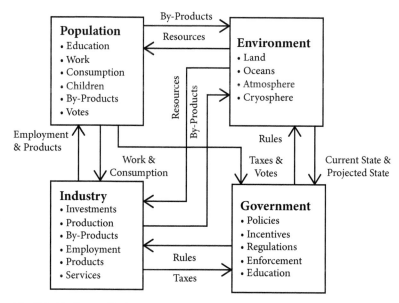

Fig. 6.1 Earth as a System

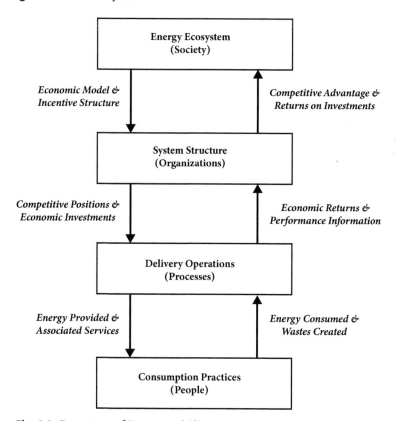

Fig. 6.2 Ecosystem of Energy and Climate

- *Organizations*: The vested interests in energy extraction, refinement, and use are enormous and are naturally inclined to sustain status quo business models, and the benefits these models provide to these organizations.
- *Processes*: Processes for extracting, refining, and utilizing fossil fuels are well developed, employ millions of people, and represent trillions of dollars of stock market capitalization.
- *People*: People have long exploited natural resources and come to depend on the benefits of these resources in terms of both consumption and employment. Changing consumption habits is very difficult.

The hierarchical representation of Figure 6.2 does not capture the fact that this is a highly distributed system, with all elements interconnected. It is difficult to solve one part of the problem, as it affects other pieces. By-products are related to population size, so one way to reduce by-products is to moderate population growth. Technology may help to ameliorate some of the by-products and their effects, but it is also possible that technology could exacerbate the effects. Clean technologies lower by-product rates but tend to increase overall use, for instance.

Sentient stakeholders include population, industry, and government. Gaining these stakeholders' support for such decisions will depend upon the credibility of the predictions of behavior, at all levels in the system. Central to this support are "space value" and "time value" discount rates. The consequences that are closest in space and time to stakeholders matter the most and have lower discount rates; attributes more distributed in time and space are more highly discounted. These discount rates will differ across stakeholders.

People will also try to "game" any strategy to improve the system, seeking to gain a share of the resources being invested in executing the transformation strategy. The way to deal with that is to make the system sufficiently transparent to understand the game being played. Sometimes gaming the system will actually be an innovation; other times, prohibitions of the specific gaming tactics will be needed.

The phenomena of central interest are depicted in Figure 6.3. Climate change is affecting the weather. More specifically, human behaviors are affecting the climate in terms of increased global warming and increased temperatures are affecting the weather.

The National Weather Service provides official definitions of climate and weather. "Weather is defined as the state of the atmosphere at a given time and place, with respect to variables such as temperature, moisture, wind speed and direction, and barometric pressure. Climate is defined as the expected frequency of specific states of the atmosphere, ocean, and land including variables such as temperature (land, ocean, and atmosphere), salinity (oceans), soil moisture (land), wind speed and direction (atmosphere), current strength and direction (oceans). Climate encompasses the weather over different periods of time and also relates to mutual interactions between the components of the earth system (e.g., atmospheric composition, volcanic

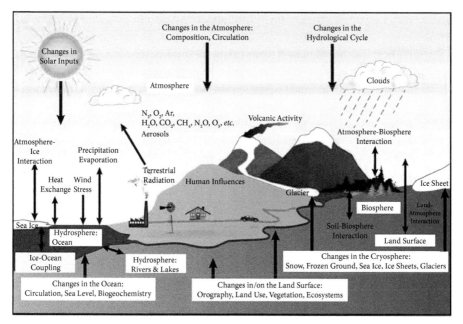

Fig. 6.3 Climate Versus Weather (NWS, 2020)

eruptions, changes in the earth's orbit around the sun, changes in the energy from the sun itself)" (NWS, 2020).

The impacts on weather are no longer hypothetical. Lenton and colleagues (2019) argue that we are already at climate tipping points in terms of Arctic warming, ice collapses, and ocean heat waves. Waterman (2019) reports on emerging consequences for U.S. national parks in terms of climate change and invasive species, as well as overcrowding and money woes. The consequences of global warming are no longer hypothetical.

Lightbody and colleagues (2019) consider flood mitigation efforts across the U.S. and argue for the cost effectiveness of mitigation. Lempert and colleagues (2018) focus on climate restoration. As compelling as such proposals may be, they face fundamental economic hurdles.

Flavelle and Mazzei (2019) recently reported on efforts to estimate the costs of raising roads in the Florida Keys to escape rising ocean levels. Route 1 in the Keys is 113 miles long. Raising all of it by 1.3 feet by 2025 will cost $2.8 billion; elevating it by 2.2 feet by 2045 will cost $4.8 billion; and by 2060 the cost would be $6.8 billion. With 13,300 people living in the Keys, this amounts to a range of $215,000 to $523,000 per person. They conclude that, "As sea levels rise, some places can't be saved."

Prospective owners of coastal homes in the U.S. will no longer be able to get 30-year mortgages as financiers can no longer predict long-term risks. Similarly, owners will no longer be able to afford increasingly expensive flood insurance. This means, the companies offering these insurances will go out of business (Flavelle, 2020).

Extreme heat has started to melt roads in states experiencing record level high temperatures. Applying an additional rubberized layer to roads helps with this, but the higher road levels result in trucks not being able to go under many bridges (Alderton, 2020).

Recent fires in California, Oregon and Washington have ravaged millions of acres, forced hundreds of thousands from their homes, and destroyed thousands of buildings. 20–30 million acres in California need to be cleared of combustible tinder, a task that has been avoided for a century. This will cost roughly $1,000 per acre. Clearing 1 million acres per year will cost $1 billion per year for 20–30 years. That a big number, but the Wine Country fires in 2017 did $9 billion in damage in one month (Temple, 2020).

Temperature rises have caused warm water fish to migrate to Northeast waters in the U.S., while resulting in cold water fish moving further north. The New England fishermen are catching foreign fish and no one in their markets has ordered them for dinner (Samenow & Freedman, 2020).

On a longer term, it is projected that between 2040 and 2060, the Southeastern and Southwestern U.S. will become uninhabitable due to temperatures and fires that humans, livestock, and crops cannot endure. Many large cites on the Eastern U.S. seaboard will be underwater. Mass migration to more hospitable places in the U.S. will be likely (Xu, et al., 2020). Large migrations north will include more than fish.

The implications are clear. We cannot deal with global warming by simply restoring everything that is damaged, and then restoring it again after the next flood, for example. We either have to stem the use of fossil fuels or prepare for disruptive and eventually very different living conditions.

Beyond the inconvenience and expense of floods, fires, etc., there is an overall stream of consequences leading from carbon to food supply and health:

- Burning of fossil fuels increases CO2
- Deforestation increases CO2 in atmosphere
- Greenhouse warming increases
- Earth's temperature increases
- Extreme weather increases
- Ice melting and sea level rise
- Salinization of groundwater and estuaries
- Decrease in freshwater availability
- Ocean acidification affects sea life
- Food supply and health degraded

The threats to life and civilization are very real and possibly devastating.

Stakeholders

Table 6.1 lists stakeholders and examples initially discussed in Chapter 2. Expanding a few of these categories of stakeholders, the number of stakeholders becomes substantially larger.

John Browne and Daniel Yergin, in their respective recent books, provide a panoramic view of the energy industry, its evolution, and challenges. They portray a sweeping landscape of stakeholders and vested interests, while also projecting how the ecosystem will eventually move beyond fossil fuels.

Browne is former CEO of BP and President of the Royal Academy of Engineering. His book (Browne, 2019) provides a well-written easily digestible tour of the history and future of engineering. He uses the terms make, think, connect, build, energize, move, defend and survive to characterize the contributions of engineering to society. His characterization of the role, history and future of energy is obviously his strong suit.

Daniel Yergin is a leading authority on energy, geopolitics, and the global economy. A bestselling author and winner of the Pulitzer Prize, he is Vice Chairman of information provider IHS MARKIT. Yergin's book (2020) is profound. When I finished reading it, I felt that I just completed a graduate course on energy, geopolitics, and climate change.

Yergin elaborates "maps" of the economics and politics of energy in the U.S., Russia, China, the Middle East, and the developing world. Energy has long been central to economic development and, for Russia and the Middle East, dominant in terms of contributions to GDP.

Table 6.1 Stakeholders in Energy and Climate.

Stakeholder	Examples
Constituencies	Congress, Public
Government Agencies	Department of Energy, Environmental Protection Agency, National Oceania and Atmospheric Administration, Federal Emergency Management Agency, States, Cities
Agencies Workforce	Employees, Unions
Industry & Institutions	Coal, Oil, Gas Companies & Related Services, Mining Companies, Renewable Energy Companies
Industry Workforce	Employees, Unions
Oversight Organizations	Government Accountability Office, Federal Energy Regulatory Commission, International Atomic Energy Agency
Advocacy Groups	Intergovernmental Panel on Climate, Change, Environmental Defense Fund, Nature Conservancy, Natural Resources Defense Council, World Wide Fund for Nature, etc.

Reductions of consumption of fossil fuels, particularly dirty fuels like coal, will help the environment but also undermine economies where populations depend on, in effect, energy stipends for their livings. Economic development in poorer countries is likely to depend on dirty, inexpensive, and plentiful fuels—like coal.

Yergin's projections of the likely adoption of renewables, mobility services, and driverless cars are prudent and clearly make the case that a carbon-free future is not just around the corner. The vested interests in the extraction industries and the millions employed in these industries present enormous challenges.

Past Innovations

United States Weather Bureau (1890)

In 1849, the Smithsonian Institution supplied weather instruments to telegraph companies and established an extensive observation network. Observations were submitted by telegraph to the Smithsonian, where weather maps were created. By the end of 1849, 150 volunteers throughout the United States were reporting weather observations to the Smithsonian regularly. By 1860, 500 stations were furnishing daily telegraphic weather reports to the **Washington Evening Star**, and as the network grew, other existing systems were gradually absorbed, including several state weather services (USWB, 2020).

The ability to observe and display simultaneously observed weather data, through the use of the telegraph, quickly led to initial efforts toward the next logical advancement, the forecasting of weather. However, the ability to observe and forecast weather over much of the country, required considerable structure and organization, which could be provided through a government agency.

The weather service is first identified as a civilian agency in 1890 when Congress, at the request of President Benjamin Harrison, passed an act transferring the meteorological responsibilities of the Signal Service to the newly-created U.S. Weather Bureau in the Department of Agriculture.

The bureau was renamed the National Weather Service when it became part of NOAA in 1970.

National Oceanic and Atmospheric Administration (NOAA) (1970)

In 1807, President Thomas Jefferson founded the U.S. Coast and Geodetic Survey (as the Survey of the Coast) to provide nautical charts to the maritime community for safe passage into American ports and along our extensive coastline. The Weather Bureau was founded 1870 and, one year later, the U.S. Commission of

Fish and Fisheries was founded. Individually, these organizations were America's first physical science agency, America's first agency dedicated specifically to the atmospheric sciences, and America's first conservation agency.

The cultures of scientific accuracy and precision, service to protect life and property, and stewardship of resources of these three agencies were brought together (by President Nixon) in 1970 with the establishment of NOAA, an agency within the Department of Commerce. (NOAA, 2020)

NOAA bills itself as "America's environmental intelligence agency."

NOAA has had a few troubles lately, ranging from its dispute over President Trump's personal weather forecast to his conflicts with the agency's executive leadership. For example, Trump replaced the agency's chief scientist with an individual who denies the reality of climate change (Flavelle & Friedman, 2020).

Environmental Protection Agency (EPA) (1970)

The American conversation about protecting the environment began in the 1960s. Rachel Carson had published her attack on the indiscriminate use of pesticides, **Silent Spring**, in 1962. Concern about air and water pollution had spread in the wake of disasters. An offshore oil rig in California fouled beaches with millions of gallons of spilled oil. Near Cleveland, Ohio, the Cuyahoga River, choking with chemical contaminants, had spontaneously burst into flames. Astronauts had begun photographing the Earth from space, heightening awareness that the Earth's resources are finite.

In early 1970, as a result of heightened public concerns about deteriorating city air, natural areas littered with debris, and urban water supplies contaminated with dangerous impurities, President Richard Nixon presented the House and Senate a groundbreaking message on the environment. He created a council to consider how to organize federal government programs designed to reduce pollution, so that those programs could efficiently address the goals laid out in his message on the environment. Following the council's recommendations, the president sent to Congress a plan to consolidate many environmental responsibilities of the federal government under one agency, a new Environmental Protection Agency. (EPA, 2020a, b)

The Trump administration worked to reverse many of the EPA's achievements.

The bulk of the rollbacks identified by the Times have been carried out by the Environmental Protection Agency, which has weakened Obama-era limits on planet-warming carbon dioxide emissions from power plants and from cars and trucks; removed protections from more than half the nation's wetlands; and withdrawn the legal justification for restricting mercury emissions from power plants. At the same time, the Interior Department has worked to open up more land for oil and gas leasing by limiting wildlife protections and weakening environmental requirements for projects. (Popovich, et al., 2020)

Corporate Average Fuel Economy (CAFE) Standards (1975)

Congress first established Corporate Average Fuel Economy (CAFE) standards in 1975, principally in response to the 1973 oil embargo. These standards were intended to roughly double the average fuel economy of the new car fleet within 20 years. These standards were enacted under President Nixon and are administered by the National Highway Traffic and Safety Administration within the Department of Transportation.

"The CAFE standards not only improve energy efficiency of the Nation's fleet, but also:

- Reduce our petroleum consumption
- Increase the availability of alternative fuel vehicles
- Promote the advancement of innovative technologies
- Lower greenhouse gas emissions, both helping to mitigate climate change and improve air quality.

NHTSA's standards since 1978 have saved (and will continue to save) many billions of gallons of fuel for American drivers" (DOT, 2020).

It is interesting how policies can sometimes interact. The federal government and state of California have offered significant incentives for consumers to purchase battery electric vehicles (BEVs). Working with General Motors, we undertook a study to project market adoption both during and after government incentives (Liu, Rouse & Hanawalt, 2018). We found that sustaining the market after the BEV incentives ended would require substantial company investments.

In the process of this study, we learned that the incentives were luring customers away from high fuel-efficiency internal combustion (IC) vehicles. As a consequence, in order to meet CAFÉ targets, automobile manufacturers were lowering prices on the IC vehicles to increase sales volumes. They were actually selling these vehicles at a significant loss per vehicle. Companies had to increase sales of large SUVs and pickup trucks to make up for these losses.

Thus, the BEV incentive policies and the CAFÉ policies were working against each other. To make matters worse, as later discussed, we assessed whether the BEVs were helping the environment. If the electricity used to charge the BEVs was from coal-fired power plants, there was no environmental benefit due to moving from IC vehicles to BEVs. The interactions of policies can be rather subtle and complicated.

Intergovernmental Panel on Climate Change (1988)

The United Nations Environment Programme (UNEP) and the World Meteorological Organization (WMO) established the Intergovernmental Panel on Climate Change (IPCC) in 1988. Its assignment was "to prepare a comprehensive review and recommendations with respect to the state of knowledge of the science of climate change; the social and economic impact of climate change, and potential response strategies and elements for inclusion in a possible future international convention on climate" (IPCC, 2020).

The IPCC has "had five assessment cycles and delivered five Assessment Reports, the most comprehensive scientific reports about climate change produced worldwide. In 2007, the IPCC and U.S. Vice-President Al Gore were jointly awarded the Nobel Peace Prize "for their efforts to build up and disseminate greater knowledge about man-made climate change, and to lay the foundations for the measures that are needed to counteract such change". (IPCC, 2020)

The U.S. was a major contributor of funds to IPCC efforts until this commitment was ended in 2017 (Ekwurzel, 2017). Both President Reagan (1980–1988) and President Bush (1988–1992) supported addressing climate change and its impacts. John McCain, running for President in 2008, supported this as well. More recently, the fossil fuel industry, with President Trump as chief cheerleader, has invested enormous sums trying to debunk science and convince people that either climate change is a hoax, or that the economic investments needed to address it would be overwhelming (Davenport & Lipton, 2017).

Potential Innovations

My earliest involvement is this ecosystem focused on automobiles. Fuel economy was a priority in several studies, a few of which are noted in the case studies that follow. Electric vehicles and autonomous vehicles have been recent objects of study.

I have been involved in several relevant National Academy studies, one of which I chaired on population growth. Energy and climate change have been on the agendas of several recent meetings. A significant percentage of Academy members have argued for more proactive initiatives in this arena.

I invested increasing attention to this topic in preparing my book on *Failure Management* (Rouse, 2021). This book comprehensively addresses our abilities and inclinations to prepare for and respond to malfunctions of technologies, organizations, and society. Climate change is one of the case studies.

Throughout the process of researching climate change, I regularly published blog posts on *Rouse on Transformation*. My posting on the Oxford University Press blog titled "There Will Be No Vaccine for Rising Sea Levels" received considerable attention with others embracing this title as a byline for their initiatives.

Case Studies

The first case study addresses innovations in the automobile industry in terms of the reasons cars succeed or fail in the marketplace, and recent technologies for electric and autonomous vehicles. This sets the stage for a case study on driverless cars for disabled and older adults. I then move on to how society can anticipate and respond to failures with emphasis on failures precipitated by climate change. The final case study considers how to design policy portfolios for mitigating global warming and its impacts.

The four case studies of potential innovations in the energy and climate ecosystem discussed in this chapter include:

- Innovations in the Automobile Industry
- Driverless Cars for Disabled and Older Adults
- Managing Failures
- Designing Policy Portfolios

Each of these case studies of potential innovations is rather substantial. Consequently, a full section of this chapter is devoted to each case.

Innovations in the Automobile Industry

The largest source of greenhouse gas emissions in the U.S. is transportation (28 percent) followed by electricity production (27 percent) and industrial production (22 percent). Thus, 77 percent of emissions come from three sources (EPA, 2020b). Battery electric vehicles (BEVs) are projected to dramatically decrease emissions. However, as noted above, moving to electric vehicles will not change these impacts if these vehicles are charged from electricity produced by coal-fired power plants (Liu, Rouse & Hanawalt, 2018).

This led us to ask how does innovation happen in the U.S. automobile industry? To address this question, we studied past innovations as well as failed attempts to innovate. This pursuit began with a study for General Motors (GM) of the best ten and worst ten cars, industry wide, over the past 50 years (Hanawalt & Rouse, 2010). GM's executives and managers chose the 20 cars, shown in Table 6.2. The question was, "How were the decisions made to put these cars into the market and what distinguished successes from failures?

Answering this question required quite a bit of sleuthing. Beyond looking at production and sales numbers, we found a wealth of interviews of automotive executives and chief engineers, as well as published reviews of these cars.

Using various survey methods and statistical analyses, we concluded that central success factors included:

Table 6.2 Ten Product Successes and Ten Product Failures.

Product Successes	Product Failures
1955 Chevrolet	1958 Edsel
1964 Pontiac GTO	1960 Chevrolet Corvair
1964 Ford Mustang	1971 Chevrolet Vega
1974 Volkswagen Rabbit	1971 Ford Pinto
1984 Chrysler Minivan	1975 AMC Pacer
1986 Ford Taurus	1981 DeLorean DMC-12
1998 Lincoln Navigator	1982 Cadillac Cimarron
1998 Toyota Prius	1988 GM10 Program
2001 Chrysler PT Cruiser	1990 Saturn
2003 Cadillac CTS	2001 Pontiac Aztec

- Correct assumptions about the target segment of a new entry in the automotive market several years in the future
- Employing a vehicle development process that could reliably and efficiently yield the vehicle envisioned
- Designers and developers being able to adapt to changing economic conditions in the marketplace

Leadership also played a role, especially when capricious decisions were made, which tended to throw the evolution of the vehicle off track. The Pontiac Aztec is a good example, where a last-minute decision was made to put the vehicle on a minivan chassis, without redesigning the body due to this change. The result was "the ugliest car on the road," according to various pundits including *Car Talk*. One GM executive commented to me, "It is really not a bad car when you are driving it." I responded, "The best thing about driving it is that you then cannot see it."

Another management fiasco was the Cadillac Cimarron, which was basically a Chevrolet Cavalier with a Cadillac badge, selling for $10,000 more than the Chevrolet. GM apparently thought that customers would only see the badge. Most auto publications quickly labeled the Cimarron a complete flop. Sales were far below expectations.

There are two bottom line lessons to be learned. First, cars should be targeted at markets as they will be when the cars hit the market. Edsel was targeted at an upscale market but appeared during the 1957 recession. Second, the product development process should yield the desired car, with sufficient discipline to minimize capricious management decisions.

The results of this study caused us to wonder why cars are removed from the market. We studied the twelve cars in Table 6.3 that were withdrawn from the market in the 1930, 1960s, and 2000s (Liu, Rouse & Yu, 2015). Using the same methodology as used for the earlier study, we assessed influences at the levels of economy, market, company, and vehicle.

Table 6.3 Twelve Vehicles Withdrawn from the Market.

Year	Vehicle
1937	Duesenberg
1937	Cord
1938	Pierce-Arrow
1940	LaSalle
1958	Packard
1960	DeSoto
1966	Studebaker
1969	Rambler
2001	Plymouth
2004	Oldsmobile
2010	Pontiac
2010	Mercury

Factors that had a pervasive influence included economic crises, market declines, poor management, external competitors, and company financial problems. The vehicle itself, particularly in terms of quality, was only a pervasive issue in the 2000s, when global competitors provided much higher quality vehicles.

These failures reflected, to a great extent, inabilities to balance the tension between differentiated offerings and economies of scale or market demands. This was quite clear among U.S. auto brands during the 2000s. GM, for example, sought economies of scale by making the Chevrolet, Pontiac, Oldsmobile, and Buick brands virtually identical except for their badges. Brand loyalty progressively became meaningless.

What is clear from these two studies is that the success of a vehicle depends on much more than just the vehicle. Success is influenced by those technologies that are adopted and subsequently embraced by the marketplace. However, poor management and bad financial decisions can undermine these advantages. Economic crises and wars can further worsen the state of enterprises.

Battery Electric Vehicles

Substantial environmental and energy challenges are driving the pursuit of alternative powertrain technologies, which nominally includes engine, transmission, drive shafts, differentials and the final drive. Emerging alternative fuel vehicles are showing their potential to address these challenges. However, diffusion of new technologies has many complications. We investigated the impacts of individual and organizational parameters of the adoption of battery electric vehicles (BEVs).

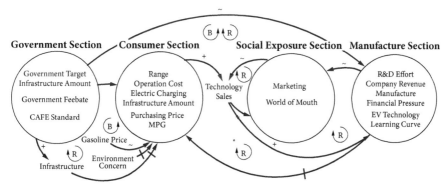

Fig. 6.4 Systems Dynamics Model of BEV Adoption (Liu, Rouse & Hanawalt, 2018)

We employed system dynamics modeling to create the representation in Figure 6.4. Mathematical relationships among different variables were derived. The impacts of government rebates, manufacturer willingness, and consumer purchasing preferences on economic and environmental issues were addressed using scenario analysis.

Three major stakeholders in the California automobile market were considered (government, manufacturer, and consumer). The types of powertrain systems considered included small/mid-size ICE, large size ICE, hybrid, EV, and fuel cell electric vehicles. Near-term impacts of government rebates, both federal and state, were found to be important to launch the market.

However, the model suggested that long term impacts will come primarily from product familiarity, consumer preference and technology competitiveness. This supports the importance of investments in R&D and advertising. Such investments could be augmented by government support of manufacturers or related research organizations. Rather than depending on short-term rebates to consumers, fundamental improvements of technology and infrastructure, e.g., charging stations, are more resilient ways to achieve a new technology's long-term self-growth.

Battery electric vehicles were found to be significantly more environmentally friendly if, as indicated above, the electricity used to charge the vehicles was not produced by coal-fired electric plants. Green electricity generation will lead to larger and more stable environmental improvements in the long term. Furthermore, pure green electricity production affects CO_2 emissions beyond just the vehicles. However, totally switching to green energy production in a short time is highly unlikely. Nevertheless, the model suggests the importance and value of paying more attention to changing production to green energy methods.

Autonomous Vehicles

The transportation industry is facing a revolution similar to when machines replaced animals one century ago. Humans may for the first time be fully out of the control loop of personal transportation. However, this revolution involves considerable disruption and uncertainty. Nevertheless, autonomous vehicles (AVs) will increasingly impact the automobile market.

We mapped various causal relationships during this significant transition to understand the impacts of different phenomena. The systems dynamic model in Figure 6.5 was constructed including two different transportation methods (personal owned vehicle and car services) and three autonomy levels (non, semi, and fully).

Consumer choices, product familiarity and acceptance were modeled to represent purchasing behavior. The U.S. auto insurance industry is likely to be substantially impacted by autonomous vehicles. Vehicle crash rate and loss ratio were considered

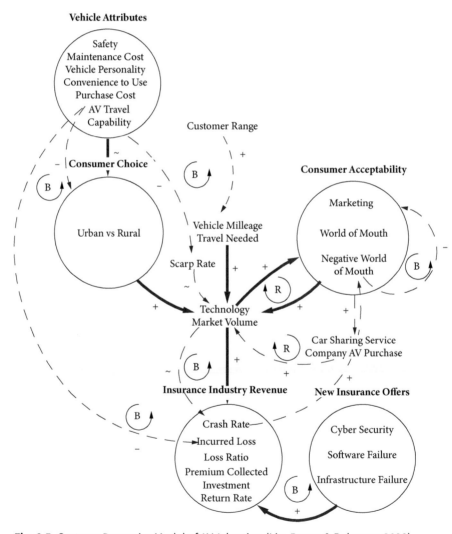

Fig. 6.5 Systems Dynamics Model of AV Adoption (Liu, Rouse & Belanger, 2020)

to calculate the insurance industry's premium collections. Different scenarios were quantified and discussed with key stakeholders. Several important causal loops were identified that will help achieve the faster growth of the technology.

With gradually improving vehicle driving assistance technologies, AVs are expected to debut in this decade. As a revolutionary way of personal transportation, it is very promising from various perspectives, including enriching personal mobility, reducing energy consumption and dramatically decreasing vehicle accidents. Yet, not everyone will see economic gains.

A primary motivation for this effort was to understand the impacts of AVs on the insurance industry. Every state in the U.S. has regulations that limit auto insurance premiums to the costs of insurance claims. Thus, insurance companies do not make profits on premiums. They make money by investing the premium monies until these funds are needed to pay claims.

The model predicts that insurance industry premiums collected will continue growing until the penetration rate of AVs becomes significant. At that point, the frequency of accidents and hence claims will decrease. Once the AV technology takes off, the industry premiums collected will be dramatically reduced.

Another consideration is the likelihood that people will use car services that own AVs rather than own the vehicles themselves. As these vehicles will be highly utilized, the total number of vehicles on the road will be reduced. Thus, the economic scale of the insurance industry will be further reduced, which will lead to decreased premiums collected. Reduced accidents and fewer cars on the road combine to result in substantial reductions of insurance premiums collected.

Summary

From an energy and climate perspective, BEVs and AVs, which will also be electric, will reduce emissions per vehicle and reduce the number of vehicles, contingent on moving away from coal-fired electricity power plants. These automotive innovations will also have substantial additional benefits, as the next case study illustrates.

Driverless Cars for Disabled and Older Adults

In Chapter 4, I described the needs of the 100 million disabled and older adults in the U.S. in the context of app-based assistive technologies to enable the disabled to work and the elderly to age in place. In this section, I build on the AV case study just discussed to consider how this technology might transform the lives of disabled and older adults.

How does this relate to energy and climate change? As noted earlier, transportation is the largest contributor to climate-threatening emissions. This case study focuses on transportation services for disabled and older adults. As I will detail, the economic consequences of this transformation are substantial and illustrate the potential cross-cutting nature of transformation.

The Auto Alliance hosted a series of three workshops on "AVs & Increased Accessibility" (Auto Alliance, 2019). I helped plan and conduct these workshops. The first workshop addressed needs of disabled and older adults. The second workshop focused on technologies to meet needs. The third addressed the policy and economic implications of the findings of the first two workshops.

Participants in Workshop 1 suggested a large number of needs. I clustered these needs into 20 categories. Eight categories covered 70% of the suggestions. Definitions of these categories are as follows:

- **Displays and controls** concern information that users can see, hear, touch, etc. and actions they can take
- **Locating and identifying vehicle** concerns users knowing where their ride is waiting and recognizing the particular vehicle
- **Passenger profiles** include secure access to information about passengers, in particular their specific needs
- **Emergencies** concern events inside and outside the vehicle that may require off-normal operations and user support
- **Adaptation to passengers** involves adjusting the human-machine interface to best support particular users with specific needs
- **Easy and safe entry and egress** concerns getting into and out of the vehicle as well as safety relative to the vehicle's external environment
- **Trip monitoring and progress** relates to providing information as the trip proceeds, particularly with regard to route and schedule disruptions
- **Onboard safety** concerns what happens in the vehicle as the trip proceeds, assuring minimal passenger stress and injury avoidance

An example mapping from needs to technologies is shown in Table 6.4. Technologies required include hardware, software, sensing, networks, and especially enhanced human-machine interfaces. Human-machine interfaces need to enable requesting vehicle services, locating and accessing vehicles, monitoring trip progress, and egressing at destinations to desired locations.

The wealth of AT and supporting technologies in Table 6.4 suggest a substantial need for seamless technology integration to avoid overwhelming disabled and older adults, or indeed anybody. We expect that AI-based cognitive assistants as discussed in Chapter 4 may be central to such integration. The question of who might provide which pieces of an overall integrated solution is addressed in the case study.

Table 6.4 Needs Versus Technologies.

Needs	Technologies				
	Hardware	Software	Sensors	Networks	HMI
Displays & Controls	Hardware for Displays & Controls	Tutoring System for HMI Use	Use and Misuse of Displays & Controls	Access to Device Failure Information	Auditory, Braille, Haptic, Tactile & Visual Displays
Locating & Identifying Vehicle	Vehicle-Mounted Sensors	Recognition Software	Integration of Sensed Information	Sensors of External Networks	Portrayal of Vehicle & Location
Passenger Profiles, Privacy	Phone or Smart Phones, Tablets	App to Securely Provide Profile Information	Recognition of Passenger	Access to Baseline Info. on Disabilities	Portrayal to Assure Recognition
Emergencies	Controls to Stop Vehicle & Move to Safe Space	Recognition & Prediction of Situation	Surrounding Vehicles, People & Built Environ.	External Services—Police, Fire, Health	Portrayal of Vehicle Situation
Adaptation to Passengers	Adjusting Entry, Egress, Seating	Learning Passenger Preferences	Sensing Reactions to Adaptations	Access to Baseline Info. on Adaptations	Portrayal to Enable Change Confirmations
Easy & Safe Entry & Egress	Sufficient Space to Maneuver	Capturing Data on Space Conflicts	Surrounding Vehicles, People & Built Environ.	Networked Access to, e.g., Bldg. Directions	Portrayal of Surrounding Objects
Trip Monitoring & Progress	Speedometer, GPS, Maps	Predictions of Progress, Points of Interest	Surrounding Vehicles, People & Built Environ.	Access to Traffic Information, e.g., Accidents	Portrayal of Trip & Progress
Onboard Safety	Securement of Wheelchairs & Occupants	Capturing Data on Securement Conflicts	Sensing & Recording Safety Risks	Access to Best Practices on Safety Risks	Portrayal of Securement Status

Model-Based Approach

There are three models involved in our integrated approach to developing market strategies for assistive technologies for disabled and older adults (Rouse & McBride, 2019; Rouse & McBride, 2021; Rouse & McBride, 2022). Figure 6.6 shows how these three models fit together. We were interested in several questions:

- What does this market want?
- What is the likely economic value of providing it?
- What competitive strategies are most attractive?
- What investments are required to execute chosen strategies?

In answering these questions, several tradeoffs were addressed. What market needs should a vehicle or service provider choose to target in terms of risks vs. returns? As is later discussed, the greatest economic opportunities were found to be too risky, requiring non-core competencies.

How might one hedge by partnering for total solutions. What revenues and profits would one likely sacrifice to the partners? The most appealing partnership might not happen. Hence a second hedge is formulated to address the risks that preferred partners choose other alliances.

Who will one likely compete with in terms of one's competencies vs. their competencies? Competitors' brands may be seen as more innovative, but have no vehicle manufacturing experience. At least one strategy in the portfolio needs to leverage manufacturing competencies.

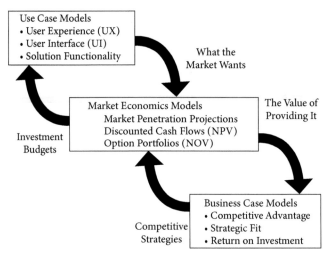

Fig. 6.6 Integrated Model-Based Approach (Rouse & McBride, 2022)

Models of Use Cases

We modeled the needed functionality using stories of humans interacting with AI-based cognitive assistants. We have employed this technique in several domains including team-based cancer care (Rouse & Johns, 2018), automotive engineering (Rouse, 2020), and this application addressing disabled and older adults (Rouse & McBride, 2018). The latter resulted in the story of Fred and Alice.

Fred is a young man with Asperger's who works as a software programmer and uses a driverless car service to get to and from work. Alice is his AI-based cognitive assistant, who is with him regardless of the particular vehicle he is in. She also evolves to help him with organizational issues at work.

This four-page story served to illustrate to stakeholders our vision for how AI would help someone like Fred. Stakeholders included advocates for disabled and older adults, health professionals, and automotive executives. They critiqued the story, made suggestions, and wanted to know when such capabilities would be available.

We have had similar responses from stakeholders in the other domains studied. Story-based models are much more compelling to a wider range of stakeholders than block diagrams and lists of functions. Once a story is finished, we analyze it in detail to determine what the cognitive assistant needs to know and needs to be able to do. Many of the insights in Table 6.4 resulted from this analysis

Models of Market Economics

I approached this analysis using the economic modeling methods and tools discussed in Chapter 2. A very significant issue in these types of analyses is the distinction between who bears the costs of investments and who realizes the returns on these investments. If it is the same entity, interpretation of the results is fairly straight-forward. In contrast, if one entity invests and a different entity realizes the returns, the investing entity will tend to see expenditures as costs and try to minimize them (Rouse, 2010). This likely may be the situation in this case study.

There is a range of economic issues associated with the impacts of AT on disabled and older adults. First, consider savings due to more people with disabilities working and increased numbers of older adults aging in place. Roughly 25 percent of people with disabilities receive benefits from the Social Security Disability Insurance (SSDI) Program; one in nine also receive benefits from the Social Security Supplemental Income (SSI) Program (SSA, 2018, 2019). The average total benefit is $1,335 per month. The total for all beneficiaries is $162 billion annually.

Among adults over 65 years old, 1.4 percent live in assisted living facilities at an average monthly cost of $3,600 and 4.2 percent live in residential nursing homes at an average monthly cost of $8,100 (NCHS, 2019). Total annual costs are $281 billion. Medicaid pays roughly half of this amount. Medicare pays for the first 100 days.

AT can enable people with disabilities to work and, therefore, no longer qualify for SSDI and SSI, creating savings for SSA (Social Security Administration). These forms of AT can also enable older adults to age in place and avoid, or at least delay, assisted living or nursing homes, resulting in savings to CMS (Centers for Medicare and Medicaid Services).

The annual total savings range from $44 billion to $222 billion for AT utilization ranging from 10 percent to 50 percent. We do not expect that AT will enable every person with disabilities to work, nor every older adult to avoid assisted living or nursing homes. However, something in the 10–30 percent range may be achievable.

Next, consider the revenue generated by the AT. People with disabilities, as well as their caregivers now working, will generate income, and pay at least Federal Insurance Contributions Act taxes. In 2016, the median earnings of people with disabilities ages 16 and over in the U.S. was $22,047, about two-thirds of the median earnings of people without disabilities, $32,479 (Kraus, et al., 2018). At the lower income, 2018 income taxes were 10 percent plus 7.65 percent for FICA and Medicare. For the caregiver earning the higher amount, 2018 incomes taxes were 12 percent plus 7.65 percent for FICA and Medicare.

Thus, the disabled person, now employed, will pay the Internal Revenue Service (IRS) $3,891 (17.65 percent x $22,047) in taxes, while the caregiver returning to employment will pay $6,382 (19.65 percent x $32,479) in taxes. Together they pay $10,273 in taxes. Thus, they were receiving $16,020 (12 months x $1335) in benefits and are now paying $10,273, an annual swing of $26,293 due to employment. This is complicated by the fact that savings are for SSA and the gains are for the IRS.

Substantial revenues will come from sales of vehicle services, vehicle maintenance, and vehicles. These high-tech vehicles will be expensive, but services dominate revenues because a fare must be paid with each use. Hundreds of millions of trips per week easily add up to billions of annual revenues as shown in Figure 6.7.

This is clearly an enormous opportunity, with revenue potentially approaching $1 trillion annually if one or more players can successfully address this large underserved market. The successful competitors will earn in the order of $100 billion profits annually, yielding over $20 billion in corporate tax revenues. Further, the $900 billion in costs to a great extent represent salaries and wages that will generate perhaps $200 billion in personal tax revenues. Of course, it is important to keep in mind that it will likely take several years to achieve the levels of market penetration needed to yield these results.

In terms of discounted cash flows, the net present value (NPV) for mobility services is $1,136 billion. Consider the federal tax revenues that would likely results from these revenues, assuming current corporate and personal tax rates, the NPV tax revenues would be $227 billion for mobility services. These revenues, when combined with the projected savings discussed earlier, make a strong case for societal investment in AT for disabled and older adults.

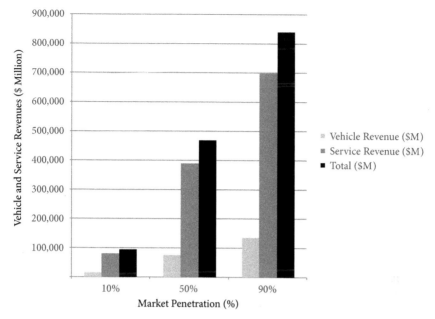

Fig. 6.7 Vehicle and Service Revenues versus Market Penetration (Rouse & McBride, 2022)

Investment Strategies

These are impressive numbers, but the key question, at this point, is what investments would be required to secure these results. Further, this opportunity is laced with uncertainties. We are least uncertain about whether people would benefit from mobility services. We are somewhat uncertain about how long it will take for adoption to become substantial. We are most uncertain about which players will dominate, particularly for mobility services.

Will it be Ford or GM, Uber or Lyft, or Amazon, Apple, Google, or Microsoft—or somebody else? The great size of the market is obvious, but who will dominate. This substantial uncertainty suggests that none of these players should "bet the company" on their assumed success. A more prudent strategy is warranted.

Buying "options" on possible futures makes sense when there is great uncertainty and many competing players. Options can be "purchased" by investing in R&D, alliances, acquisitions, etc. These options can be "exercised," or not, at a later date when uncertainties are better understood. Thus, purchasing an option, as explained in Chapter 2, gives one the right but not the requirement to later exercise the option.

Our investment portfolio included positions in two market segments—mobility services, and vehicle sales. We formulated options for each of these investments as follows:

- Mobility Services: Option purchase of $1000 million per year for Years 1 and 2; option exercise of $4000 million per year for Years 3 and 4; 25 percent profits for Years 5–14.
- Vehicle Sales: Option purchase of $500 million per year for Years 1 and 2; option exercise of $2500 million per year for Years 3 and 4; 25 percent profits for Years 5–14.

Economic projections show that mobility services are clearly superior investments to vehicle sales. Of course, the vehicles are needed to enable the mobility services.

The NPV for vehicle sales is negative while NOV is positive. This is due, in part, to the capitally intensive nature of vehicle development. The NOV is positive, about $1 billion, because the option approach explicitly represents the possibility of exiting the investment (not exercising the option) after Year 2 if technical and/or market uncertainties are unacceptable going forward. As noted in Chapter 2, NPV assumes you proceed regardless of these assessments.

If one were an automotive OEM (original equipment manufacturer), the investments in core competencies of vehicle design, development, and manufacturing might be key to participating in the other market segment. On the other hand, a technology company might lead with mobility services, perhaps with one or more vehicle partners.

In summary, at least one of the two market segments is quite attractive. The vehicle sales segment is less attractive, but a necessary piece of the puzzle. Nevertheless, the overall value proposition suggests that disabled and older adults are very likely to have their needs met.

Models of Business Cases

At this point we know that the market opportunity is very attractive, but also highly uncertain in terms of numerous competitors and when key technologies will be sufficiently mature to achieve significant market penetration.

In Chapter 2, I discussed our integrated framework for addressing uncertain markets with uncertain technologies. The business case of primary concern is how an automotive OEM (original equipment manufacturer) should position itself in this market and the associated investments needed. OEMs are interested in three primary attributes:

- Competitive Advantage (CA): To what extent will the investment of interest enable value-added pricing, reduce production costs, reduce operating costs, and leverage existing capacities?
- Strategic Fit (SF): To what extent will the investment of interest leverage technology competencies, exploit current delivery architectures, complement

existing value propositions, exploit current partnerships and infrastructure, and provide other opportunities for exploitation?

- Return on Investment (ROI): What capital expenditures, technology acquisition costs, and labor expenses will be needed? What revenue and profits will likely result?

The hypothetical OEM wants to consider five alternative solutions, or scenarios, because each includes a market strategy as well as a solution.

1. Provide total vehicle package
2. Provide vehicle platform to host intelligent software
3. Provide vehicle platform to host user-centered HMI
4. Provide vehicle platform without alliance
5. Provide integrated mobility services

These scenarios represent five alternative models of business cases. Based on discussion with automotive executives, utility functions were assessed for CA, SF, and ROI and probabilities were established.

Weightings on the three utility functions were varied in sensitivity analyses. Three scenarios survived this analysis. Scenario 4 was retained as a status quo investment. Scenarios 2 and 3 were retained as hedges. These scenarios are risky, as the cultivation of partners may not succeed. However, the upside is substantial if these options end up "in the money."

Policy Implications

There are a variety of policy implications that need to be addressed. Several issues surround the legal and ethical implications of disabled and older adults availing themselves of mobility services. What if users are injured while using mobility services? What training is provided to help users avoid such consequences?

Perhaps the biggest policy issue is payment for these services. The targeted populations have limited abilities to pay the full costs. Such services, albeit much lower tech, are often subsidized by various levels of government. For example, public transit for older adults in Washington, DC is one dollar per trip. However, few municipalities could afford the costs underlying the revenue projections shown earlier.

The needed monies exist, but they are not in the right buckets. Savings of $100–200 billion for SSA and CMS are easily imaginable. Tax revenues to the IRS are clearly of the same order of magnitude. But, translating these monies to subsidies for disabled and older adults will be far from straightforward. I expect that legislation will be needed to enable this.

The traditional overarching question for investments such as outlined in this case study is, "Who benefits and who pays?" Clearly, disabled and older adults will be enormous beneficiaries in terms of enhancing their sense of purpose, maintaining social connections, and staying mobile. Assistive technologies will be key enablers of these benefits.

The economy and society will also benefit from addressing this underserved market. Millions of jobs will be created. For example, driverless cars will likely need daily maintenance to calibrate sensors as well as clean these sensors. At the end of each day of use, probably late at night or very early in the morning, each vehicle will find its way back to a maintenance depot for inspection and recalibration. This may be partially automated but eventually maintaining millions of vehicles per day will require people highly skilled with using this automation and interpreting measurements.

Vehicle and service providers will greatly benefit from this opportunity, but maybe not all of them. As noted earlier, it could be Ford or GM, Uber or Lyft, or Amazon, Apple, Google, or Microsoft—or somebody else. There is enormous uncertainly in this nascent market. Some companies will be big winners; perhaps the ones that best know how to manage the inherent uncertainty.

Who pays? We need a systemic perspective on costs, savings and revenues. The resulting payers will probably include a mix of employers, government agencies, and individuals. However, a significant portion of people may have limited abilities to contribute. It seems reasonable to argue that a portion of savings and revenues should contribute to payment, perhaps only indirectly, e.g., via taxes.

Somewhat simplistically, the bottom line is 100 million people see enhanced quality of life; perhaps 1 million new jobs are created, and up to $1 trillion is added to the annual GDP. Yet, a prudent automotive OEM should not bet the company on this opportunity. The models discussed in this case study enable evidence-based formulation of a portfolio of traditional investments and options that hedge the contingencies of this market.

Managing Failures

In a recent book, (Rouse, 2021), I addressed failure management in the context of malfunctions of technologies, organizations, and society. Eighteen well-known case histories were analyzed across nuclear power, space and marine operations; photography, computing, and communications industries; and the economy, health, population growth, and climate change. The proximate, distal, and ultimate causes of these failures were characterized within the multi-level framework discussed in Chapter 2.

It is important to distinguish accident prevention from failure management. Prevention is a great goal, but there will inevitably be failures that are not prevented. The challenges of energy and climate change are examples of failing to prevent consequences which we now need to remediate. An approach to failure management is needed.

Failure Management Tasks

There are four tasks associated with failure management:

- Detection: Determination that the state of the system is off normal
- Diagnosis: Determination of the cause(s) of the off normal states
- Compensation: Controlling the system to achieve acceptable states
- Remediation: Repairing or countering the cause(s) of the failure

Early detection, rapid (correct) diagnosis, timely compensation, and eventual remediation are key. These things could have been done better for the current challenges of energy and climate change. Societal safety could have been addressed earlier and better.

I will define safety as assurance of the acceptability of future states of systems, as well as the consequences of these states. What is a safe health system, economy, or environment? I think the same definition of safety applies. Millions of people dying, losing their homes, and being inundated by rising sea levels reflect unsafe ecosystems. The surveillance mechanisms discussed below are able to detect the emergence of unsafe system states. However, we seem willing to let bad things happen and try to fix them later, often much later.

Failure Surveillance and Control

We would like to design systems, enterprises, and ecosystems that anticipate the possibility of failures and incorporate mechanisms for managing these failures. The goal is resilience. We need approaches for dealing with failures of systems for which there are no blueprints, i.e., systems that were not really designed.

Surveillance of the state of the system focuses on detecting anomalies, i.e., unexpected system states. There can be passive, active, or predictive surveillance, as well as predictive control. With passive surveillance, off-normal situations are detected and reported, inherently after the fact. Active surveillance involves proactively probing systems looking for emergent anomalies. This enables reporting trends that possibly portend failures. In other words, passive and active surveillance measure what *has* happened.

Predictive surveillance focuses on what *might* happen. Predictive surveillance uses a model of the system to predict outputs. This evolving system model is of great interest to management because it informs them of the nature of the system, what actually is happening versus what they thought would happen. They might learn, for example, that the performance characteristics of their system have degraded, or perhaps the nature of the environment has changed.

The precipitation of population and climate failures reflects people not understanding the consequences of their actions. Large families and consumption of fossil fuels were not intended to undermine economies and environments. They were local decisions about economic needs and priorities that had consequences that few people imagined. They were just living their lives and trying to get by. Of course, citizens, managers, and politicians do this all the time.

Complications

There are various complications that make failure management more difficult. Failures that emerge over time where, for example, a subsystem degrades for a period before it fails, e.g., a slow leak that eventually ruptures. Another complication is multiple failures where more than one thing goes wrong, often independently, although this may not be readily apparent.

We also need to consider the possibility of malicious failures, situations where competitors, adversaries, or villains consciously cause systems to fail. We have, of late, seen numerous instances of such failures. This possibility does not seem to really change surveillance, detection, and diagnosis. One still has to determine what went wrong and why.

However, compensation and remediation are likely to be quite different. One has to counter the adversary, both to eliminate the current threat and minimize the likelihood of similar future threats. This is still about safety, as broadly defined above, but also includes the design of countermeasure to thwart adversaries. Cybersecurity is, of course, a major example of such threats.

These phenomena might not seem to apply to energy and climate change. Who would want to aggravate climate change and extreme events? This might not be their intent, but there are certainly forces that hope to impede the transition from a fossil fuel economy to a green economy. It is not clear if there are limits to their disruption strategies and tactics.

Integrated Decision Support

Integrated decision support for failure management must achieve several objectives, First, it has to represent both running the enterprise you have while trying to create the enterprise you want. In other words, keeping the current engine running while you design and deploy the future engine.

There are three levels of operations of interest. Level four provides societal context:

- Plans for future operations
- Current operations
- Detection & diagnosis within current operations

Failure management has to balance all three levels of operations, while monitoring level four (society) for changes of the rules of the game. This balance is very difficult to achieve—the present almost always dominates the future.

Figure 6.8 portrays these three levels of support. This integrated decision support concept was motivated, in part, by a much more constrained view of integration in a production system setting (Rouse, 1988). The findings for the 18 case studies in Rouse (2021) were the primary drivers of the functionality depicted in Figure 6.8.

The dashed lines differentiate the three levels. The roles of the three levels are:

- The top level monitors the "market" and "enterprise" and invests accordingly, with market and enterprise broadly defined
- The second level executes the top-level plans, employing existing and new capacities, the latter due to the above investments
- The lowest level addresses anomalies, decides whether something has failed, diagnoses sources of failures, which contributes to situation assessment

What does "failure" mean in this depiction? Failure to acknowledge and deter phenomena and often delayed failure management are central to energy and climate change. These are the proximate causes of failures. Distal or ultimate causes include:

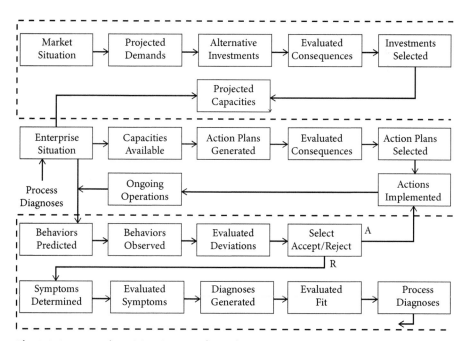

Fig. 6.8 Integrated Decision Support for Failure Management

- Failures to correctly assess markets and enterprise situations and trends
- Failures to invest appropriately in products and processes, including training, procedures, etc., where products and processes include interventions, e.g., drugs, regulations, incentives
- Failures to recognize situations and act despite compelling evidence of the need to respond

These distal or ultimate causes often resulted in transforming easily managed failures into complex, high consequence problems epitomized by the cases discussed in Rouse (2021).

What does this decision support system monitor? A good start is the United Nations' Intergovernmental Panel on Climate Change (IPCC) discussed earlier in this chapter. The IPCC provides access to observed data covering the physical climate (e.g., global distributions temperature and rainfall), atmospheric composition, socio-economic information (e.g. national population and income data), and impacts of climate change (IPCC, 2019). Their reports include:

- Data Compilations
  - o Climate System Scenario Tables
  - o Climate Observations: Global mean temperature, climatology data set
  - o Carbon Dioxide: Observed atmospheric concentrations
  - o Socio-Economic Baseline Dataset
  - o Observed Climate Change Impacts:
- Computational Models
  - o Climate System Scenario Tables
  - o Emissions Scenarios from Integrated Assessment Models
  - o Carbon Dioxide: Projected emissions and concentrations
  - o Global Climate Model Outputs: Period averages & global means

There is a range of models needed in addition to those provided by the IPCC to make the integrated decision support concept fully functional. Many of these are available, in multiple versions, in the broad community.

Summary

A central premise of this case study is that failure management can be pursued in an integrated manner, regardless of the specific context. The thinking need not change, although the specific interventions will obviously be context dependent. In other words, the conceptual design of integrated decision support can be generalized, while the detailed design of the support depends on the context.

The integrated decision support concept presented here broadly applies to various aspects of energy and climate change. The concept is general; the specifics are context dependent. This case study has articulated a technical solution to the broad problem of failure management. It would be straightforward to argue the economic benefits of this approach but beyond the scope of this exposition.

Designing Policy Portfolios

This case study addresses alternative policy interventions to address global warming, as well as the impacts of global warming (Rouse & Verma, 2022). A portfolio of interventions is needed rather than an integrated "solution"—there is no silver bullet, no vaccine for sea level rise. I consider a range of interventions, each with one or more potential implementation mechanisms. Each member of the portfolio has associated uncertainties in terms of the effectiveness of interventions and mechanisms, and required investments. I discuss preferred strategies for dealing with the uncertainties associated with each member of the portfolio.

Policy Levers

Consider the policy levers most likely to mitigate global warming, as well as mitigate the impacts of global warming. This section considers 20 possible interventions, ten for mitigating global warming and ten for mitigating the impacts of global warming. I also consider five policy mechanisms for implementing these interventions.

Interventions. Table 6.5 summarizes the 20 policy interventions in terms of which of five mechanisms are likely to be employed to implement each policy. The first three interventions to mitigate global warming are not surprising—decrease use of fossil fuels, decrease methane emissions, and eliminate coal-fired power plants. The next three emphasize increasing use of alternatives, including increased use of renewable energy, investing in home energy efficiency, and investing in clean energy public transit. The next two interventions address encouraging support of the changes implied by the first six including transitioning people to clean jobs and increasing education for these clean jobs. Finally, the last two interventions have longer-term payoffs including increased consumption of plant-based food and investing in reforestation.

The next ten interventions concern the impacts of global warming, particularly flooding, high temperatures, and fires. The first three interventions include deterring building in flood plains, encouraging flood proofing homes, and encouraging flood proofing businesses. The next three concern dealing with water and wind in terms of investing in dikes, levees, etc., investing in wetlands to absorb hurricanes, and investing in means to project "where the water will be," which has been shown to help those affected to react more appropriately.

Table 6.5 Interventions vs. Mechanisms for Mitigating Global Warming.

	Intervention	Communicate	Educate	Incentivize	Invest	Regulate
Mitigating Global Warming	Decrease use of fossil fuels	✓				✓
	Decrease methane emissions	✓				✓
	Eliminate coal-fired power plants	✓				✓
	Increase use of renewable energy	✓		✓	✓	✓
	Invest in home energy efficiency	✓		✓	✓	✓
	Invest in clean energy public transit	✓		✓	✓	
	Transition to clean jobs	✓	✓	✓	✓	
	Increase education for clean jobs	✓	✓	✓		
	Increase consumption of plant-based food	✓	✓	✓		✓
	Invest in reforestation	✓		✓	✓	✓
Mitigating Impacts of Global Warming	Deter building in flood plains	✓		✓		✓
	Encourage flood proofing homes	✓		✓	✓	✓
	Encourage flood proofing businesses	✓		✓	✓	
	Invest in dikes, levees, etc.	✓		✓	✓	
	Invest in wetlands to absorb hurricanes	✓		✓	✓	
	Invest in means to project "where the water will be"	✓		✓	✓	
	Invest in raising roads to enable continuity of access			✓	✓	✓
	Invest in means to address high temperatures and fires			✓	✓	✓
	Invest in educating K–12 and the whole population to understand threats	✓	✓		✓	
	Invest in developing jobs and training to respond to environmental threats and events	✓	✓	✓	✓	

Considering the impacts of high temperatures as well as flooding, the next two interventions concern investing in raising roads to enable continuity of access and investing in means to address high temperatures and fires. Longer-term interventions include investing in educating K-12 and the whole population to understand threats and investing in developing jobs and training to respond to environmental threats and events.

Mechanisms. As indicated, there are five mechanisms for implementing the 20 possible interventions. The simplest mechanism is communication, as USDA does to farmers and CDC does to the public in general. The next level of investment is education, both face-to-face and online. The classic example is the USDA Extension Services.

Beyond information and education, incentives can be provided to incentivize people's behaviors. As discussed earlier, a good example is federal and state rebates for buying battery electric vehicles (Liu, Rouse & Hanawalt, 2018). A higher level of commitment is investing in, for instance, funding education about clean energy jobs. Good examples are strongly increasing job opportunities for solar panel installation and wind turbine repair (BLS, 2018).

A final mechanism is regulation. NHTSA's Corporate Average Fuel Economy (CAFE) standards regulate how far our vehicles must travel on a gallon of fuel. EPA Emission Standards Regulations provide another example. One benefit of this mechanism is the ability of the Executive Branch of the Federal Government to unilaterally issue regulations.

Strategies

Before deciding which interventions to include in the policy portfolio, we need to consider the nature of the investments of interest. As discussed in Chapter 2, we have found that there are four basic investment strategies that decision-makers can use: optimize, adapt, hedge, and accept.

- If the success of investments of interest is certain, then there is little chance that decision- makers will be surprised. Consequently, these investments should be optimized. If the unexpected cannot happen, then there is no chance of failure
- If the investments of interest are not highly predictable, but can be appropriately modified when necessary, it may be in the best interest for decision-makers to plan to adapt investments as warranted, i.e., not make major investments now
- If the investments of interest are not very predictable and the decision-makers have limited abilities to adapt and respond, it may be best to invest in hedges, i.e., make small investments in options available for later larger investments
- If the investments of interest are totally unpredictable and there is no viable way to respond, then decision-makers have no choice but to not invest, i.e., accept the status quo

	Not Feasible	Possibly Feasible	Fully Feasible
Definite Success	Hedge Via Partnership	Hedge Via Larger Investment	Optimize Intervention Investment
Possible Success	Hedge Via Partnership	Hedge Via Smaller Investment	Adapt If Opportunity Emerges
Unlikely Success	Accept Current Situation	Accept Current Situation	Adapt If Opportunity Emerges

Intervention Uncertainty (vertical axis). Mechanism Uncertainty (horizontal axis).

Fig. 6.9 Strategies Versus Uncertainties

These four strategies are differentially relevant for different areas of an uncertainty space with axes involving uncertainties around the requirements, and the ability to meet those requirements. Figure 6.9, focuses on uncertainties in the effectiveness of interventions and uncertainties in the effectiveness of mechanisms.

Decision-Making

The goal is to decide which interventions to include in the policy portfolio. We can address these decisions using multi-stakeholder, multi-attribute utility theory as discussed in Chapter 2. The attributes of interest include:

- Intervention Effectiveness (IE): How well will the interventions work?
- Mechanism Effectiveness (ME): How likely will the mechanisms work?
- Required Investment (RI): How large investments will success require?

The expected utility of each intervention $E[U_T]$ can be calculated using

$$E[U_T] = W_{IE}xP_{IE}xU_{IE} + W_{ME}xP_{ME}xU_{ME} + W_{RI}xP_{RI}x(1 - U_{RI}) \quad (6.1)$$

where $W_{IE} + W_{ME} + W_{RI} = 1$ and P_{IE}, P_{ME}, and P_{RI} are the probabilities of achieving U_{IE}, U_{ME}, and U_{RI}, respectively. $E[U_T]$ increases with IE and ME, but decreases with RI, hence the term $(1-U_{RI})$ is employed to represent desires for smaller investments.

Table 6.6 summarizes IE, ME and RI for each intervention, assuming the mechanisms in Table 6.5 are employed. The entries in this table reflect the product of probabilities and utilities in the following ways:

Table 6.6 Interventions vs. Attributes.

	Intervention	Intervention Effectiveness	Mechanism Effectiveness	Required Investment
Mitigating Global Warming	Decrease use of fossil fuels	High	High	Low
	Decrease methane emissions	High	High	Low
	Eliminate coal-fired power plants	High	Moderate	Low
	Increase use of renewable energy	High	Moderate	Moderate
	Invest in home energy efficiency	High	Moderate	Moderate
	Invest in clean energy public transit	High	Moderate	High
	Transition to clean jobs	Moderate	Moderate	High
	Increase education for clean jobs	Moderate	Moderate	High
	Increase consumption of plant-based food	Low	High	Low
Mitigating Impacts of Global Warming	Invest in reforestation	Moderate	Moderate	Moderate
	Deter building in flood plains	High	Moderate	Low
	Encourage flood proofing homes	High	Moderate	Low
	Encourage flood proofing businesses	High	Moderate	Low
	Invest in dikes, levees, etc.	High	Moderate	High
	Invest in wetlands to absorb hurricanes	High	Moderate	Moderate
	Invest in means to project "where the water will be"	Moderate	High	Low
	Invest in raising roads to enable continuity of access	High	Moderate	High
	Invest in means to address high temperatures and fires	High	Moderate	High
	Invest in educating K-12 and the whole population to understand threats	High	Moderate	Low
	Invest in developing jobs and training to respond to environmental threats and events	Moderate	Moderate	High

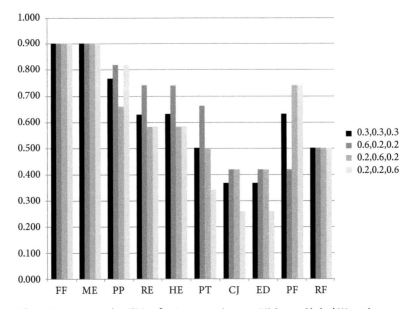

Fig. 6.10 Expected Utilities for Interventions to Mitigate Global Warming

- IE is high if the effects are direct and timely.
- ME is high if no Congressional authorizations and appropriations are required.
- RI directly reflects the level of investment needed.

Figure 6.10 summarizes the expected utilities for the ten interventions intended to mitigate global warming. Figure 6.11 summarizes the expected utilities for the ten interventions intended to mitigate the impacts of global warming. The weights (W_{IE}, W_{ME} and W_{RI}) vary from equal (all 0.333) to 0.6 for the most important attribute to 0.2 for the other two attributes.

The resulting policy portfolio includes those interventions with highest expected utilities. Six interventions (FF, ME, PP, FP, PH, PB) are high, almost independent of the weights because they have direct impacts, are easy to execute, and require low investments. These interventions are:

- Decrease use of fossil fuels (FF)
- Decrease methane emissions (ME)
- Eliminate coal-fired power plants (PP)
- Deter building in flood plains (FP)
- Encourage flood-proofing homes (PH)
- Encourage flood-proofing businesses (PB)

Three interventions (PF, WW, EP) have high utilities for certain weightings. They have indirect impacts, but are easy to execute and require low investments. These interventions are:

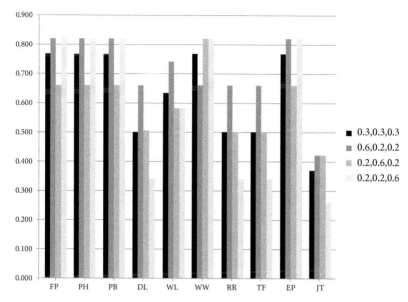

Fig. 6.11 Expected Utilities for Interventions to Mitigate Impacts of Warming

- Increase consumption of plant-based food (PF)
- Invest in means to project "where the water will be" (WW)
- Invest in educating K-12 and whole population to understand threats (EP)

Thus, the policy portfolio includes 9 interventions of the original 20. The 11 interventions excluded suffered from requiring high investment and/or needing Congressional approval.

How should one invest in these nine interventions? For the top 6, optimization is appropriate if feasible, especially since the investments required are low. The adapt strategy would needlessly delay action. For the bottom 3, a hedge strategy is appropriate in terms of investing in R&D and pilot projects to determine how best to refine these interventions. The accept strategy does not apply here, in part because we have been accepting global warming far too long.

Influencing Change

The success of the interventions depends on change at several levels as outlined throughout this chapter:

- Government: Countries' consumption and production of energy, including key technologies and materials (Economist, 2020)
- Organizations: Companies' investments and competitive positions in alternative energy sources

Table 6.7 Influencing People to Change.

Lever of Influence	Focus & Situation	
	Personal Benefit (Not Necessarily in Crisis)	Societal Benefit (Especially in Crisis)
Education & Evidence	Diet	War
Rules & Regulations	Smoking	Depression
Social Pressure	Exercise	Pandemic
Financial Incentives	Environment	Climate Change

- Processes: Infrastructure for storing and delivering energy, including charging stations
- People: Willingness and abilities to change energy consumption habits and preferences, as well as employment aspirations

Changes at all levels are important, but the focus here will be on the people level. Table 6.7 summarizes four levers of influence as they apply to the focus of change and the situation. Education and evidence provide important levers as they did for the health risks of smoking. Rules and regulations, e.g., prohibiting smoking in restaurants helped as well. Social pressures from non-smokers contributed. Finally, the steadily increasing prices of cigarettes, due to greatly increased taxes, provided another incentive to quit smoking.

Societal benefits, especially during crises, can be leveraged in the same ways. People tend to come together over time as crises worsen. We have experienced this with wars, financial crises, and health crises. A consensus on global warming has yet to emerge, in part because many leaders have discounted or dismissed the evidence.

However, it is difficult to ignore hurricanes, flooding, and fires. Similarly, it is beyond belief to deny the seriousness of the pandemic with over 900,000 deaths in the U.S. Fortunately, one of the interventions in the policy portfolio is "invest in educating K-12 and the whole population to understand threats."

At this point, we have assessed the expected utilities of the twenty interventions, and the extent to which these assessments are sensitive to the weights in the multi-attribute utility function. It would be helpful to know how these interventions interact in terms of impact and possible synergies among mechanisms. Such interactions could be addressed using a computational model, perhaps developed on the basis of the conceptual model in Figure 6.2. This model could be hosted in an interactive visualization facility such as discussed in Chapter 2.

Summary

The methodology employed in this case study was also employed in the earlier case study in this chapter focused on assessing alternative strategies for automotive OEMs (original equipment manufacturers) to address the market for driverless cars for disabled and older adults. The application in this case study does not involve a technology platform. It involves a portfolio of policies, pursed by federal, state, and local governments, to mitigate global warming. The absence of an integrated technology platform does not mean that the notion of design is not relevant. Investment portfolios should be designed.

The interventions considered here were gleaned from a broad review of relevant literature. However, the analysis reported cannot be deemed fully evidence based. Data on the effectiveness of the interventions and mechanisms, as well as their likely costs, need to be compiled and analyzed. Values, concerns, and perceptions of a broad set of important stakeholders need to be assessed and incorporated in multi-stakeholder, multi-attribute utility functions. This will lead to refinement of the policy portfolio presented here.

Nevertheless, this case study has demonstrated that a very complex policy problem can be approached comprehensively and systematically. The next step is to create an evidence-based interactive computational model that enables stakeholders to explore refinement and extension of the policy portfolio. This should lead to well-informed and well-articulated advocacy of the investments needed to execute the interventions that can significantly mitigate global warming.

Approach to Transformation

Transforming the energy and climate ecosystem faces enormous challenges, especially to move from a carbon economy to a green economy. We did it before when we replaced horses with electric streetcars, private automobiles and trucks. However, the "horse lobby" was not a powerful force then.

We also have challenges of solar, wind, and nuclear energy. Solar and wind have become less and less expensive, but are inherently intermittent. Nuclear power plants could easily assume base loads, but the public is still reluctant to trust nuclear power. Three Mile Island and Chernobyl provided chilling illustrations of what could go wrong (Rouse, 2021).

What are the incentives for vested interests to change? They have already demonstrated willingness to invest enormous amounts in lobbying, election contributions, and disinformation campaigns. I think the government will likely have to buy their assets stranded by this transformation. They can either wait for their assets to be worthless or sell them for acceptable prices.

How will displaced workforces react? Not positively. However, the energy industry is a leading creator of new, well-paying jobs. We can create job training and, at least in the transition, perhaps preferential recruitment for displaced workers to become solar panel installers and wind turbine maintainers, two of the fastest growing, well-paid jobs in the U.S. economy.

We need broad-based support for a shared understanding of the challenges and the strategies we have as a society for addressing these challenges. The following three strategies are likely to enable addressing the challenges of climate change and its consequences:

- *Share Information*: Broadly share credible information so all stakeholders understand the situation.
- *Create Incentives*: Develop long-term incentives to enable long-term environmental benefits while assuring short-terms gains for stakeholders.
- *Create an Experiential Approach*: Develop an interactive visualization of these models to enable people to see the results.

An experiential approach can be embodied in a "policy flight simulator" that includes large interactive visualizations that enable stakeholders to take the controls, explore options, and see the sensitivity of results to various decisions (Rouse, 2014b). The central idea is to create the means for all stakeholders to experience the phenomena associated with climate change and explore alternative means for managing these phenomena.

I can imagine a CNN special where interactive visualizations are available to support audience participation in exploration, discussion and debate of the nature of the problems, the alternative solutions of the problems, and consequences of the alternatives. Of course, the usefulness of this approach totally depends on the level of trust people have with these mechanisms. This is a central challenge that I return to in Chapter 8.

Economic Valuation

The economic analysis outlined in the second case study of driverless cars for disabled and older adults illustrates the difficulty of accounting for all costs and benefits across the energy and climate ecosystem and the other three ecosystems discussed in this book. Such analysis is complicated by revenues and costs being associated with both private and public sectors.

There are private sector revenues and costs associated with creating and providing systems and products, as well as service revenues and costs. The companies involved compensate employees, provide benefits, and pay federal, state, and local taxes. These monies are spent and provide income to others who pay taxes, etc.

The public sector revenues and costs include both actual revenues and those attributed to savings, as was emphasized in the aforementioned case study. The intensity of hurricanes and flooding, as well as fires and other heat damage, impose enormous financial burdens on society. Investments in mitigating the frequency and intensity of these consequences can result in substantial savings. These savings can be balanced against the investments needed to enable such mitigation.

We need a broader view of the long-term economics of energy and climate, broader in the sense of how revenues and costs accrue across ecosystems, and longer in terms of several decades rather than a few years. The benefits and burdens of moving to a green economy should be equitably shared across society. This transformed economy will result in millions of new well-paid jobs and wealth accumulation that is hopefully broadly shared.

To make the case for this future, we need to account for investment costs, revenues, operating costs, and profits in ways that make sense for both public and private participants. This will require working across resource silos in government organizations. For example, here are three cross-cutting tallies needed:

- Reduced social security and health outlays due to disabled adults working and paying taxes, as well as elderly adults aging in place rather than in expensive residential care, should be tallied together.
- Increased personal incomes due to investments in education, consequent reductions of child health deficiencies, and the resulting increased tax revenues should be tallied together.
- Reduced costs of remediating the consequences of extreme weather events and increased incomes and taxes paid due to millions of new well-paid jobs should be tallied together.

I return to this idea in Chapter 7.

Conclusions

The energy and climate ecosystem is amazingly complex. The need for energy is pervasive, affecting everyone. Vested interests in energy resources by companies and consumption by everyone need to be transformed to mitigate climate change and its impacts. Mooney (2020) argues that will require "massive and rapid changes, from your kitchen to your carport." By 2050, everything will need to be electric.

As noted above, this will be wrenching, particularly for those stakeholders in the fossil fuel industry. Yet, we have done this before. Stagecoaches and canal boats were displaced by railroads, followed by trucks for other than bulk products. Electric lighting displaced whale oil and kerosene lighting, and electric motors later displaced steam power. In the process, financial resources were redeployed and new jobs emerged. I expect that we will look back in 2050 and marvel at what we have accomplished.

References

Alderton, M. (2020). Why climate change is about to make your bad commute worse. *Washington Post*, August 8

Anon. (2020). The changing geopolitics of energy. *The Economist*, September 17

Auto Alliance (2019). *Assessing Transportation Needs of People with Disabilities and Older Adults: Report of Workshop 1*, Washington, DC: Auto Alliance

BLS (2018). *Fastest Growing Occupations*. https://www.bls.gov/ooh/fastest-growing.htm

Browne, J. (2019). *Make, Think, Imagine: Engineering the Future of Civilization*. New York: Pegasus Books

Davenport, C., and Lipton, E. (2017). How GOP leaders came to view climate change as fake science. *New York Times*, June 3

DOT (2020). *Corporate Average Fuel Economy (CAFE) Standards* https://www.transportation.gov/mission/sustainability/corporate-average-fuel-economy-cafe-standards

Ekwurzel, B. (2017). US Abandons global science leadership, Zeroes out IPCC funding, *Common Dreams*, August 9

EPA (2020a). *The Origins of the EPA*. https://www.epa.gov/history/origins-epa

EPA (2020b). *Inventory of US Greenhouse Emissions and Sinks: 1990-2018*. Washington, DC: Environmental Protection Industry

Flavelle, C. 2020). Rising seas threaten an American institution: the 30-year mortgage. *New York Times*, June 19

Flavelle, C., and Friedman, L. (2020). As election nears, Trump makes a final push against climate science. *New York Times*, October 28

Flavelle, C., and Mazzei, P. (2019). Florida Keys deliver a hard message: As seas rise, some places can't be saved, *New York Times*, December 5

Hanawalt, E.S., and Rouse, W.B. (2010). Car wars: Factors underlying the success or failure of new car programs, *Journal of Systems Engineering*, 13 (4), 389–404

IPCC (2019). *IPCC Data Distribution Center*, Intergovernmental Panel on Climate Change. https://www.ipcc-data.org/observ/index.html, Accessed 12-11–19

IPCC (2020). *The History of IPCC*. https://www.ipcc.ch/about/history/

Kraus, L., Lauer, E., Coleman, R., and Houtenville, A. (2018). *2017 Disability Statistics Annual Report*. Durham: Institute on Disability. University of New Hampshire

Lempert, R.J., Marangoni, G., Keller, K., and Duke, J. (2018). *Is Restoration an Appropriate Climate Policy Goal?* Santa Monica, CA: RAND

Lenton, T.M., et al. (2019). Climate tipping points—too risky to bet against. *Nature*, 575, 592–595

Lightbody, L., Fuchs, M., and Edwards, S. (2019). *Mitigation Matters: Policy Solutions to Reduce Local Flood Risk*. Philadelphia, PA: The Pew Charitable Trusts

Liu, C., Rouse, W.B., and Belanger, D. (2020). Understanding risks and opportunities of autonomous vehicle technology adoption through systems dynamic scenario modeling—The American insurance industry. *IEEE Systems Journal*, 14 (1), 1365–1374, doi: 10.1109/JSYST.2019. 2913647

Liu, C., Rouse, W.B., and Hanawalt, E. (2018). Adoption of powertrain technologies in automobiles: A system dynamics model of technology diffusion in the American market. *IEEE Transactions on Vehicular Technology*, 67 (7), 5621–5634

Liu, C., Rouse, W.B., and Yu, X. (2015). When transformation fails: Twelve case studies in the automobile industry. *Journal of Enterprise Transformation*, 5 (2), 71–112

Mooney, C. (2020). Biden wants the US to stop contributing to climate change by 2050. Here's what that would actually take. *Washington Post*. December 15

NCHS (2019). *Long-Term Care Providers and Service Users in the United States, 2015-16*. Atlanta, GA: Centers for Disease Control and Prevention. Office of Vital and Health Statistics.

NOAA (2020), *Our History*, https://www.noaa.gov/our-history

NWS (2020). *Climate Versus Weather*. https://www.weather.gov/climateservices/CvW, Accessed 11-16-20

Popovich, N., Albeck-Ripka, L., and Pierre-Louis, K. (2020). The Trump administration is reversing more than 100 environmental rules. *New York Times*, November 10

Rouse, W.B. (1988). Intelligent decision support for advanced manufacturing systems. *Manufacturing Review*, 1(4), 236–243

Rouse WB, (Ed.) (2010). *The Economics of Human Systems Integration: Valuation of Investments in People's Training and Education, Safety and Health, and Work Productivity*. New York: John Wiley

Rouse, W.B. (2014a). Earth as a system. In M. Mellody, ed., *Can Earth's and Society's Systems Meet the Needs of 10 Billion People?* (pp. 20–23). Washington, DC: National Academies Press

Rouse, W.B. (2014b). Human interaction with policy flight simulators. *Journal of Applied Ergonomics*, 45 (1), 72–77

Rouse, W.B. (2020). AI as system engineering: Augmented intelligence for systems engineers. *Insight*, 23 (1), 54–56

Rouse, W.B. (2021). *Failure Management: Malfunctions of Technologies, Organizations, and Society*. Oxford, UK: Oxford University Press

Rouse, W.B. and Johns, M.M.E. (2018). *Clinicians With Cognitive Assistants*. Atlanta, GA: School of Medicine, Emory University

Rouse, W.B. and McBride, D.K. (2018). *Fred and Alice*. Vienna, VA: SourceAmerica

Rouse, W.B. and McBride, D.K. (2019). A systems approach to assistive technologies for disabled and older adults. *The Bridge*, 49 (1), 32–38

Rouse, W.B., and McBride, D.K. (2021). Cost/benefit analysis for human systems investments: predicting and trading off economic and non-economic impacts of human factors & ergonomics. In W. Karwowski & G. Salvendy, eds, **Handbook of Human Factors & Ergonomics** (5th Edition), New York: Wiley

Rouse, W.B., & McBride, D.K., (2022). Assistive Technologies for Disabled and Older Adults: Models of Use Cases, Market Economics, and Business Cases. In A. Madni & N. Augustine, Eds., **Handbook of Model-Based Systems Engineering**. Berlin: Springer

Rouse, W.B., & Verma, D., (2022). **Methods for Integrating Dynamic Requirements**. Hoboken, NJ: Systems Engineering Research Center, Report SERC-2022-TR-01.

Samenow, J. and Freedman, A. (2020). Hot ocean waters along East Coast are drawing in weird fish and supercharging hurricane season. **Washington Post**, July 31

SSA (2018). **Annual Statistical Report on the Social Security Disability Insurance Program, 2017**. Washington, DC: Social Security Administration, Office of Retirement and Disability Policy

SSA (2019). **Annual Statistical Report on the Social Security Supplemental Security Income Program, 2018**. Washington, DC: Social Security Administration, Supplemental Security Income Program

Temple, J. (2020). Preventing fires has failed: California needs to learn how to work with them instead. **Technology Review**, 123 (6), 40–42

USWB (2020). **History of the National Weather Service**. https://www.weather.gov/timeline

Waterman, J. (2019). Our national parks are in trouble: Overcrowding, invasive species, climate change, and money woes. **New York Times Magazine**, November 22

Xu, C., Kohler, T.A., Lenton, T.M., Svenning, J-C., & Scheffer, M. (2020). Future of the human climate niche. **Proceedings of the National Academies of Sciences**, 117 (21), 11350–11355

Yergin, D. (2020). **The New Map: Energy, Climate, and the Clash of Nations**. New York: Penguin Press

7

Across Ecosystems

This chapter addresses the following questions:

- What is common across the four ecosystems?
- How can economic models be applied across the four ecosystems?
- Is an integrated approach to investing across ecosystems feasible?
- What lessons learned should inform the application of our approach?
- What is next after knowing what to do and how to do it?

Comparisons Across Ecosystems

Table 7.1 summarizes the 20 historical case studies of innovation in public-private ecosystems discussed in Chapters 3–6. The primary emphasis is on cases where government organizations initiated the changes or played a major role in their implementation. Private enterprises were almost always significantly affected.

Clearly, innovation does happen in public-private ecosystems, but not in the same, often dramatic, ways that new products can transform markets as, for example, Apple's iPhone has. Innovation in public-private ecosystems usually involves process changes such as new rules of the game and new organizational players. These changes almost always have to be socialized to gain support from existing players.

The drivers of innovation can be seen in the right column of Table 7.1:

- **Needs** for change—war, disease, energy, or organizational challenges
- **Opportunities** for change—e.g., exploiting IP, telegraph, telemedicine
- **Leaders**—presidential leadership but also champions like Bush and Perry
- **Organization**—abilities to execute and influence key stakeholders

Thus, innovative change in public-private ecosystems requires much more than just a good idea that makes sense. The complex behavioral and social systems associated with public-private ecosystems tend to be conservative in the sense of usually trying to preserve the status quo. A sense of urgency needs to be fostered.

The needs, opportunities, and leaders have to be understood, motivated, and aligned with the changes sought. For instance, many of the case studies required

Transforming Public-Private Ecosystems. William B. Rouse, Oxford University Press.
© William B. Rouse (2022). DOI: 10.1093/oso/9780192866530.003.0007

Table 7.1 Twenty Innovations in Four Ecosystems.

	Innovation	Causes & Catalysts
National Security	Defense Act (1920)	Wilson; shift from reliance on government arsenals to defense contractors
	UARCs (1942)	Roosevelt; ensuring maintenance of essential engineering and technology capabilities
	Armed Services Procurement Act (1947)	Truman; consolidation of diverse service-specific procurement rules and regulations
	DARPA (1958)	Eisenhower; agility to compete with Soviet Union in space race
	Packard Commission (1986)	Reagan, Perry; agility and affordability of acquisition of defense capabilities
Healthcare Delivery	Flexner Report (1910)	Taft; transformed the nature and process of medical education & profession of medicine
	Social Security (1935)	Roosevelt; key program of New Deal's initiatives to address the Great Depression
	Medicare & Medicaid (1965)	Johnson; remediating lack of healthcare due to poverty of a large proportion of elderly
	Affordable Care Act (2010)	Obama; providing insurance to large uninsured population
	Telemedicine (2020)	Trump; pandemic enabled payment for services not rendered in clinical offices
Higher Education	Morrill Land-Grant Acts (1862)	Lincoln; enabling public universities to add programs in agriculture & engineering
	Agricultural Extension Service (1914)	Wilson; assistance to assure food needs would be met during World War I and World War II
	GI Bill (1944)	Roosevelt; providing educational opportunities to returning veterans
	National Science Foundation (1950)	Truman, Bush; federal responsibility for financial support of basic scientific research
	Bayh-Dole Act (1980)	Carter; enabling universities to take advantage of intellectual property they create
Energy & Climate	USWB (1890)	Harrison; ability to simultaneously observe weather data, through the use of the telegraph
	NOAA (1970)	Nixon; merger of three agencies to focus on science-based protection of life and property
	EPA (1970)	Nixon; public concerns about deteriorating city air and contaminated urban water supplies
	CAFÉ Standards (1975)	Ford; reactions to 1973 oil crisis and need for less reliance on foreign energy
	IPCC (1988)	Reagan; formed by UN to provide assessments of climate change and its impacts

vigorous backing by the President of the United States and often champions "on the ground" to shepherd initiatives to success. Fundamental change seldom happens on its own.

Beyond needs, opportunities, and leaders, an organization is needed to make it happen. This organization needs to understand key stakeholders in terms of values, concerns, and perceptions, as well as the extent to which they trust what they are hearing and are confident in what they are being promised. Past misdeeds are usually well remembered. Regaining trust usually requires substantial efforts.

Transforming public-private ecosystems is much more a process than a well-reasoned solution. Consequently, the particulars of the solution will emerge from the process and be synthesized and integrated to foster the acceptance and support of the many stakeholders involved. This process typically requires strong leadership, a topic I discuss in Chapter 8.

Pursuing Cross-Cutting Transformation

Several principles apply, both within and across ecosystems. First, one has to understand stakeholders' values, concerns, and perceptions, as well as the extent they are likely to trust assessments, plans, and commitments. This, of course, starts with identifying major stakeholders. It is usually important for major stakeholder groups to know, or get to know, each other.

This can be a challenge when transformation initiatives cross ecosystems. For example, a national security technology investment may be likely to yield significant benefits for health, education, and energy. In order for these three ecosystems to be cheerleaders for security's investment, they have to know about it and know the key security stakeholders.

In many of the case studies discussed in this book we adopted the following rule of thumb. If a proposed transformation initiative results in any major stakeholder losing substantially and they are not compensated for this loss, the initiative will fail. Put another way, one needs all major stakeholders to perceive the initiative to be valid, acceptable, and viable for them. It also helps if secondary stakeholders are supportive.

One needs to take great care in formulating, communicating, and implementing interventions. Major stakeholders need to be involved in the design, deployment. and ongoing operations of initiatives. They need to feel at least partial ownership of the vision, strategy, plans, and execution. If you find that you are doing it all by yourself, you are in trouble. Transformation is a team sport, and not a spectator sport.

Means are needed to enable and motivate change. The greatest benefits of an initiative may be months or years away. Devise means for near-term benefits, even if they are quite modest. Such benefits can include opportunities to be involved at higher levels of the organization, having expenses covered that usually are not reimbursed, and co-authorship of key documents.

Be careful about expecting philosophical buy-in. Reflecting on the 16 potential innovations discussed in Chapters 3–6, an underlying theme is moving from a money-centered to a human-centered society for patients, students, and everyone in general. People do not need to embrace this theme to be valuable members of transformation teams.

Economic Valuation

Table 7.2 summarizes the economic valuation methods discussed in Chapter 2 and employed in the 16 case studies of potential innovations in Chapters 3–6. Not every method was used for every study. The nature of the questions of interest dictated the methods employed.

Table 7.2 Potential Innovations Versus Valuation Methods.

Case Study	Economic Valuation				
	Financial Projections (R & C)	Discounted Cash Flow (NPV)	Real Options (NOV)	Multi-Attribute Utility Theory (MAUT)	Multi-Stakeholder MAUT
Technology options	✓	✓	✓	✓	✓
Value-centered R&D	✓	✓	✓	✓	✓
Acquiring ships	✓	✓	✓		
Aircraft operating costs	✓	✓	✓	✓	✓
Scaling trial results	✓	✓			
Policy analysis	✓	✓		✓	✓
Population health	✓				
Assistive technology	✓	✓	✓		
Scenario strategies	✓	✓			
Resource demographics	✓	✓			
Technology investments	✓	✓	✓		
Student choice	✓	✓		✓	✓
BEV & AV vehicles	✓	✓		✓	✓
Disabled & older adults	✓	✓	✓	✓	
Managing failures	✓	✓	✓	✓	
Policy portfolios	✓	✓		✓	✓

Table 7.3 Economic Implications of Transformation.

Ecosystem	Public Sector		Private Sector	
	Revenues	Costs	Revenues	Costs
National Security	Acquisitions savings; sustainment savings	Investments in processes; operating costs of processes	Increased sales; decreased costs of securing business	Investments in processes; operating costs of processes
Healthcare Delivery	Population health cost savings; decreased costs of Medicare & Social Security	Investments in transforming processes; operating costs of process	Increased revenues for population health; decreased delivery costs	Investments in processes; operating costs of processes
Higher Education	Increased tax revenues due to enhanced STEM talent pipeline	Grants to institutions and students	Increased online program revenues; delivery cost savings	Investments in processes; operating costs of processes
Energy & Climate	Increased tax revenues due to job creation; decreased mitigation costs	Investments in transforming energy economy & incentivizing change	Increased revenues for renewable & nuclear energy	Reduced asset values for fossil fuel resources & production capacities

Table 7.3 continues the discussion in Chapter 6 regarding how the economics of transformation cross ecosystems of revenues, savings, and costs across organizational silos. The bottom lines need to be projected across siloes. We are interested in the benefit/cost projections for society, not just CMS (healthcare) IRS (tax revenues) or SSA (disability and retirement). This broader view can motivate and enable transformation. In particular, this can motivate much broader support.

We need to deal with the possible disconnect between costs incurred now and likely benefits much later. Today's costs are captured in an organization's Income Statement, or equivalent. Tomorrow's benefits do not appear at all unless the organization has a Balance Sheet that includes assets with potential to provide significant future economic value.

The transition to having both Income Statements and Balance Sheets involves differentiating operating costs from investments. It also requires translating investments into asset values. Option pricing theory can help with this, but a broader range of financial models are relevant and useful (Rouse, 2010; Sage & Rouse, 2011). The central issue is the need to differentiate how operating expenditures and investments are framed and estimated.

More fundamentally, we need to move stakeholders beyond budgets and staff to think in terms of value creation and the financial metrics that can enable investments and assess outcomes. Public-private ecosystems have emerged and evolved to create value for society, not just to keep people employed. The goal is not just the sustainability of each of these ecosystems; it is the sustainability of society.

For example, as discussed in Chapter 4, our healthcare expenditures are intended to enable a healthy workforce. Our education expenditures, discussed in Chapter 5, are intended to enable a workforce with the necessary knowledge and skills. We need to recognize these expenditures as investments in our society's current and future workforce, global competitiveness, and economic growth and prosperity.

A Broader Vision

Several phenomena cut across all ecosystems. Financial resources are major issues for all the potential innovations, as emphasized by the discussions of economic valuations for each case study. These valuations should be much more robust than simply projections of budgets. Transformation is not just a cost; it enables new futures with expanded economic benefits.

Workforce is central to all ecosystems. National security is concerned with the STEM talent pipeline. Healthcare is focused on workforce requirements to care for an aging population, not to mention an occasional pandemic. A primary role of education is to produce new members of the workforce. Both education and energy will face workforce challenges as technologies and jobs change.

Innovation is important to growth in general and security, health, education, energy in particular. Investments in innovation in any one ecosystem can pay off in all ecosystems. This is not automatic, however, and careful attention needs to be paid to identifying and leveraging innovations that have emerged elsewhere. Such leveraging happens much less than it should, mostly because there is no way to account for it and, hence, few people are paying attention to it.

Finally, growth is an essential phenomenon for all ecosystems and society in general. Several of the non-profits with whom I have consulted, including universities, have entertained potential zero-growth strategies. However, avoiding growth almost guarantees decline. Formulating hedges for possible declines almost guarantees growth. Stasis is not a stable state.

Hence, all organizations—public or private—need growth strategies. They need strategies to grow the value they provide to their constituencies. This may require increased budgets and staff, but not necessarily. Higher education, by harnessing leading-edge technologies, could provide enhanced educational value to a larger population of students while decreasing the costs of education. This would likely be disruptive in the near term, but of enormous value in the long term.

Table 7.4 summarizes factors affecting and enabled by ecosystems. It might be easy to debate the extent to which an ecosystem or phenomenon belongs or does not belong in a particular cell of this table. However, the most important conclusion one can glean from this table is the great extent to which ecosystems and phenomena are intertwined.

To a great extent, the four public-private ecosystems discussed here are managed as organizational siloes. The public agencies and private companies, as well as other non-governmental organizations within ecosystems, do interact, often intensely. However, interactions across ecosystems are much rarer. Information does not flow as easily and there are many fewer incentives.

Table 7.4 Factors Affecting and Enabled by Ecosystems.

	Affects	Enabled By
Security	Technology innovation, economic growth	Workforce, STEM talent, innovation, resources
Health	Healthy workforce, education	Workforce, innovation, resources
Education	Educated workforce, STEM talent	Health, resources
Energy	Cleaner air, milder weather, healthier population	Workforce, STEM talent, resources
Resources	Security, health, education, energy	Innovation, growth
Workforce	Security, health, education energy	Health, education, STEM talent
Innovation	Growth, resources, security, health, education, energy	Workforce, STEM talent, resources
Growth	GDP, jobs, tax revenues, budgets	Innovation

Investing Across Ecosystems

These observations suggest that we should think in terms of investing across ecosystems. Investments in enabling technologies could involve shared investments and returns on investments in terms of impacts of these technologies. Consider these four enabling technologies:

- Data integration: Healthcare delivery is investing heavily here
- Knowledge management: Higher education has long invested here
- Interactive visualizations: Health, education, and energy leverage this
- Artificial intelligence: National security is investing heavily here

Each ecosystem should consider accounting for likely returns in the other three ecosystems in their analyses of alternative investments. Thus, the investment portfolios in these four technology areas should be seen as co-owned. Consequently, all four ecosystems should co-invest. This, of course, requires substantial information sharing and a firm foundation of trust.

For this to make sense, the four ecosystems have to explicitly collaborate in making decisions and plans, as well as executing them. This suggests that there should be common decision-making technologies. The approaches from Chapter 2, as illustrated in Chapters 3–6, are good candidates. There is a wealth of concepts, principles, models, methods, and tools to draw upon. The key is to avoid everybody using something different.

Inevitably leaders in one ecosystem or another will argue that they are different and, therefore, need specialized decision-making technologies. However, as this book clearly and repeatedly illustrates, every decision is not unique. Shared metrics, methods, and tools will greatly enhance collaboration. Indeed, the choice of common concepts, principles, models, methods, and tools should be a collaborative effort in itself.

The four ecosystems can also co-invest in means to enhance decision-making technologies. For example, they can collaboratively invest in creating and refining AI-based cognitive assistants to inform and support decision-making. Thus, not all investments should focus on the specific needs and opportunities within warfighting, medicine, teaching, and energy. Some investments should address improving the functioning and value provided by the ecosystems.

I am not suggesting that such cross-pollination does not happen or has not happened. Many of the technologies I have created from national security investments were first deployed in automotive, electronics, healthcare, and semiconductor industries for non-security purposes. Thus, these investments yielded significant returns, but much more narrowly and slowly than might have happened.

It seems to me that such transitions should be institutionalized. They should not solely depend on lone entrepreneurs finding opportunities and investing energies to convince customers in disparate domains to give the new technologies a try.

Instead, the process might involve existing cross-ecosystem trusted relationships, which would even help the intrepid lone entrepreneurs to more quickly communicate their value propositions and deliver the promised benefits.

Conclusions

The four public-private ecosystems considered in this book exhibit enormous complexity. They also present enormous opportunities. Leveraging these opportunities will require us to address how we account for investments, returns on investments, and operating costs. As discussed in Chapter 6, this is complicated for energy and climate. Doing this across the four ecosystems is even more complicated.

This leads me back to a prescription articulated earlier (Rouse, 2015, 2019) and repeated in Chapter 6. We need to immerse key stakeholders in the complexity of their own worlds as well as each other's worlds. We need the following capabilities:

- *Share Information*: Broadly share credible information so all stakeholders understand the situation. Understand the basis of their credibility judgments and what influences trust.
- *Create Incentives*: Develop incentives to enable long-term benefits while assuring short-terms gains for stakeholders. Understand everyone's time scales and discount rates.
- *Create an Experiential Approach*: Develop an interactive visualization of their worlds to enable people to explore alternative futures. Encourage disparate stakeholders to discuss and debate possible futures.

Thus, I am arguing for a hands-on approach to innovation and transformation. This can transform tendencies for stakeholders to argue with each other in discussions and debates about phenomena in the computational model world, including leading indicators of possible futures and alternative hedges against the risks in these futures.

As noted earlier, transformation should not be a spectator sport. Key stakeholders need to be fully engaged in the game. In this way wicked problems can become solvable problems, albeit often only incrementally. Complete success is an elusive goal, in part because, as we get better, we move the goal posts. That is a good outcome. I suggest in Chapter 8 that transformation should become a core competency.

References

Rouse, W.B. ed. (2010). *The Economics of Human Systems Integration: Valuation of Investments in People's Training and Education, Safety and Health, and Work Productivity*. New York: John Wiley

Rouse, W.B. (2015). *Modeling and Visualization of Complex Systems and Enterprises: Explorations of Physical, Human, Economic, and Social Phenomena*. Hoboken, NJ: John Wiley

Rouse, W.B. (2019). *Computing Possible Futures: Model Based Explorations of "What if?"* Oxford, UK: Oxford University Press

Sage, A.P. and Rouse, W.B. (2011). *Economic System Analysis and Assessment*. New York: Wiley

8
Enabling Change

This chapter addresses the following questions:

- What innovations can enable change?
- How can complex adaptive systems be managed?
- How can one address adversaries?
- How are stakeholders best engaged?
- What is the role of leadership?
- What is the role of trust?
- Can abilities to change become a core competency?

Innovations to Enable Change

There are innovative ways to enable change. First and foremost, while transformation typically involves changing processes, a key enabler is changing people. In one of my consulting engagements with a European auto maker, they had rolled out large posters depicting the new processes, but they had not engaged the workforce in understanding the intent of these processes and how to execute them. My task was to unearth this problem.

As I have discussed several times, it is important to understand stakeholders' values, concerns, and perceptions, as well as the needs and beliefs that underlie these perceptions (Rouse, 1993). In a consulting engagement with a semiconductor company, I determined that the conflict surrounding their environmental strategy was complicated by many people needing to believe that they did not contribute to toxic waste.

A helpful message when addressing major changes involves emphasizing the overarching importance of fostering a healthy, educated, and productive workforce, or the population in general. One way I have articulated this is that leaders should provide a vision of where the train is going, portray what the view will be like along the way, and assure people of their seats on the train. Transformation should not be a surprise

It is also important to articulate and communicate broadly based economic arguments for change. As we have faced the pandemic at Georgetown University, the senior leadership has been very open in sharing the details of the current and

Transforming Public-Private Ecosystems. William B. Rouse, Oxford University Press.
© William B. Rouse (2022). DOI: 10.1093/oso/9780192866530.003.0008

projected economic situation of the university. This transparency has prompted much discussion among faculty members and staff, but not the animosity I have encountered elsewhere.

The usefulness of the above mechanisms totally depends on trust. I return to this topic later in this chapter after I discuss leadership. Transformation is not essentially just a technical endeavor of improving processes, e.g., supply chains, and installing information technology.

Managing Complex Systems

To some extent, complex adaptive systems can be designed. For instance, one can design enterprise-wide information capabilities for such systems (Zammuto, et al., 2007). However, these systems cannot be designed in the same sense that a vehicle or industrial process can be designed. As discussed in Chapter 2, this is due to the strong tendencies of complex adaptive systems to learn, adapt, and self-organize.

Consequently, the task of managing complex adaptive systems becomes a challenge because, in effect, the system keeps redesigning itself. In fact, the construct of "management" has to be viewed differently. Consider the management philosophy with which one approaches this task. An essential contrast is profit maximization via cost minimization vs. value maximization.

Value Philosophy

As an example, recent attempts at healthcare reform have tended, in effect, to pursue the lowest cost, acceptable healthcare for our population. In contrast, we should be pursuing the highest value healthcare. Value focuses on organizational outputs (or outcomes), rather than inputs. Thus, we should emphasize the health states (outputs) of patients rather than the revenues (inputs) of providers.

Value relates to benefits of outcomes, rather than outcomes themselves. From this perspective, we should be very interested in productivity improvements due to wellness, rather than simply the lack of sickness. In an increasingly knowledge-based economy, the intellectual assets embodied in people are central to global competitiveness and economic growth. A recent report from the Milken Institute strongly supports this assertion by showing that the costs of lost productivity are often four to five times larger than the costs of healthcare (DeVol, et al., 2007).

Finally, value implies relevant, usable, and useful outcomes. This means that stakeholders have to understand and appreciate the management philosophy and its implications. In a complex adaptive system, a lack of understanding and/or appreciation tends to result in what might be seen as dysfunctional behaviors by one or more stakeholder groups. However, these behaviors may be well intended and reasonable within these stakeholders' understanding of the ends being sought and the means that are appropriate.

Organizational Behaviors

Management of complex adaptive systems is better approached with a different set of organizational behaviors, as shown in Table 8.1 (Rouse, 2008). Adopting a human-centered perspective that addresses the abilities, limitations, and inclinations of all stakeholders suggests these differences (Rouse, 2007, 2015).

Given that no one is "in charge" of a complex adaptive system, one's approach to management should emphasize leadership rather than traditional management—using influence rather than power. Since most, and perhaps all, of the stakeholder groups are not employees, command and control have to be replaced with incentives and inhibitions. One cannot require stakeholders to comply with organizational dictates. They need to be incentivized to behave accordingly.

Most stakeholders cannot be directly observed. Thus, one cannot manage their activities; one can only assess the value of their outcomes. In a traditional system, one might attempt to optimize efficiency. The learning and adaptive characteristics of a complex adaptive system should be leveraged to foster agility rather than throttled by optimization approaches focused on inevitably out-of-date requirements.

While contractual commitments certainly exist in complex systems, the nature of these systems is such that stakeholders can fairly easily change allegiances, at least at the end of the current contract. Personal commitments can greatly diminish the risks of such behaviors. This implies much less emphasis on arms' length relationships among stakeholder groups. This usually also requires greater transparency of organizational policies, practices, and outcomes.

Work gets done by heterarchies. In contrast, permissions are granted and resources are provided by hierarchies. To the extent that the heterarchy has to stop and ask the hierarchy for permission or resources, the efficiency and effectiveness of the system

Table 8.1 Organizational Behaviors.

	Traditional System	Complex Adaptive System
Roles	Management	Leadership
Methods	Command & Control	Incentives & Inhibitions
Measurement	Activities	Outcomes
Focus	Efficiency	Agility
Relationships	Contractual	Personal Commitments
Network	Hierarchy	Heterarchy
Design	Organizational Design	Self Organization

is undermined. Decision-making authority and resources should be delegated to the heterarchy with, of course, the right incentives and inhibitions.

Finally, as noted earlier, complex adaptive systems self-organize. One cannot impose an organizational design. To the extent that one does, it will be morphed by the stakeholders as they learn and adapt to changing conditions. The result will be that the organization one thinks they are managing will not really exist. To the extent that everyone agrees to pretend that is still exists, or ever existed, this shared delusion will undermine value (Rouse, 1998).

Information Systems

Given the differences noted in Table 8.1, what information is needed to oversee the system? This information should include:

- Measurements and projections of system state in terms of current and projected value flows, as well as current and projected problems
- Measurements and projections of system performance in terms of current and projected value, costs, and metrics such as value divided by cost, as well as current and projected options for contingencies
- Observations of system stakeholders in terms of involvement of each stakeholder group and performance of each stakeholder group
- Capabilities for measurement, modeling and display of system state, including agile "What If?" experimentation and adaptation

Note that this prescription is quite consistent with the approach to failure management presented in Chapter 6.

Who would look at the types of information listed above? If we were discussing the banking system, then the answer would be the Federal Reserve Bank. The Fed does not tell banks what to do. It sets the prime interest rate and determines each bank's reserve requirements. Banks and investors then decide how they want to adapt to any changes.

There is no overseer of most ecosystems. Considering that the health of the country's ecosystems is essential to competitiveness and economic growth, perhaps there should be an overseer. What variables might this entity monitor and adjust?

Admittedly, outcomes can be difficult to characterize and calibrate, and attribution of causes of outcomes can be quite difficult due to both the involvement of multiple actors and the fact that outcomes emerge over time. Nevertheless, at the very least, we should be able to characterize and assess bad outcomes.

More controversially, an oversight organization might adjust tax rates so that the economic benefits of high-value outcomes are rewarded. I know this idea is controversial as I have presented it to various groups of thought leaders. Beyond philosophical objections to using the tax system to achieve greater public good, the most frequent criticism is that organizations cannot control outcomes—others' behaviors are central to success.

However, this phenomenon is central to most markets. The enterprises that succeed are able to convince and incentivize behaviors that co-create high-value outcomes. Of course, success with this model depends on organizations seeing themselves as being responsible for assuring high-value outcomes, rather than just being paid for the costs of their activities.

Transforming Adversaries

Important changes do happen, but it is not easy. Vested interests push back strongly if there are not significant incentives for them to change. Expect adversaries. Vested interests try to leverage popular perceptions and preferences. For example, the pushback is not about threats to revenues and profits; it is about threats to jobs.

The key is to understand the bases of the varying perceptions and creating narratives that address them. You need a better, more compelling, story than your adversaries. But, how do we get constituencies to believe these stories? Offhand, it seems to me that you need to undermine the credibility of the naysayers. You need to portray their record, relative to their claims.

Yet, we face the difficulties that their "advertisements" can say absolutely anything. They can point to your dastardly deeds with no supporting evidence. Their first amendment rights support their rights to lie, as long as it does not cause you physical harm.

Fortunately, as outlined throughout this book, there is a systematic process for addressing these challenges. First, one identifies key stakeholders and solicits their involvement. Then, one determines stakeholders' values, concerns, and perceptions. This includes understanding stakeholders' levels of trust, as is discussed later in this chapter.

The process then focuses on determining how interventions are likely to affect stakeholders. This can be assisted by immersing stakeholders in explorations of alternative paths to success. A thorough understanding of both positive and negative perceptions of alternatives is needed. Determine to the extent possible whether negative perceptions will lead to any stakeholders becoming adversaries.

I learned a valuable lesson from an early research project for the State Library of Illinois. Our computational model showed that one large library resource was undermining network performance. The State Librarian confronted the director of this organization with these findings. He said that he understood but could not resolve the issue. She said that she could accept that if he relented on another unrelated issue. He agreed.

The principle is simple. If stymied in reaching agreement over the particulars of an initiative, rather than create an adversary, broaden the scope of the negotiation to include other benefits that the stakeholders in question will see as benefits. Broaden the deal so that in some other ways these stakeholders will perceive valuable gains, not just unfortunate losses.

It can also help if the change initiative is formulated as a portfolio of sub initiatives that are staggered in time. Implement the easy to agree to pieces first. Create some early wins. Delay the contentious pieces until later if possible. Do not hide these longer-term plans, but indicate that the specifics of these plans will be reviewed later once the overall implementation process is better understood.

Role of Leadership

What competencies are needed to lead a transformation initiative successfully? What are the relative roles of technical skills versus leadership skills? I studied four transformation success stories to address these questions.

The four case studies of Lockheed Martin, Newell-Rubbermaid, Reebok, and UPS provided the basis for assessing the necessary competencies for transforming an enterprise. To make this assessment, all initiatives and tasks performed by these four companies were copied into a spreadsheet with main categories from the cases, i.e., drivers, approach, customers, efficiency, culture, and execution.

For each task or initiative, one or more competencies needed for success were identified. Competency, relative to a task, was defined as sufficient knowledge, ability, and expertise to enable successful completion of that task. No attempt was made to classify competencies as individual or organizational, in part because the source data would not support such an assessment. Further, no attempt was made to assess the relative importance of these competencies, again because the source data would not support such an assessment.

Assessment of Competencies

I performed the assessment of competencies, having worked with these executives to varying extents, as well as having extensive experience with a large number of other companies involved in fundamental change initiatives. The result of this assessment was 125 matches of initiatives and/or tasks to 18 competencies. It is important to note that the set of competencies emerged from the assessment and was not defined in advance. Further, while the research literature on these competencies influenced these assessments, there was no attempt to conform to any particular research paradigms.

The resulting data set was then sorted by competencies. The juxtaposition of instances of competencies resulted in many re-wordings, re-definitions, and subsequent resortings. Without this rework, the set of competencies would have been much larger than 18. Figure 8.1 summarizes the process and results.

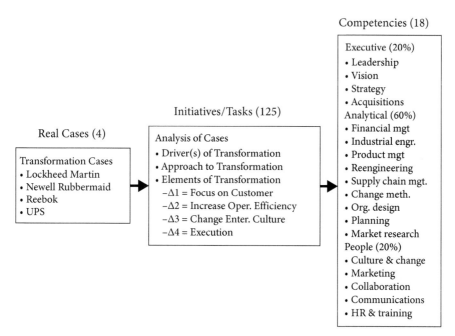

Fig. 8.1 Overall Process for Competency Assessment

Analytical competencies accounted for 73 of 125 instances (58 percent). These competencies included financial management, industrial engineering, product management, reengineering, supply chain management, change methodology, organizational design, planning, and market research. People competencies accounted for 27 of 125 instances (22 percent) including culture and change, marketing, collaboration, communications, and human resources (HR) and training. Finally, executive competencies accounted for 25 of the 125 instances (20 percent) including leadership, vision, strategy and acquisitions.

Note that the percentages of each competency cluster—roughly 20 percent, 60 percent, and 20 percent—do not necessarily relate to the importance or criticality of each cluster or each competency. They simply reflect the frequency with which the authors of the referenced source documents discussed particular initiatives and tasks. These discussions reflected the authors' reports of what the companies did in the process of successfully transforming their enterprises.

Validation Surveys

Two online validation surveys were conducted. Both focused on competencies that fast-rising middle managers need to gain if they are be able to lead successful enterprise transformation initiatives later in their careers. The first was a pilot survey with the 18 members of the Advisory Board of the Tennenbaum Institute at Georgia

Tech, yielding 10 responses for a 56 percent response rate. The subsequent full survey went to 385 executives and senior managers who had earlier expressed interest in enterprise transformation, yielding 57 completed responses for a 16 percent response rate. All of the people surveyed were in positions, or had been in positions, where they could designate and support middle managers to gain the competencies of interest.

They were asked to rate the extent to which candidate competencies were important for leading fundamental organizational change in general, not for the four case studies presented here, and not in terms of particular aspects of transformation. Thus, while the target audience for gaining these competencies was characterized as currently middle managers, respondents were asked to rate the competencies that should be gained by the time people became leaders of transformation initiatives, despite the reality of their not currently being in such leadership positions.

Overall Findings

Respondents rated competencies on a 5-point Likert scale: not important, somewhat important, important, very important, and extremely important. There were very few ratings of unimportant or somewhat important for any of the competencies. Figure 8.2 shows the percentage of respondents that rated each competency very important or extremely important. (Note that, based on a pilot test of the survey, the "HR and training" competency in Figure 8.1 was, for the survey, separated into two competencies—"Human Resources" and "Training and Education." Thus, Figure 8.2 differs slightly from Figure 8.1.)

The results are quite clear. Respondents were less concerned with more operational competencies such as supply chain management and industrial engineering. In contrast, they placed great emphasis on leadership, vision, planning, strategy, culture and change, and collaboration, teamwork, and social networking. This is quite consistent with the literature on leadership and change. All in all, the set of executive competencies were strongly endorsed, while the analytic and people competencies received less support, albeit roughly 40–60 percent of responders rated them highly.

Nevertheless, understanding and communicating the drivers of transformation, formulating and employing a well-defined approach to transformation, understanding and enabling the cultural changes needed, and focusing on execution are viewed as crucial. It is reasonable to argue that competencies associated with a customer focus and efficiency are necessary for transformation, but by no means sufficient. Without the more highly rated competencies, an enterprise is likely to try to get better and better at what they are already doing.

This finding is consistent with the conclusions of Charan and Colvin (1999). They reported that 70 percent of high-profile chief executives that were fired could not be attributed to a lack of customer-driven vision, strategy, and plans. Instead, these CEOs were fired because they could not get their organizations to embrace the

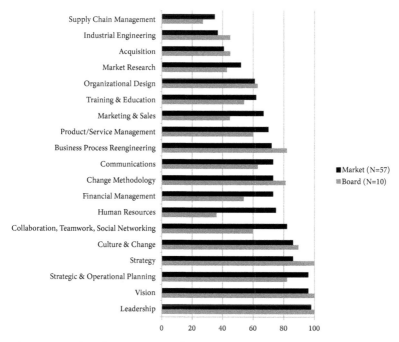

Fig. 8.2 Results of Two Surveys of Executives and Senior Managers (Rouse, 2011)

necessary changes and execute the plans for accomplishing them. They had some of the necessary ingredients for change, but they lacked sufficient ingredients as embodied in the highly rated competencies discussed here.

The competencies identified, as well as their relative importance, raise the question of how one could assess the extent to which an individual or organization possesses these competencies. Indeed, the competencies rated as relatively less important are those that are most easy to assess, e.g., the extent to which an individual has or has not mastered particular analytical skills. In contrast, assessing the extent to which an individual is, or can be, a visionary is a subject of much debate.

A related question concerns how best to foster these competencies, both individually and organizationally. What pedagogical or experiential approaches are likely to be most successful in creating people skilled in these competencies? What are the relative costs and benefits of these approaches? We are much better at teaching people in ways that they gain analytical competencies than we are at teaching people to be leaders and especially visionaries.

Nevertheless, we now know what competencies are needed to successfully transform an enterprise. The critical research questions are how to assess whether an individual or organization has these competencies and how best to foster these competencies when needed. A further research issue concerns the nature of work support needed to enhance people's abilities to exhibit the needed competencies as well as overcome their limitations relative to these competencies.

Examples of Success

Transformation can be successfully pursued and achieved, as the three examples that were discussed earlier illustrate. IBM moved from relying on mainframe computer sales to selling software and services. Microsoft moved beyond milking Windows and Microsoft Office to embrace the Internet. Apple transformed itself from selling computers to providing elegant digital devices.

- IBM had its highest share price in 1990, but was on the path to losing billions in 1993. Louis Gerstner, IBM CEO, is widely credited with transforming IBM into a customer-focused global enterprise dedicated to leadership in services and technology.
- Microsoft at first dismissed the Internet and Netscape's web browser, introduced in 1994. By May of 1995, however, Microsoft CEO Bill Gates had thrown his company wholeheartedly into joining the "Internet tidal wave."
- Apple was on the brink of fizzling out, struggling to find a consistently profitable source of revenue. Instead of continuing to aimlessly pursue marginal product ideas, Apple, with Steve Jobs again leading, began to focus once more on creating beautiful consumer electronics.

There are also great examples of public sector trailblazers leading fundamental change. Abraham Lincoln led the country through the Civil War and emancipated enslaved blacks. Theodore Roosevelt championed the Progressive Era. Franklin Roosevelt's New Deal helped pull the country out of the Great Depression. Table 7.1 summarizes many other examples.

Trust

Trust is a major issue in society today. The Pew Research Center reports that U.S. trust in government has dropped from almost 80 perccentduring the Johnson administration to 17 percent today (Pew, 2019a). Americans trust scientists and the military at 80 percent or better, but distrust elected officials (Pew 2019b). "Higher levels of familiarity with the work of scientists are associated with more positive and more trusting views of scientists regarding their competence, credibility and commitment to the public."

The Organization for Economic Cooperation and Development. has reported on an extensive study of trust (OECD, 2018). The main results were:

- "Self-reported measures of trust in others capture a belief about trustworthiness, as well as altruistic preferences.
- Experimental measures capture willingness to cooperate and one's own trust-worthiness. Therefore, both measures are loosely related.
- Perceptions of institutional performance strongly correlate with both trust in government and trust in others.
- Perceived government integrity is the strongest determinant of trust in government.
- Indicators associated with social capital, such as neighborhood connectedness and attitudes towards immigration, perceived satisfaction with public services, social preferences and expectations matter for trust in others.
- An increase in all significant determinants of trust in government by one standard deviation may be conducive to an increase in trust by 30 to 60 percent."

Data reported by *Frontiers in Public Health* (Rijs & Fenter, 2020) is shown in Figure 8.3. The differences between New Zealand and the United States, for example, are rather astounding. It is likely just a coincidence, but this difference parallels

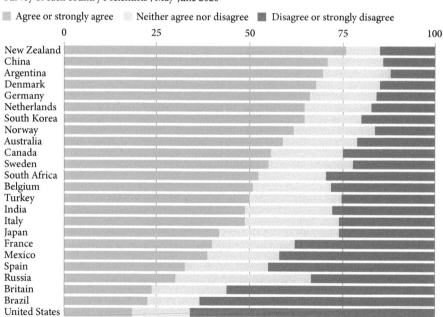

*25,307 researchers affiliated with Frontiers, a Swiss publisher of scientific journals

Fig. 8.3 Perceptions of Role of Scientific Advice by Country (Rijs & Fenter, 2020)

the difference in how the two countries have handled the pandemic. Clearly, the phenomenon of mistrust is substantial in the U.S.

Why? The OECD study suggests that mistrust of government is due to a lack of perceived government integrity, as well as perceptions of poor institutional performance. Taking these results as a whole, people trust the evidence that scientists report, but they do not trust how government translates this evidence into policy. I expect that Americans very much distrust how lobbyists and campaign contributions affect legislation, regulations, and policy in general.

How might this be mitigated? My sense is that transparency is the answer. The recent 6,000-page coronavirus relief bill passed by the US Congress is not an example of transparency. It represents opaqueness and obscuration, par excellence. It is laced with $100 billion or so of appropriations that have nothing to do with coronavirus relief.

Transparency involves open sharing data, assumptions, and predictions. It involves public knowledge of who benefits, who sacrifices, and how such tradeoffs were addressed. It also requires acknowledgement of indirect consequences such as foregone tax revenues that could have funded other important needs. This is required for a human-centered society rather than a money-centered winner takes all society.

Discussion

Overall, transformation is a process rather than a solution. Thus, the specific nature of the eventual solution will inherently emerge over time, with stakeholders understanding how the pieces of the puzzle emerged and seeing how their contributions affected the outcomes.

What are the consequences if the people given control over our government have no idea how it works? In *The Fifth Risk*, Michael Lewis (2018) takes us into the engine rooms of a government under attack by its own leaders. Presidential appointees during the Trump administration were shockingly uninformed about the functions of their new workplace. Some even threw away the briefing books that had been prepared for them.

At the Department of Agriculture, the funding of vital programs like food stamps and school lunches was slashed. The Commerce Department apparently did not have enough staff to conduct the 2020 Census properly. The Department of Energy, where international nuclear risk is managed, did not have enough inspectors to track and locate black market uranium before terrorists do.

Willful ignorance plays a role in these looming disasters. If your ambition is to maximize short-term gains without regard to the long-term cost, you are better off not knowing those costs. If you want to preserve your personal immunity to the hard problems, it is better to never really understand those problems. There is upside to ignorance, and downside to knowledge.

If there are dangerous fools in Lewis' book, there are also heroes, unsung, of course. They are the linchpins of the system—those public servants whose knowledge, dedication, and proactivity keep the machinery running. Michael Lewis finds them, and he asks them what keeps them up at night. These linchpins are central to successful transformation of public-private ecosystems.

Conclusions

Fundamental change is at the core of our society and it always has been, albeit at a bit faster pace of late. Joel Mokyr's *The Lever of Riches: Technological Creativity and Economic Progress* (1990) makes a compelling historical case for the enormous value of technological change. Near-term disruption leads to long-term growth and prosperity. Of course, it can be rather troublesome in the transition.

Can we, as a society, absorb and leverage constant technological disruption? Why might the answer be "No"? Might the mechanisms whereby we mitigate change and its consequences be our undoing? That is a distinct possibility.

Joseph Tainter's *The Collapse of Complex Societies* (Cambridge University Press, 1988) presaged Jared Diamond's *Collapse: How Societies Choose to Fail or Succeed* (Viking Press, 2004). Both books provide vivid explanations of how societies fail and why.

Societies create mechanisms to deal with new challenges. Walls are built to thwart Mongol hoards. Regulations are created to deter fraud and corruption. Programs are designed to assure equity of access to education and health. Each of these initiatives leads to a new layer of societal complexity.

Each of these layers creates a set of vested interests in the operations of the layer and the economic benefits of these operations. Consequently, it is very difficult to eliminate layers, even if the original motivation for the layer has disappeared.

Adding layers is much easier. The benefits of the layer, to both those targeted to receive these benefits and those compensated to provide these benefits, can be quite substantial. That's why they are very reluctant to forego these benefits, even if the provision of these benefits no longer makes sense.

So, societies keep adding layers that consume resources. Eventually, a new challenge emerges—a pandemic, climate change or alien invaders—and there are no resources to invest in a new layer. All resources are being consumed to support earlier layers of complexity. This is a harbinger of societal failure.

Where do we currently stand? There are layers that many people do not realize exist. For example, the blog on Downsizing the Federal Government indicates, "The federal government spends more than $20 billion a year on subsidies for farm businesses. About 39 percent of the nation's 2.1 million farms receive subsidies, with the lion's share of the handouts going to the largest producers of corn, soybeans, wheat, cotton, and rice."

Transportation subsidies are probably the largest, with public transit receiving $50 billon per year. Airplanes, aluminum, athletic shoes, automotive, microelectronics, and oil are among the largest corporate recipients of subsidies, with the top 10 recipients receiving $30–40 billion per year. Layers of bureaucracy administer all of these subsidies. There is a labyrinth of vested interests, advocates, and lobbyists.

We also have layers that administer Social Security, Medicare, and Medicaid, as well as layers that regulate agriculture, aviation, banking, education, energy, environment, finance, healthcare, transportation, etc. These activities create economic value in the sense that the millions of employees involved translate their salaries and wages into consumption.

The complexity is staggering during "normal" times, but can become overwhelming during crises such as the mortgage meltdown (2007–2010) and the current pandemic. The impacts of climate change are lurking around the corner, which over the coming years will consume an increasing portion of global GDP.

Might the layer of complexity added to address the impacts of climate change precipitate societal failure? The risk of this is sufficient to warrant careful and thoughtful anticipation of this possibility and careful consideration of mechanisms to mitigate this outcome. Our typical approach of "too little, too late" is no longer viable. Actually, it never was but we muddled through. Muddling is now a sure way to guarantee enormous negative societal consequences.

We need to pursue transparency, as just discussed, to make complexity visible. Then, we need to work to eliminate unwarranted complexity. Elimination should be prioritized before elaboration. We need less process, and these processes should be easily understandable and easily scrutinized. Put simply. transformation needs to be a core competency of our society. We need to do change well and repeatedly.

References

Charan, R. and Colvin, G. (1999, June 21). Why CEOs fail. *Fortune*, 68–78.

Devol, R., Bedroussian, A., Charuworn, A., Chatterjee, A., Kim, I., Kim, S., and Klowden, K. (2007). *An Unhealthy America: The Economic Burden of Chronic Disease*. Santa Monica, CA: Milken Institute, October.

Diamond, J. (2004). *Collapse: How Societies Choose to Fail or Succeed* New York: Viking Press.

Lewis, M. (2018). *The Fifth Risk*. New York: Norton.

Mokyr, J. (1990). *The Lever of Riches: Technological Creativity and Economic Progress*. Oxford, UK: Oxford University Press.

OECD (2018). *Trust and Its Determinants: Evidence from the Trustlab Experiment*. Paris, France: Organization for Economic Cooperation and Development.

Pew (2019a). *Public Trust in Government: 1958–2019*. Washington, DC: Pew Research Center, April 11.

Pew (2019b). *Trust and Mistrust in Americans' Views of Scientific Experts*. Washington, DC: Pew Research Center, August 2.

Rijs, C. and Fenter, F. (2020). The academic response to COVID-19. *Frontiers Public Health*, October 28.

Rouse, W.B. (1993). *Catalysts for Change: Concepts and Principles for Enabling Innovation*. New York: Wiley

Rouse, W.B. (1998). *Don't Jump to Solutions: Thirteen Delusions that Undermine Strategic Thinking*. San Francisco, CA: Jossey-Bass.

Rouse, W.B. (2007). *People and Organizations: Explorations of Human-Centered Design*. New York: Wiley.

Rouse, W.B. (2008). Healthcare as a complex adaptive system: Implications for design and management. *The Bridge*, 38 (1), 17–25.

Rouse, W.B. (2011). Necessary competencies for transforming an enterprise, *Journal of Enterprise Transformation*, 1 (1), 71–92.

Rouse, W.B. (2015). *Modeling and Visualization of Complex Systems and Enterprises: Explorations of Physical, Human, Economic, and Social Phenomena*. New York: Wiley.

Tainter, J. (1988). *The Collapse of Complex Societies*. Cambridge, UK: Cambridge University Press.

Zammuto, R.F., Griffith, T.L., Majchrzak, A., Dougherty, D.J., and Faraj, S. (2007). Information technology and the changing fabric of organization. *Organization Science*, 18 (5), 749–762.

Index